HIDDEN TREASURES

Senior Authors

Roger C. Farr

Dorothy S. Strickland

Authors

Richard F. Abrahamson ◆ Alma Flor Ada ◆ Barbara Bowen Coulter

Bernice E. Cullinan ◆ Margaret A. Gallego

W. Dorsey Hammond

Nancy Roser ◆ Junko Yokota ◆ Hallie Kay Yopp

Senior Consultant

Asa G. Hillard III

Consultants

Kanani Choy ◆ Lee Bennett Hopkins ◆ Stephen Krashen ◆ Rosalia Salinas

Harcourt Brace & Company

Orlando Atlanta Austin Boston San Francisco Chicago Dallas New York Toronto London

Requests for permission to make copies of any part of the work should be mailed to: Permissions Department, Harcourt Brace & Company, 6277 Sea Harbor Drive, Orlando, Florida 32887-6777.

HARCOURT BRACE and Quill Design is a registered trademark of Harcourt Brace & Company.

Acknowledgments appear in the back of this work.

Printed in the United States of America

ISBN 0-15-306405-6

1 2 3 4 5 6 7 8 9 10   048   99 98 97 96

Dear Reader,

When you open **Hidden Treasures**, you open doors to discovery. Behind one door you'll find the hidden treasures of ancient Egypt. Behind others you'll see how one ancient Roman city was built and how another was destroyed by the terrible force of a volcano.

During the year, you will learn how people lived in ancient Greece and how Arctic wolves survive at the top of the world. You will also come to understand how people find hidden strengths within themselves. You will read of Tuan Nguyen, a Vietnamese boy, who must learn to adapt to life in America and of Joan Benoit Samuelson, a long-distance runner who struggles to keep her Olympic dream alive.

So join us now in search of excitement, adventure, and hidden treasures.

Sincerely,

The Authors

The Authors

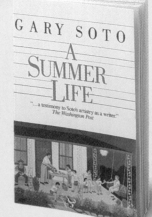

Contents

Meeting Challenges

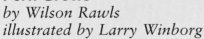

BEHIND THE SEALED DOOR

The Discovery of the Tomb and Treasures of Tutankhamun

THE
GOLDEN GOBLET

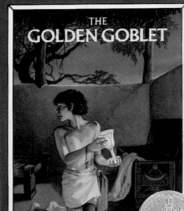

...GRAW

KIDS
DISCOVER

PREMIER ISSUE

Pyramids

TUT'S
GOLD

Shen of the Sea
Chinese Stories for Children

By Arthur Bowie Chrisman
Illustrated by Else Hasselriis

WALLS
DEFENSES
THROUGHOUT
HISTORY
BY JAMES CROSS GIBLIN

Ancient Civilizations

CONTENTS

THE WORDS OF
MARTIN LUTHER KING, JR.

HELLO,
MY NAME IS
SCRAMBLED
EGGS

THE
VIETNAMESE
IN AMERICA

The Star Fisher
LAURENCE YEP

NUMBER THE STARS
a novel by Lois Lowry

Celebrating Differences

Stories of Ten Remarkable Athletes

CHAMPIONS

BY *Bill Littlefield*

PAINTINGS BY *Bernie Fuchs*

With a Foreword by Fr

KIDS DISCOVER

Ancient Greece

NIKE
Sneaker
or
god
?

Olympic
Dirty
Tricks!

Horse outsmarts town!

ANCIENT
GREEK
WISDOM
He
who
flies
falls
!

AQUATHINKING

WHAT
ARCHIMEDES
LEARNED
IN THE
BATHTUB
!

CITY

A Story of Roman Planning and Construction
DAVID MACAULAY

THE
GOLDEN FLEECE
AND THE
HEROES
WHO LIVED
BEFORE
ACHILLES
BY PADRAIC
COLUM

Inside illustrations
by Willy Pogany

SCHOLASTIC

A TIME QUEST BOOK

THE SECRETS OF
VESUVIUS
by Sara C. Bisel

Exploring the mysteries of an ancient buried city

SCHOLASTIC

TURNING POINTS

CONTENTS

FOCUS: Five Women Photographers

JULIA MARGARET CAMERON · MARGARET BOURKE-WHITE
FLOR GARDUÑO · SANDY SKOGLUND · LORNA SIMPSON

Sylvia Wolf

DIEGO RODRIGUEZ DE SILVA Y
VELASQUEZ
By Ernest Raboff

ART FOR CHILDREN

I, Juan de Pareja

Elizabeth Borton de Treviño

The Will and the Way

PAUL R. WILLIAMS, ARCHITECT

Karen E. Hudson

Rizzoli

MASTERPIECES

CONTENTS

13

CONFRONTING NATURE

CONTENTS

Theme
Meeting
Challenges

Our relationships and experiences teach us about ourselves. The boys and girls in the next selections learn that they have the determination and self-reliance to meet new challenges, fulfill dreams, and survive on their own.

17

Contents

Theme
Meeting
Challenges

19

Bookshelf

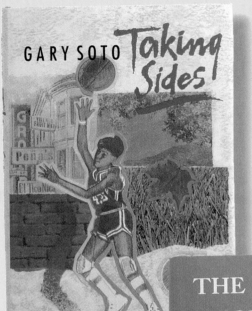

Taking Sides
by Gary Soto

Linc Mendoza is struggling to fit in at his new school. He finds his loyalties divided though, when he plays in a basketball game against his former teammates.
Award-Winning Author
Signatures Library

The Phantom Tollbooth
by Norton Juster
illustrated by Jules Feiffer

Milo feels hopelessly bored with his life until the day he receives a mysterious package.
Award-Winning Author
Signatures Library

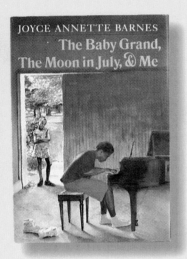

The Baby Grand, the Moon in July, and Me
by Joyce Annette Barnes

Annie's brother Mattie causes an uproar when he buys a piano on credit, and it's up to Annie to help her parents appreciate her brother's musical talent.

Apple Is My Sign
by Mary Riskind

As the deaf child of deaf parents, Harry Berger must make adjustments when he attends a boarding school in the "hearing world."
ALA Notable Book

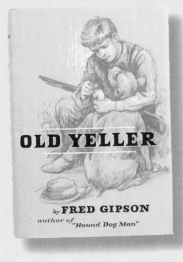

Old Yeller
by Fred Gipson

Travis and his dog, Old Yeller, together face the dangers and responsibilities of life on the Texas frontier of 1860.
Newbery Honor

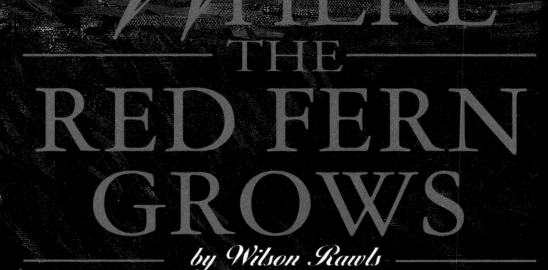

WHERE THE RED FERN GROWS

by *Wilson Rawls*

illustrated by *Larry Winborg*

During the Great Depression, Billy Coleman lived in a beautiful valley in the Ozark Mountains of Oklahoma. One day he became infected with what he called "the dog-wanting disease." He didn't want just any breed of dog either. He wanted expensive hounds—coon hounds—and he wanted two of them. But his parents were poor and he tried for a long time not to pester them about the dogs.

Award-Winning
Author

The dog-wanting disease never did leave me altogether. With the new work I was doing, helping Papa, it just kind of burned itself down and left a big sore on my heart. Every time I'd see a coon track down in our fields, or along the riverbanks, the old sore would get all festered up and start hurting again.

Just when I had given up all hope of ever owning a good hound, something wonderful happened. The good Lord figured I had hurt enough, and it was time to lend a helping hand.

It all started one day while I was hoeing corn down in our field close to the river. Across the river, a party of fishermen had been camped for several days. I heard the old Maxwell car as it snorted and chugged its way out of the bottoms. I knew they were leaving. Throwing down my hoe, I ran down to the river and waded across at a place called the Shannon Ford. I hurried to the camp ground.

It was always a pleasure to prowl where fishermen had camped. I usually could find things: a fish line, or a forgotten fish pole. On one occasion, I found a beautiful knife stuck in the bark of a sycamore tree, forgotten by a careless fisherman. But on that day, I found the greatest of treasures, a sportsman's magazine, discarded by the campers. It was a real treasure for a country boy. Because of that magazine, my entire life was changed.

I sat down on an old sycamore log, and started thumbing through the leaves. On the back pages of the magazine, I came to the "For Sale" section—"Dogs for Sale"—every kind of dog. I read on and on. They had dogs I had never heard of, names I couldn't make out. Far down in the right-hand corner, I found an ad that took my breath away. In small letters, it read: "Registered redbone coon hound pups—twenty-five dollars each."

The advertisement was from a kennel in Kentucky. I read it over and over. By the time I had memorized the ad, I was seeing dogs, hearing dogs, and even feeling them. The magazine was forgotten. I was lost in thought. The brain of an eleven-year-old boy can dream some fantastic dreams.

How wonderful it would be if I could have two of those pups. Every boy in the country but me had a good hound or two. But fifty dollars—how could I ever get fifty dollars? I knew I couldn't expect help from Mama and Papa.

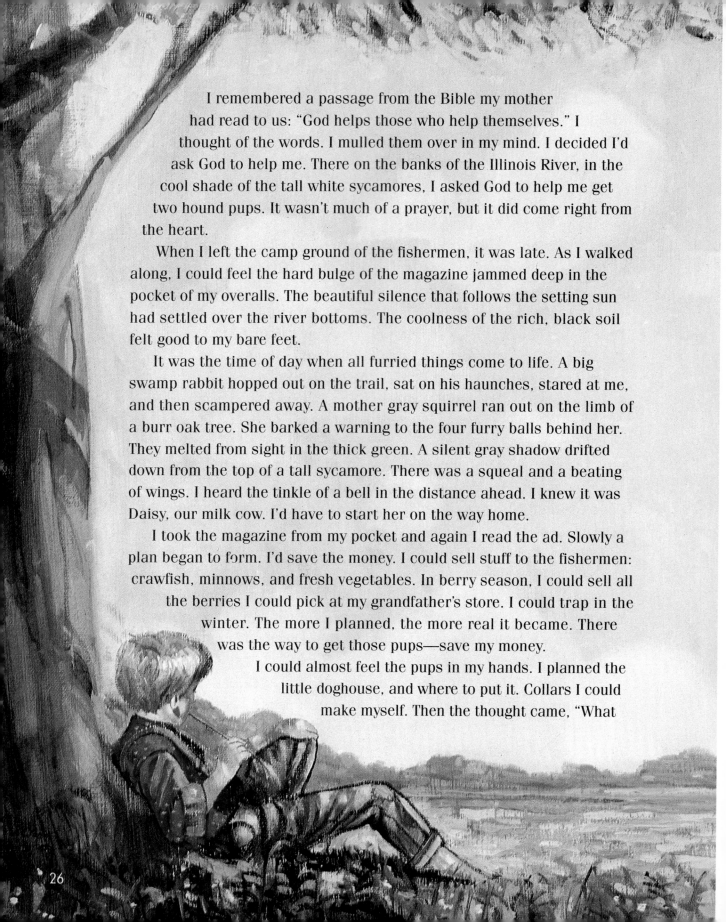

I remembered a passage from the Bible my mother
had read to us: "God helps those who help themselves." I
thought of the words. I mulled them over in my mind. I decided I'd
ask God to help me. There on the banks of the Illinois River, in the
cool shade of the tall white sycamores, I asked God to help me get
two hound pups. It wasn't much of a prayer, but it did come right from
the heart.

When I left the camp ground of the fishermen, it was late. As I walked
along, I could feel the hard bulge of the magazine jammed deep in the
pocket of my overalls. The beautiful silence that follows the setting sun
had settled over the river bottoms. The coolness of the rich, black soil
felt good to my bare feet.

It was the time of day when all furried things come to life. A big
swamp rabbit hopped out on the trail, sat on his haunches, stared at me,
and then scampered away. A mother gray squirrel ran out on the limb of
a burr oak tree. She barked a warning to the four furry balls behind her.
They melted from sight in the thick green. A silent gray shadow drifted
down from the top of a tall sycamore. There was a squeal and a beating
of wings. I heard the tinkle of a bell in the distance ahead. I knew it was
Daisy, our milk cow. I'd have to start her on the way home.

I took the magazine from my pocket and again I read the ad. Slowly a
plan began to form. I'd save the money. I could sell stuff to the fishermen:
crawfish, minnows, and fresh vegetables. In berry season, I could sell all
the berries I could pick at my grandfather's store. I could trap in the
winter. The more I planned, the more real it became. There
was the way to get those pups—save my money.

I could almost feel the pups in my hands. I planned the
little doghouse, and where to put it. Collars I could
make myself. Then the thought came, "What

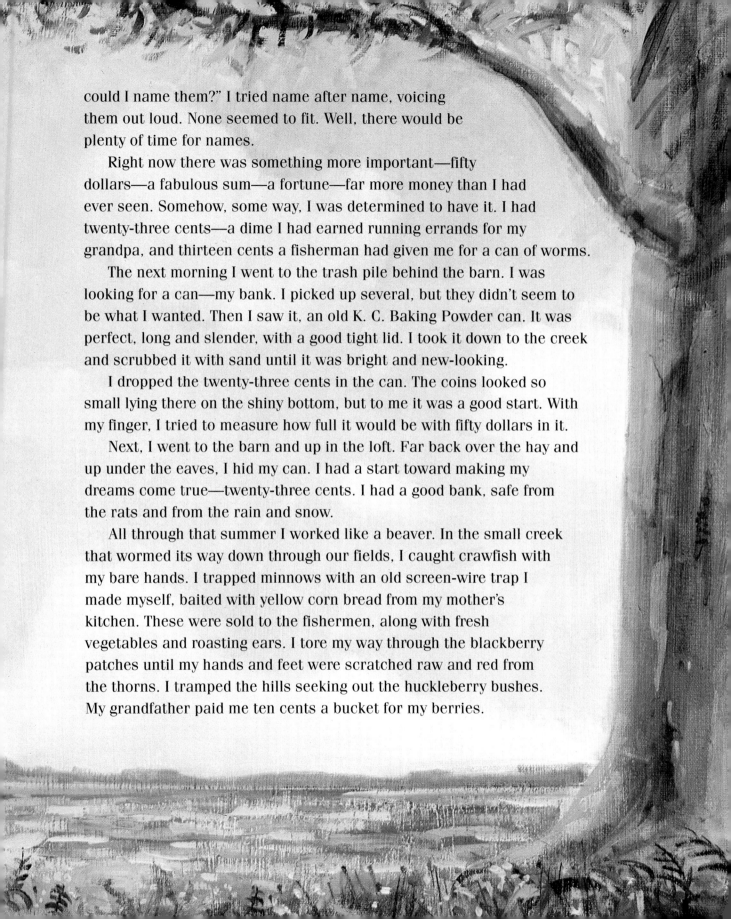

could I name them?" I tried name after name, voicing them out loud. None seemed to fit. Well, there would be plenty of time for names.

Right now there was something more important—fifty dollars—a fabulous sum—a fortune—far more money than I had ever seen. Somehow, some way, I was determined to have it. I had twenty-three cents—a dime I had earned running errands for my grandpa, and thirteen cents a fisherman had given me for a can of worms.

The next morning I went to the trash pile behind the barn. I was looking for a can—my bank. I picked up several, but they didn't seem to be what I wanted. Then I saw it, an old K. C. Baking Powder can. It was perfect, long and slender, with a good tight lid. I took it down to the creek and scrubbed it with sand until it was bright and new-looking.

I dropped the twenty-three cents in the can. The coins looked so small lying there on the shiny bottom, but to me it was a good start. With my finger, I tried to measure how full it would be with fifty dollars in it.

Next, I went to the barn and up in the loft. Far back over the hay and up under the eaves, I hid my can. I had a start toward making my dreams come true—twenty-three cents. I had a good bank, safe from the rats and from the rain and snow.

All through that summer I worked like a beaver. In the small creek that wormed its way down through our fields, I caught crawfish with my bare hands. I trapped minnows with an old screen-wire trap I made myself, baited with yellow corn bread from my mother's kitchen. These were sold to the fishermen, along with fresh vegetables and roasting ears. I tore my way through the blackberry patches until my hands and feet were scratched raw and red from the thorns. I tramped the hills seeking out the huckleberry bushes. My grandfather paid me ten cents a bucket for my berries.

Once Grandpa asked me what I did with the money I earned. I told him I was saving it to buy some hunting dogs. I asked him if he would order them for me when I had saved enough. He said he would. I asked him not to say anything to my father. He promised me he wouldn't. I'm sure Grandpa paid little attention to my plans.

Little by little, the nickels and dimes added up. The old K. C. Baking Powder can grew heavy. I would heft its weight in the palm of my hand. With a straw, I'd measure from the lip of the can to the money. As the months went by, the straws grew shorter and shorter.

The next summer I followed the same routine.

"Would you like to buy some crawfish or minnows? Maybe you'd like some fresh vegetables or roasting ears."

The fishermen were wonderful, as true sportsmen are. They seemed to sense the urgency in my voice and always bought my wares. However, many was the time I'd find my vegetables left in the abandoned camp.

There never was a set price. Anything they offered was good enough for me.

A year passed. I was twelve. I was over the halfway mark. I had twenty-seven dollars and forty-six cents. My spirits soared. I worked harder.

Another year crawled slowly by, and then the great day came. The long hard

grind was over. I had it—my fifty dollars! I cried as I counted it over and over.

As I set the can back in the shadowy eaves of the barn, it seemed to glow with a radiant whiteness I had never seen before. Perhaps it was all imagination. I don't know.

Lying back in the soft hay, I folded my hands behind my head, closed my eyes, and let my mind wander back over the two long years. I thought of the fishermen, the blackberry patches, and the huckleberry hills. I thought of the prayer I had said when I asked God to help me get two hound pups. I knew He had surely helped, for He had given me the heart, courage, and determination.

Early the next morning, with the can jammed deep in the pocket of my overalls, I flew to the store. As I trotted along, I whistled and sang. I felt as big as the tallest mountain in the Ozarks.

Arriving at my destination, I saw two wagons were tied up at the hitching rack. I knew some farmers had come to the store, so I waited until they left. As I walked in, I saw my grandfather behind the counter. Tugging and pulling, I worked the can out of my pocket and dumped it out in front of him and looked up.

Grandpa was dumbfounded. He tried to say something, but it wouldn't come out. He looked at me, and he looked at the pile of coins. Finally, in a voice much louder than he ordinarily used, he asked, "Where did you get all this?"

"I told you, Grandpa," I said, "I was saving my money so I could buy two hound pups, and I did. You said you would order them for me. I've got the money and now I want you to order them."

Grandpa stared at me over his glasses, and then back at the money.

"How long have you been saving this?" he asked.

"A long time, Grandpa," I said.

"How long?" he asked.

I told him, "Two years."

His mouth flew open and in a loud voice he said, "Two years!"

I nodded my head.

The way my grandfather stared at me made me uneasy. I was on needles and pins. Taking his eyes from me, he glanced back at the money. He saw the faded yellow piece of paper sticking out from the coins. He worked it out, asking as he did, "What's this?"

I told him it was the ad, telling where to order my dogs.

He read it, turned it over, and glanced at the other side.

I saw the astonishment leave his eyes and the friendly-old-grandfather look come back. I felt much better.

Dropping the paper back on the money, he turned, picked up an old turkey-feather duster, and started dusting where there was no dust. He kept glancing at me out of the corner of his eye as he walked slowly down to the other end of the store, dusting here and there.

He put the duster down, came from behind the counter, and walked up to me. Laying a friendly old work-calloused hand on my head, he changed the conversation altogether, saying, "Son, you need a haircut."

I told him I didn't mind. I didn't like my hair short; flies and mosquitoes bothered me.

He glanced down at my bare feet and asked, "How come your feet are cut and scratched like that?"

I told him it was pretty tough picking blackberries barefoot.

He nodded his head.

It was too much for my grandfather. He turned and walked away. I saw the glasses come off, and the old red handkerchief come out. I heard the good excuse of blowing his nose. He stood for several seconds with his back toward me. When he turned around, I noticed his eyes were moist.

In a quavering voice, he said, "Well, Son, it's your money. You worked for it, and you worked hard. You got it honestly, and you want some dogs. We're going to get those dogs.

He walked over and picked up the ad again, asking, "Is this two years old, too?"

I nodded.

"Well," he said, "the first thing we have to do is write this outfit. There may not even be a place like this in Kentucky any more. After all, a lot of things can happen in two years."

Seeing that I was worried, he said, "Now you go on home. I'll write to these kennels and I'll let you know when I get an answer. If we can't get the dogs there, we can get them someplace else. And I don't think, if I were you, I'd let my Pa know anything about this right now. I happen to know he wants to buy that red mule from Old Man Potter."

I told him I wouldn't, and turned to leave the store.

As I reached the door, my grandfather said in a loud voice, "Say, it's been a long time since you've had any candy, hasn't it?"

I nodded my head.

He asked, "How long?"

I told him, "A long time."

"Well," he said, "we'll have to do something about that."

Walking over behind the counter, he reached out and got a sack. I noticed it wasn't one of the nickel sacks. It was one of the quarter kind.

My eyes never left my grandfather's hand. Time after time, it dipped in and out of the candy counter: peppermint sticks, jawbreakers, horehound, and gumdrops. The sack bulged. So did my eyes.

Handing the sack to me, he said, "Here. First big coon you catch with those dogs, you can pay me back."

I told him I would.

On my way home, with a jawbreaker in one side of my mouth and a piece of horehound in the other, I skipped and hopped, making half an effort to try to whistle and sing, and couldn't for the candy. I had the finest grandpa in the world and I was the happiest boy in the world.

I wanted to share my happiness with my sisters but decided not to say anything about ordering the pups.

Arriving home, I dumped the sack of candy out on the bed. Six little hands helped themselves. I was well repaid by the love and adoration I saw in the wide blue eyes of my three little sisters.

Day after day, I flew to the store. Grandpa would shake his head. Then on a Monday, as I entered the store, I sensed a change in him. He was in high spirits, talking and laughing with half a dozen farmers. Every time I caught his eye, he would smile and wink at me. I thought the farmers would never leave, but finally the store was empty.

Grandpa told me the letter had come. The kennels were still there, and they had dogs for sale. He said he had made the mail buggy wait while he made out the order. And, another thing, the dog market had gone downhill. The price of dogs had dropped five dollars. He handed me a ten-dollar bill.

"Now, there's still one stump in the way," he said. "The mail buggy can't carry things like dogs, so they'll come as far as the depot at Tahlequah, but you'll get the notice here because I ordered them in your name."

I thanked my grandfather with all my heart and asked him how long I'd have to wait for the notice.

He said, "I don't know, but it shouldn't take more than a couple of weeks."

I asked how I was going to get my dogs out from Tahlequah.

"Well, there's always someone going in," he said, "and you could ride in with them."

That evening the silence of our supper was interrupted when I asked my father this question: "Papa, how far is it to Kentucky?"

I may as well have exploded a bomb. For an instant there was complete silence, and then my oldest sister giggled. The two little ones stared at me.

With a half-hearted laugh, my father said, "Well, now, I don't know, but it's a pretty good ways. What do you want to know for? Thinking of taking a trip to Kentucky?"

"No," I said. "I just wondered."

My youngest sister giggled and asked, "Can I go with you?"

I glared at her.

Mama broke into the conversation, "I declare, what kind of a question is that? How far is it to Kentucky? I don't know what's gotten into that mind of yours lately. You go around like you were lost, and you're losing weight. You're as skinny as a rail, and look at that hair. Just last Sunday they had a haircutting over at Tom Rolland's place, but you couldn't go. You had to go prowling around the river and the woods."

I told Mama that I'd get a haircut next time they had a cutting. And I just heard some fellows talking about Kentucky up at the store, and wondered how far away it was. Much to my relief, the conversation was ended.

The days dragged by. A week passed and still no word about my dogs. Terrible thoughts ran through my mind. Maybe my dogs were lost; the train had a wreck; someone stole my money; or perhaps the mailman lost my order. Then, at the end of the second week, the notice came.

My grandfather told me that he had talked to Jim Hodges that day. He was going into town in about a week and I could ride in with him to pick up my dogs. Again I thanked my grandfather.

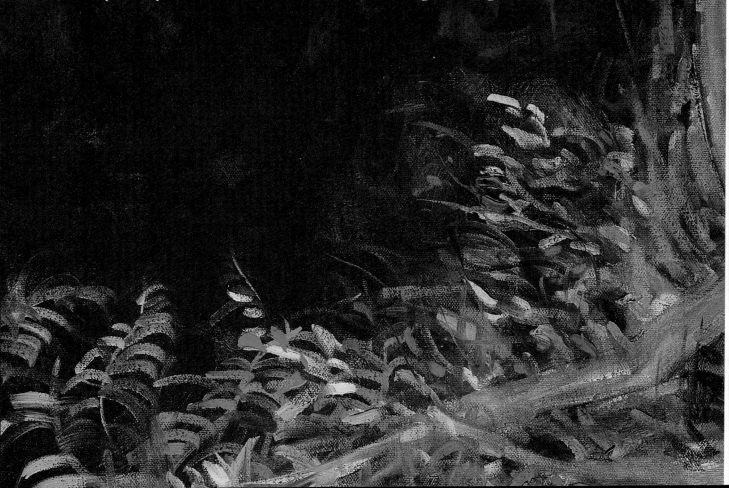

I started for home. Walking along in deep thought, I decided it was time to tell my father the whole story. I fully intended to tell him that evening. I tried several times, but somehow I couldn't. I wasn't scared of him, for he never whipped me. He was always kind and gentle, but for some reason, I don't know why, I just couldn't tell him.

That night, snuggled deep in the soft folds of a feather bed, I lay thinking. I had waited so long for my dogs, and I so desperately wanted to see them and hold them. I didn't want to wait a whole week.

In a flash I made up my mind. Very quietly I got up and put on my clothes. I sneaked into the kitchen and got one of Mama's precious flour sacks. In it I put six eggs, some leftover corn bread, a little salt, and a few matches. Next I went to the smokehouse and cut off a piece of salt pork. I stopped at the barn and picked up a gunny sack. I put the flour sack inside the gunny sack. This I rolled up and crammed lengthwise in the bib of my overalls.

I was on my way. I was going after my dogs.

Tahlequah was a small country town with a population of about eight hundred. By the road it was thirty-two miles away, but as the crow flies, it was only twenty miles. I went as the crow flies, straight through the hills.

On arriving at the depot, my nerve failed me. I was afraid to go in. I didn't know what I was scared of, but I was scared.

Before going around to the front, I peeked in a window. The stationmaster was in his office looking at some papers. He was wearing a funny little cap that had no top in it. He looked friendly enough but I still couldn't muster up enough courage to go in.

I cocked my ear to see if I could hear puppies crying, but could hear nothing. A bird started chirping. It was a yellow canary in a cage. The stationmaster walked over and gave it some water. I thought, "Anyone that is kind to birds surely wouldn't be mean to a boy."

With my courage built up I walked around to the front and eased myself past the office. He glanced at me and turned back to the papers. I walked clear around the depot and again walked slowly past the office. Glancing from the corner of my eye, I saw the stationmaster looking at me and smiling. He opened the door and came out on the platform. I stopped and leaned against the building.

Yawning and stretching his arms, he said, "It sure is hot today. It doesn't look like it's ever going to rain."

I looked up at the sky and said, "Yes, sir. It is hot and we sure could do with a good rain. We need one bad up where I come from."

He asked where I lived.

I told him, "Up the river a ways."

"You know," he said, "I have some puppies in there for a boy that lives up on the river. His name is Billy Colman. I know his dad, but never have seen the boy. I figured he would be in after them today."

On hearing this remark, my heart jumped clear up in my throat. I thought surely it was going to hop right out on the depot platform. I looked up and tried to tell him who I was, but something went wrong. When the words finally came out they sounded like the squeaky old pulley on our well when Mama drew up a bucket of water.

I could see a twinkle in the stationmaster's eyes. He came over and laid his hand on my shoulder. In a friendly voice he said, "So you're Billy Colman. How is your dad?"

I told him Papa was fine and handed him the slip my grandpa had given me.

"They sure are fine-looking pups," he said. "You'll have to go around to the freight door."

I'm sure my feet never touched the ground as I flew around the building. He unlocked the door, and I stepped in, looking for my dogs. I couldn't see anything but boxes, barrels, old trunks, and some rolls of barbed wire.

The kindly stationmaster walked over to one of the boxes.

"Do you want box and all?" he asked.

I told him I didn't want the box. All I wanted was the dogs.

"How are you going to carry them?" he asked. "I think they're a little too young to follow."

I held out my gunny sack.

He looked at me and looked at the sack. Chuckling, he said, "Well, I guess dogs can be carried that way same as anything else, but we'll have to cut a couple of holes to stick their heads through so that they won't smother."

Getting a claw hammer, he started tearing off the top of the box. As nails gave way and boards splintered, I heard several puppy whimpers. I didn't walk over. I just stood and waited.

After what seemed like hours, the box was open. He reached in, lifted the pups out, and set them down on the floor.

"Well, there they are," he said. "What do you think of them?"

I didn't answer. I couldn't. All I could do was stare at them.

They seemed to be blinded by the light and kept blinking their eyes. One sat down on his little rear and started crying. The other one was waddling around and whimpering.

I wanted so much to step over and pick them up. Several times I tried to move my feet, but they seemed to be nailed to the floor. I knew the pups were mine, all mine, yet I couldn't move. My heart started acting like a drunk grasshopper. I tried to swallow and couldn't. My Adam's apple wouldn't work.

One pup started my way. I held my breath. On he came until I felt a scratchy little foot on mine. The other pup followed. A warm puppy tongue caressed my sore foot.

I heard the stationmaster say, "They already know you."

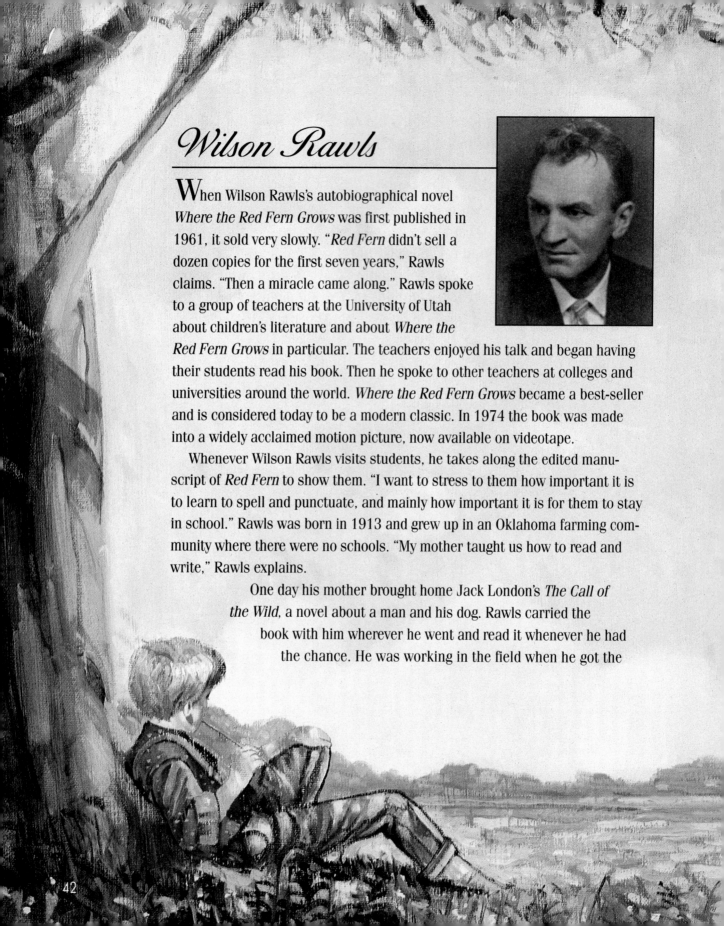

Wilson Rawls

When Wilson Rawls's autobiographical novel *Where the Red Fern Grows* was first published in 1961, it sold very slowly. "*Red Fern* didn't sell a dozen copies for the first seven years," Rawls claims. "Then a miracle came along." Rawls spoke to a group of teachers at the University of Utah about children's literature and about *Where the Red Fern Grows* in particular. The teachers enjoyed his talk and began having their students read his book. Then he spoke to other teachers at colleges and universities around the world. *Where the Red Fern Grows* became a best-seller and is considered today to be a modern classic. In 1974 the book was made into a widely acclaimed motion picture, now available on videotape.

Whenever Wilson Rawls visits students, he takes along the edited manuscript of *Red Fern* to show them. "I want to stress to them how important it is to learn to spell and punctuate, and mainly how important it is for them to stay in school." Rawls was born in 1913 and grew up in an Oklahoma farming community where there were no schools. "My mother taught us how to read and write," Rawls explains.

One day his mother brought home Jack London's *The Call of the Wild*, a novel about a man and his dog. Rawls carried the book with him wherever he went and read it whenever he had the chance. He was working in the field when he got the idea to write his own book, something like *The Call of the Wild*. That idea later became *Where the Red Fern Grows*.

"When speaking in the schools," he says, "I tell youngsters to keep reaching out for whatever goals they set for themselves. As long as they are honest and truthful and don't hurt anyone along the way, they will have help in reaching their goal. I know I did."

Larry Winborg

Growing up in Idaho Falls, Idaho, Larry Winborg spent time in his father's automobile repair shop. Though his father wanted Larry to follow in his footsteps and take over the business, Larry had decided by the first grade that he wanted to become an artist. One day when Larry was about fourteen, a gentleman came into the shop. Larry's brother nudged him excitedly. "That's Wilson Rawls! He wrote *Where the Red Fern Grows*." Larry Winborg thinks back fondly to his encounter with the famous author who had moved to Idaho Falls to be near the good fishing. "It's quite a coincidence that I'm illustrating this story today," says Larry. Larry has since left Idaho and now lives on a mountainside in Utah with his wife, who is a weaver, and their four children. Besides illustrating for magazines, Larry paints landscapes from a wealth of subjects right around his home. "When you look out a window in my house, it's like looking at a postcard."

Winborg

CREATE AN AD

TO BUY OR NOT TO BUY

Pets for sale are advertised in different ways. Write a magazine advertisement describing a particular pet for sale. Illustrate your ad to attract buyers. Ask a partner to tell whether, based on your ad, he or she would purchase the pet and why or why not.

MAKE A SAVINGS PLAN

A PENNY SAVED IS A PENNY EARNED

Imagine that you have saved $5. An item you want to buy costs $20. Develop a plan for earning and saving the needed amount. List chores or activities you could do to earn money. What amount should you charge for each job or activity?

RESPONSE

MAKE A WISH LIST

THE DOG-WANTING DISEASE

Billy says he has the "dog-wanting disease." What do you think he means by that? Work with a small group to discuss things you think are worth working hard for. What "wanting diseases" do members of your group have?

WHAT DO YOU THINK?

- What kind of person is Billy? Describe him by using incidents from the story.

- Would you like to know Billy? Why or why not?

- Have you ever worked hard for something the way Billy did? Tell about it.

CORNER

Last Summer with Maizon

by Jacqueline Woodson

Illustrated by Alaiyo Bradshaw

"Sure wish you weren't going away," Margaret said, choking back tears for what seemed like the millionth time. They were sitting on the M train, crossing the Williamsburg Bridge, and Margaret shivered as the train passed over the water. The L train would have made the trip easier but the L didn't go over the bridge and Maizon had wanted to ride over it once more before she left.

Maizon sat nervously drumming her fingers against the windowpane. "Me too," she said absently.

Margaret looked over at Mama and Grandma. Grandma stared out of her window. She looked old and out of place on the train.

"Maizon?" Margaret said, turning back toward her.

"Hmm?" Maizon frowned. She seemed to be concentrating on something in the water. It rippled and danced below them.

"Even though I wrote you those two letters, you only have to write me one back if you don't have a lot of time or something." Margaret looked down at her fingers. She had begun biting the cuticles, and now the skin surrounding her nails was red and ragged.

"I'll write you back," Maizon promised.

"Maizon . . ."

"What, Margaret!"

Margaret jumped and looked at Maizon. There was an uneasiness in her eyes she had never seen before.

"Forget it," she said.

Ms. Tory leaned over. "We'll be getting off in a few stops."

They rode the rest of the way in silence. At Delancey Street they changed for another train and a half hour later they were at Penn Station.

"I guess now we'll have to call each other to plan the same outfits," Maizon said as they waited for her train. Her voice sounded forced and fake, Margaret thought, like a grown-up trying to make a kid smile.

"I guess," Margaret said. The conductor called Maizon's train.

"I guess I gotta go," Maizon said softly, and Margaret felt a lump rise in her throat.

"I'll write you back, Margaret. Promise. Thanks for letting me keep the double-dutch trophy even if it is only second place." They hugged for a long time. Maizon sniffed loudly. "I'm scared, Margaret," she whispered.

Margaret didn't know what to say. "Don't be."

"Bye, Ms. Tory."

Margaret's mother bent down and hugged Maizon. "Be good," she said as Maizon and her grandmother made their way toward the train.

"Mama," Margaret said as they watched Maizon and her grandmother disappear into the tunnel.

"What, dear?"

"What's the difference between a best friend and an old friend?"

"I guess . . ." Her mother thought for a moment. "I guess an old friend is a friend you once had and a best friend is a friend you'll always have."

"Then maybe me and Maizon aren't best friends anymore."

"Don't be silly, Margaret. What else would you two be? Some people can barely tell you apart. I feel like I've lost a daughter."

"Maybe . . . I don't know . . . Maybe we're old friends now. Maybe this was our last summer as best friends. I feel like something's going to change now and I'm not going to be able to change it back."

Ms. Tory's heels made a clicking sound through the terminal. She stopped to buy tokens and turned to Margaret.

"Like when Daddy died?" she asked, looking worried.

Margaret swallowed. "No. I just feel empty instead of sad, Mama," she said.

Her mother squeezed her hand as they waited for the train. When it came, they took seats by the window.

Ms. Tory held on to Margaret's hand. "Sometimes it just takes a while for the pain of loss to set in."

"I feel like sometimes Maizon kept me from doing things, but now she's not here. Now I don't have any"—Margaret thought for a moment, but couldn't find the right words—"now I don't have any excuse not to do things."

When the train emerged from its tunnel, the late afternoon sun had turned a bright orange. Margaret watched it for a moment. She looked at her hands again and discovered a cuticle she had missed.

Margaret pressed her pencil to her lips and stared out the classroom window. The school yard was desolate and gray. But everything seemed that way since Maizon left. Especially since a whole week had passed now without even a letter from her. Margaret sighed and chewed her eraser.

"Margaret, are you working on this assignment?"

Margaret jumped and turned toward Ms. Peazle. Maizon had been right—Ms. Peazle was the crabbiest teacher in the school. Margaret wondered why she had been picked to teach the smartest class. If students were so smart, she thought, the least the school could do was reward them with a nice teacher.

"I'm trying to think about what to write, Ms. Peazle."

"Well, you won't find an essay on your summer vacation outside that window, I'm sure. Or is that where you spent it?"

The class snickered and Margaret looked down, embarrassed. "No, ma'am."

"I'm glad to hear that," Ms. Peazle continued, looking at Margaret over granny glasses. "And I'm sure in the next ten minutes you'll be able to read your essay to the class and prove to us all that you weren't just daydreaming. Am I right?"

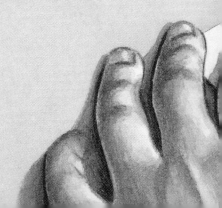

"I hope so, ma'am," Margaret mumbled. She looked around the room. It seemed everyone in 6-1 knew each other from the previous year. On the first day, a lot of kids asked her about Maizon, but after that no one said much to her. Things had changed since Maizon left. Without her, a lot of the fun had gone out of sitting on the stoop with Ms. Dell, Hattie, and Li'l Jay. Maybe she could write about that. No, Margaret thought, looking down at the blank piece of paper in front of her. It was too much to tell. She'd never get finished and Ms. Peazle would scold her—making her feel too dumb to be in 6-1. Margaret chewed her eraser and stared out the window again. There had to be something she could write about quickly.

"Margaret Tory!" Ms. Peazle warned. "Am I going to have to change your seat?"

"Ma'am? I was just . . ."

"I think I'm going to have to move you away from that window unless you can prove to me that you can sit there without being distracted."

"I can, Ms. Peazle. It helps me write," she lied.

"Then I take it you should be ready to read your essay in"—Ms. Peazle looked at her watch—"the next seven minutes."

Margaret started writing frantically. When Ms. Peazle called her to the front of the room, her sheet of notebook paper shook in her hand. She pulled nervously at the hem of the maroon dress she and Maizon had picked out for school and tried not to look out at the twenty-six pairs of eyes she knew were on her.

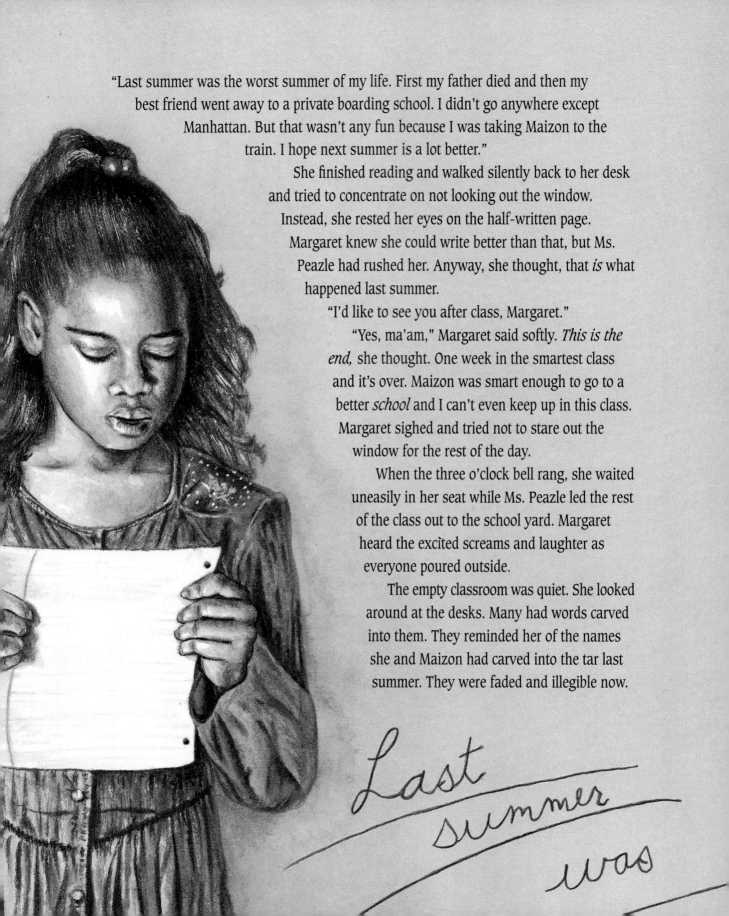

"Last summer was the worst summer of my life. First my father died and then my best friend went away to a private boarding school. I didn't go anywhere except Manhattan. But that wasn't any fun because I was taking Maizon to the train. I hope next summer is a lot better."

She finished reading and walked silently back to her desk and tried to concentrate on not looking out the window. Instead, she rested her eyes on the half-written page. Margaret knew she could write better than that, but Ms. Peazle had rushed her. Anyway, she thought, that *is* what happened last summer.

"I'd like to see you after class, Margaret."

"Yes, ma'am," Margaret said softly. *This is the end,* she thought. One week in the smartest class and it's over. Maizon was smart enough to go to a better *school* and I can't even keep up in this class. Margaret sighed and tried not to stare out the window for the rest of the day.

When the three o'clock bell rang, she waited uneasily in her seat while Ms. Peazle led the rest of the class out to the school yard. Margaret heard the excited screams and laughter as everyone poured outside.

The empty classroom was quiet. She looked around at the desks. Many had words carved into them. They reminded her of the names she and Maizon had carved into the tar last summer. They were faded and illegible now.

Last summer was

Ms. Peazle came in and sat at the desk next to Margaret's. "Margaret," she said slowly, pausing for a moment to remove her glasses and rub her eyes tiredly. "I'm sorry to hear about your father . . ."

"That's okay." Margaret fidgeted.

"No, Margaret, it's not okay," Ms. Peazle continued, "not if it's going to affect your schoolwork."

"I can do better, Ms. Peazle, I really can!" Margaret looked up pleadingly. She was surprised at herself for wanting so badly to stay in Ms. Peazle's class.

"I know you can, Margaret. That's why I'm going to ask you to do this. For homework tonight . . ."

Margaret started to say that none of the other students had been assigned homework. She decided not to, though.

"I want you to write about your summer," Ms. Peazle continued. "I want it to express all of your feelings about your friend Maizon going away. Or it could be about your father's death and how you felt then. It doesn't matter what you write, a poem, an essay, a short story. Just so long as it expresses how you felt this summer. Is that understood?"

"Yes, ma'am." Margaret looked up at Ms. Peazle. "It's understood."

Ms. Peazle smiled. Without her glasses, Margaret thought, she wasn't that mean-looking.

"Good, then I'll see you bright and early tomorrow with something wonderful to read to the class."

Margaret slid out of the chair and walked toward the door.

"That's a very pretty dress, Margaret," Ms. Peazle said.

Margaret turned and started to tell her that Maizon was wearing the same one in Connecticut, but changed her mind. What did Ms. Peazle know about best friends who were almost cousins, anyway?

"Thanks, ma'am," she said instead, and ducked out of the classroom. All of a sudden, she had a wonderful idea!

the worst summer of my life

The next morning Ms. Peazle tapped her ruler against the desk to quiet the class. "Margaret," she asked when the room was silent. "Do you have something you want to share with us today?"

Margaret nodded and Ms. Peazle beckoned her to the front of the room.

"This," Margaret said, handing Ms. Peazle the sheet of looseleaf paper. It had taken her most of the evening to finish the assignment.

Ms. Peazle looked it over and handed it back to her.

"We're ready to listen," she said, smiling.

Margaret looked out over the class and felt her stomach slide up to her throat. She swallowed and counted to ten. Though the day was cool, she found herself sweating. Margaret couldn't remember when she had been this afraid.

"My pen doesn't write anymore," she began reading.

"I can't hear," someone called out.

"My pen doesn't write anymore," Margaret repeated. In the back of the room, someone exaggerated a sigh. The class chuckled. Margaret ignored them and continued to read.

"It stumbles and trembles in my hand.
If my dad were here—he would understand.
Best of all—It'd be last summer again.

But they've turned off the fire hydrants
Locked green leaves away.
Sprinkled ashes on you
and sent you on your way.

I wouldn't mind the early autumn
if you came home today
I'd tell you how much I miss you
and know I'd be okay.

Mama isn't laughing now
She works hard and she cries
she wonders when true laughter
will relieve her of her sighs
And even when she's smiling
Her eyes don't smile along
her face is growing older
She doesn't seem as strong.
I worry cause I love her
Ms. Dell says, 'where there is love,
there is a way.'

It's funny how we never know
exactly how our life will go
It's funny how a dream can fade
With the break of day.

I'm not sure where you are now
though I see you in my dreams
Ms. Dell says the things we see
are not always as they seem.

So often I'm uncertain
if you have found a new home
and when I am uncertain
I usually write a poem.

Time can't erase the memory
and time can't bring you home
Last summer was a part of me
and now a part is gone."

The class stared at her blankly, silent. Margaret lowered her head and made her way back to her seat.

"Could you leave that assignment on my desk, Margaret?" Ms. Peazle asked. There was a small smile playing at the corners of her mouth.

"Yes, ma'am," Margaret said. Why didn't anyone say anything?

"Now, if everyone will open their history books to page two seventy-five, we'll continue with our lesson on the Civil War."

Margaret wondered what she had expected the class to do. Applaud? She missed Maizon more than she had in a long time. *She would know what I'm feeling,* Margaret thought. And if she didn't, she'd make believe she did.

Margaret snuck a look out the window. The day looked cold and still. *She'd tell me it's only a feeling poets get and that Nikki Giovanni feels this way all of the time.* When she turned back, there was a small piece of paper on her desk.

"I liked your poem, Margaret," the note read. There was no name.

Margaret looked around but no one looked as though they had slipped a note on her desk. She smiled to herself and tucked the piece of paper into her notebook.

The final bell rang. As the class rushed out, Margaret was bumped against Ms. Peazle's desk.

"Did you get my note?" Ms. Peazle whispered. Margaret nodded and floated home.

Ms. Dell, Hattie, and Li'l Jay were sitting on the stoop when she got home.

"If it weren't so cold," she said, squeezing in beside Hattie's spreading hips, "it would be like old times."

"Except for Maizon," Hattie said, cutting her eyes toward her mother.

"Hush, Hattie," Ms. Dell said. She shivered and pulled Li'l Jay closer to her. For a moment, Margaret thought she looked old.

"It's just this cold spell we're having," Ms. Dell said. "Ages a person. Makes them look older than they are."

Margaret smiled. "Reading minds is worse than eavesdropping, Ms. Dell."

"Try being her daughter for nineteen years," Hattie said.

"Hattie," Margaret said, moving closer to her for warmth. "How come you never liked Maizon?"

"No one said I never liked her."

"No one had to," Ms. Dell butted in.

"She was just too much ahead of everyone. At least she thought she was."

"But she was, Hattie. She was the smartest person at P.S. 102. Imagine being the smartest person."

"But she didn't have any common sense, Margaret. And when God gives a person that much brain, he's bound to leave out something else."

"Like what?"

Ms. Dell leaned over Li'l Jay's head and whispered loudly, "Like the truth."

She and Hattie laughed but Margaret couldn't see the humor. It wasn't like either of them to say something wrong about a person.

"She told the truth . . ." Margaret said weakly.

Ms. Dell and Hattie exchanged looks.

"How was school?" Hattie asked too brightly.

"Boring," Margaret said. She would tuck what they said away until she could figure it out.

"That's the only word you know since Maizon left. Seems there's gotta be somethin' else going on that's not so *boring* all the time," Ms. Dell said.

"Well, it's sure not school. I read a poem to that stupid class and no one but Ms. Peazle liked it." She sighed and rested her chin on her hand.

"That's the chance you gotta take with poetry," Ms. Dell said. "Either everybody likes it or everybody hates it, but you hardly ever know, 'cause nobody says a word. Too afraid to offend you or, worse yet, make you feel good."

Margaret looked from Ms. Dell to Hattie then back to Ms. Dell again.

"How come you know so much about poetry?"

"You're not the first li'l black girl who wanted to be a poet."

"And you can bet your dress you won't be the last," Hattie concluded.

"You wanted to be a poet, Hattie??!!"

"Still do. Still make up poems in my head. Never write them down, though. The paper just yellows and clutters useful places. So this is where I keep it all now," she said, pointing to her head.

"A poem can't exist inside your head. You forget it," Margaret said doubtfully.

"Poems don't exist, Miss Know-It-All. Poems live! In your head is where a poem is born, isn't it?"

Margaret nodded and Hattie continued. "Well, my poetry chooses to live there!"

"Then recite one for me, please." Margaret folded her arms across her chest the way she had seen Ms. Dell do so many times.

"Some poems aren't meant to be heard, smarty-pants."

"Aw, Hattie," Ms. Dell interrupted, "let Margaret be the judge of that."

"All right. All right." Hattie's voice dropped to a whisper. "Brooklyn-bound robin redbreast followed me from down home / Brooklyn-bound robin, you're a long way from your own / So fly among the pigeons and circle the sky with your song."

They were quiet. Ms. Dell rocked Li'l Jay to sleep in her arms. Hattie looked somberly over the block in silence and Margaret thought of how much Hattie's poem made her think of Maizon. What was she doing now that the sun was almost down? she wondered. Had she found a new best friend?

"Maybe," she said after a long time. "Maybe it wasn't that the class didn't like my poem. Maybe it was like your poem, Hattie. You just have to sit quietly and think about all the things it makes you think about after you hear it. You have to let . . . let it sink in!"

"You have to feel it, Margaret," Hattie said softly, draping her arm over Margaret's shoulder.

"Yeah. Just like I felt when I wrote my poem, or you felt when you found a place for that one in your head!"

"Margaret," Ms. Dell said, "you gettin' too smart for us ol' ladies."

followed me from down home Brooklyn~bound

Margaret leaned against Hattie and listened to the fading sounds of construction. Soon the building on Palmetto Street would be finished. She closed her eyes and visions of last summer came into her head. She saw herself running down Madison Street arm in arm with Maizon. They were laughing. Then the picture faded into a new one. She and Maizon were sitting by the tree watching Li'l Jay take his first steps. He stumbled and fell into Maizon's arms. Now it all seemed like such a long time ago.

When she opened her eyes again, the moon was inching out from behind a cloud. It was barely visible in the late afternoon. The sky had turned a wintry blue and the streetlights flickered on. Margaret yawned, her head heavy all of a sudden from the long day.

"Looks like your mother's workin' late again. Bless that woman's heart. Seems she's workin' nonstop since your daddy passed."

"She's taking drawing classes. She wants to be an architect. Maybe she'll make a lot of money."

"Architects don't make a lot of money," Hattie said. "And anyway, you shouldn't be worrying your head over money."

"She has a gift," Ms. Dell said. "All of you Torys have gifts. You with your writing, your mama with her drawings, and remember the things your daddy did with wood. Oh, that man was something else!"

"What's Li'l Jay's going to be?"

Ms. Dell stood up and pressed Li'l Jay's face to her cheek.

"Time's gonna tell us, Margaret. Now, come inside and do your homework while I fix you something to eat. No use sitting out in the cold."

Margaret rose and followed them inside.

"You hear anything from Maizon yet?" Hattie asked.

Margaret shook her head. If only Maizon were running up the block!

"I wrote her two letters and she hasn't written me one. Maybe she knows we're not really best friends anymore." Margaret sighed. She had been right in thinking she and Maizon were only old friends now, not the friends they used to be. "Still, I wish I knew how she was doing," she said, turning away so Hattie wouldn't see the tears in her eyes.

"We all do, honey," Hattie said, taking Margaret's hand. "We all do."

Two weeks later, Margaret sat at the kitchen table, scribbling furiously into her diary. When she looked up, the clock on the kitchen wall said ten thirty. She couldn't believe she had spent three hours writing. She flipped back to where she had begun and counted. Fifteen pages! Margaret heard her mother's key in the lock and quickly stuffed the diary back into her bookbag.

"Margaret," her mother said, coming into the kitchen, "what are you doing up? It's after ten o'clock."

"I wanted to stay up to tell you the news," Margaret said. Her mother sat across from her. "Ms. Peazle entered my poem in a contest! If I win, I get scholarship money and I get to read it in front of the mayor!"

Ms. Tory smiled and Margaret almost laughed with pleasure at the pride in her mother's eyes. "That's wonderful, Margaret," she said, rising to give Margaret a hug.

Margaret shivered a little. They had never sat like this before, just the two of them in the soft quiet light of the kitchen. The feeling was new and strange. She felt closer to her mother all of a sudden. And the closeness felt grown-up and good.

"That would have made your daddy proud," her mother said softly.

Margaret swallowed. She hadn't thought about her father all day and now, looking away from the sadness in her mother's eyes, she saw her father clearly, smiling proudly down at her.

"He is proud, Mama," Margaret whispered. "From his place in heaven, he's real proud."

Her mother shook her head and dabbed at her eyes quickly, then rose. "Want to have some tea with me to celebrate?" she asked, going over to the stove. Not waiting for an answer, she put the teabags in cups and turned on the fire beneath the kettle. "You hear anything from Maizon?"

Margaret looked down at the table. The cloth blurred a little. Maizon had left a month ago. She shook her head.

Her mother turned back to the stove and poured the water into the cups. "I guess Blue Hill must be pretty hard. It's not like Maizon not to let anyone know how she's doing." She brought the cups over to the table. Margaret blew at the cloud of steam above her cup. "Have you spoken to her grandmother? Maybe she's heard something."

Margaret shook her head again. "I haven't been by there since Maizon left." All of a sudden she felt guilty. "It would just make me miss her more."

"She must be pretty lonely in that big house by herself," her mother said, reading her thoughts.

Margaret took a small sip of tea. It was minty and almost bitter. "I'll go see her after school tomorrow."

The kitchen fell silent. "You think Maizon forgot about Madison Street, Mama?"

Her mother laughed a little uncertainly. "It would take a lot to forget Madison Street."

"I was talking to some girls in school and they said they like me better since Maizon left. They said she was bossy and snotty."

Her mother looked up. "What did you say to them?"

Margaret picked nervously at the vinyl checkered tablecloth. The small hole wore away to a bigger one.

"Don't, Margaret," her mother said gently.

"I didn't say anything," she admitted.

"Don't let them say bad things about her when she's not here to defend herself. That's not what a real friend would do."

Margaret swallowed and took a quick sip of tea. The hot liquid washed the sadness back down for a moment.

"I wanted to tell them that Maizon's not like that, that they didn't know her like I did," she said quietly.

Her mother laid her hand on top of Margaret's. "Why didn't you? It's not like you not to."

Margaret shrugged. "The words got stuck. Those girls never paid any attention to me. I wanted them to keep liking me. I don't hardly have any friends in school." She looked up at her mother helplessly. "I felt real bad when I walked away, though."

Her mother shook her head. "It's hard to know what to do," she said, almost to herself. "I miss your father and I want to talk about him with a friend sometimes, but then I don't want anyone to remind me how empty I feel." She sniffed and gave Margaret a weak smile. "You better get to bed. School tomorrow."

"You okay, Mama?" She felt as though a strong wind had blown in between them, pulling them further and further apart. The closeness she had felt a moment ago was gone.

"It's going to take time, Margaret. Everything will fall into place. But it's going to take time."

Margaret hugged her. "We have a lot of time, Mama."

Jacqueline Woodson

Jacqueline Woodson was born in Ohio, grew up in South Carolina, and later moved with her family to Brooklyn, New York. Brooklyn became the setting for her trilogy of books about Maizon and Margaret: *Last Summer with Maizon, Maizon at Blue Hill,* and *Between Madison and Palmetto.*

Many of Jacqueline Woodson's story ideas come from her own experiences helping people in trouble. She has worked as a drama therapist in New York City's shelters, helping runaway teens and homeless people cope with their problems. She writes about African American young people and the different issues they struggle with. *Maizon at Blue Hill,* for example, focuses on the struggles of a gifted Black child. "These issues were absent in literature I read growing up," she says, "issues I want my own children to grow up enlightened about."

Woodson has taught writing at Goddard College in Vermont and has visited classrooms to speak to children about writing. "I write remembering the child I was, am still, will always be," she says. "You can't write a book without putting a little of yourself into it. You mix a bit of yourself up with your imagination."

Alaiyo Bradshaw

Alaiyo Bradshaw was born in London, England, and now lives in Brooklyn, New York. She likes going to the movies, shopping, and reading, but mostly she loves to paint using watercolors. She currently teaches art at both the Newark School of Fine and Industrial Arts in New Jersey and at Parsons School of Design in New York City.

Alaiyo

RESPONSE CORNER

LEAN ON ME

Margaret asks her mother about the difference between an *old* friend and a *best* friend. How would you define each? Write a short essay comparing and contrasting the two types of friends.

68

SCHOOL'S OUT!

Draw an outline of a large window on a sheet of paper. Inside the window frame, write a poem about a vacation from school. Decorate the window, and display your poem in the classroom.

PLAYFUL POETRY

Why does Margaret like poetry by Nikki Giovanni? Work with a group to find some poems by the poet. Talk about what seems important to her. Have members of your group take turns reading the poems to the rest of the class while others act them out.

WHAT DO YOU THINK?

- Why does Margaret feel that Maizon has become an old friend rather than a best friend?

- Have you ever felt sad and lonely like Margaret? What did someone else do or say to make you feel better?

- Do you think that by the end of the story Margaret has moved toward accepting her father's death and Maizon's absence?

Art and Literature

In this theme, you read of characters who learn something about themselves as they meet challenges. What traits might the young men in the painting share with the characters in the stories? Why do you think so? What does the painting show you about meeting challenges?

The Biglin Brothers Racing (1873)
by Thomas Eakins

Thomas Eakins studied mathematics and medicine as well as art. This background helped him paint figures in motion that were almost as lifelike as those in photographs. In The Biglin Brothers Racing, *Eakins shows two of his friends sculling, or rowing, in a race on the Schuylkill River in Pennsylvania.*

70

LENGE

Award-Winning
Author

FROM *LOCAL NEWS*

by Gary Soto

ILLUSTRATED BY
MIKE REED

For three weeks José tried to get the attention of Estela, the new girl at his middle school. She's cute, he said to himself when he first saw her in the cafeteria, unloading her lunch of two sandwiches, potato chips, a piece of cake wrapped in waxed paper, and boxed juice from a brown paper bag. "Man, can she grub!"

On the way home from school he walked through the alleys of his town, Fresno, kicking cans. He was lost in a dream, trying to figure out a way to make Estela notice him. He thought of tripping in front of her while she was leaving her math class, but he had already tried that with a girl in sixth grade. All he did was rip his pants and bruise his knee, which kept him from playing in the championship soccer game. And that girl had just stepped over him as he lay on the ground, the shame of rejection reddening his face.

He thought of going up to Estela and saying, in his best James Bond voice, "Camacho. José Camacho, at your service." He imagined she would say, "Right-o," and together they would go off and talk in code.

He even tried doing his homework. Estela was in his history class, and so he knew she was as bright as a cop's flashlight shining in your face. While they were studying Egypt, José amazed the teacher, Mrs. Flores, when he scored twenty out of twenty on a quiz—and then eighteen out of twenty when she retested him the same day because she thought that he had cheated.

"Mrs. Flores, I studied hard—¡de veras![1] You can call my mom," he argued, his feelings hurt. And he *had* studied, so much that his mother had asked, "¿Qué pasó? What's wrong?"

"I'm going to start studying," he'd answered.

His mother bought him a lamp because she didn't want him to strain his eyes. She even fixed him hot chocolate and watched her son learn about the Egyptian god Osiris, about papyrus and mummification. The mummies had scared her so much that she had heated up a second cup of chocolate to soothe herself.

But when the quizzes had been returned and José bragged, "Another A-plus," Estela didn't turn her head and ask, "Who's that brilliant boy?" She just stuffed her quiz into her backpack and left the classroom, leaving José behind to retake the test.

One weekend he had wiped out while riding his bike, popping up over curbs with his eyes closed. He somersaulted over his handlebars and saw a flash of shooting stars as he felt the slap of his skin against the asphalt. Blood rushed from his nostrils like twin rivers. He bicycled home, his blood-darkened shirt pressed to his nose. When he examined his face in the mirror, he saw that he had a scrape on his chin, and he liked that. He thought Estela might pity him. In history class she would cry, "Oh, what happened?" and then he would talk nonsense about a fight with three *vatos*.[2]

But Estela had been absent the Monday and Tuesday after his mishap. By the time she returned on Wednesday his chin had nearly healed.

José figured out another way to get to know her. He had noticed the grimy, sweat-blackened handle of a racket poking out of her backpack. He snapped his fingers and said to himself, "Racquetball. I'll challenge her to a game."

---

[1] de veras (dā·bā´räs): truly

[2] vatos (bä´tōs): guys

He approached her during lunch. She was reading from her science book and biting into her second sandwich, which was thick with slabs of meat, cheese, and a blood-red tomato. "Hi," José said, sitting across the table from her. "How do you like our school?"

Estela swallowed, cleared her throat, drank from her milk carton until it collapsed, and said, "It's OK. But the hot water doesn't work in the girls' showers."

"It doesn't work in ours either," he remarked. Trying to push the conversation along, he continued, "Where are you from?"

"San Diego," she said. She took another monstrous bite of her sandwich, which amazed José and made him think of his father, a carpenter, who could eat more than anyone José knew.

José, eager to connect, took a deep breath and said, "I see that you play racquetball. You wanna play a game?"

"Are you good?" Estela asked flatly. She picked up a slice of tomato that had slid out of her sandwich.

"Pretty good," he said without thinking as he slipped into a lie. "I won a couple of tournaments."

He watched as the tomato slice slithered down Estela's throat. She wiped her mouth and said, "Sure. How about after school on Friday."

"That's tomorrow," José said.

"That's right. Today's Thursday and tomorrow's Friday." She flattened the empty milk carton with her fist, slapped her science book closed, and hurled the carton and her balled-up lunch bag at the plastic-lined garbage can.

"What's your name?"

"Camacho. José Camacho."

"I'm Estela. My friends call me Stinger."

"Stinger?"

"Yeah, Stinger. I'll meet you at the courts at 3:45." She got up and headed toward the library.

After school José pedaled his bike over to his uncle Freddie's house. His uncle was sixteen, only three years older than José. It made José feel awkward when someone, usually a girl, asked, "Who's that hunk?" and he would have to answer, "My uncle."

"Freddie," José yelled, skidding to a stop in the driveway.

Freddie was in the garage lifting weights. He was dressed in sweats and a Raiders sweatshirt, the hem of his T-shirt sticking out in a fringe. He bench-pressed 180 pounds, then put the weights down and said, "Hey, dude."

"Freddie, I need to borrow your racquetball racket," José said.

Freddie rubbed his sweaty face on the sleeve of his sweatshirt. "I didn't know you played."

"I don't. I got a game tomorrow."

"But you don't know how to play."

José had been worrying about this on his bike ride over. He had told Estela that he had won tournaments.

"I'll learn," José said.

"In one day? Get serious."

"It's against a girl."

"So. She'll probably whip you twenty-one to *nada*."[3]

"No way."

But José's mind twisted with worry. What if she did, he asked himself. What

---

[3] nada (nä´dä): nothing

if she whipped him through and through. He recalled her crushing the milk carton with one blow of her fist. He recalled the sandwiches she downed at lunch. Still, he had never encountered a girl who was better than he was at sports, except for Dolores Ramirez, who could hit homers with the best of them.

Uncle Freddie pulled his racket from the garage wall. Then he explained to José how to grip the racket. He told him that the game was like handball, that the play was off the front, the ceiling, and the side walls. "Whatever you do, don't look behind you. The ball comes back—fast. You can get your *ojos*⁴ knocked out."

"Yeah, I got it," José said vaguely, feeling the weight of the racket in his hand. He liked how it felt when he pounded the sweet spot of the strings against his palm.

---

⁴ ojos (ō´ hōs): eyes

Freddie resumed lifting weights, and José biked home, swinging the racket as he rode.

That night after dinner José went outside and asked his father, "Dad, has a girl ever beaten you at anything?"

His father was watering the grass, his shirt off and a stub of cigarette dangling from his mouth. His pale belly hung over his belt, just slightly, like a deflated ball.

"Only talking," he said. "They can outtalk a man any day of the week."

"No, in sports."

His father thought for a while and then said, "No, I don't think so."

His father's tone of voice didn't encourage José. So he took the racket and a tennis ball and began to practice against the side of the garage. The ball raced away like a rat. He retrieved it and tried again. Every time, he hit it either too softly or too hard, and he couldn't get the rhythm of a rally going.

"It's hard," he said to himself. But then he remembered that he was playing with a tennis ball, not a racquetball. He assumed that he would play better with a real ball.

The next day school was as dull as usual. He took a test in history and returned to his regular score of twelve out of twenty. Mrs. Flores was satisfied.

"I'll see you later," Estela said, hoisting her backpack onto one shoulder, the history quiz crumpled in her fist.

"OK, Estela," he said.

"Stinger," she corrected.

"Yeah, Stinger. 3:45."

José was beginning to wonder whether he really liked her. Now she seemed abrupt, not cute. She was starting to look like Dolores "Hit 'n' Spit" Ramirez—tough.

After school José walked slowly to the outdoor three-walled courts. They were empty, except for a gang of sparrows pecking at an old hamburger wrapper.

José practiced hitting the tennis ball against the wall. It was too confusing. The ball would hit the front wall, then ricochet off the side wall. He spent most of his time running after the ball or cursing himself for bragging that he had won tournaments.

Estela arrived, greeting José with a jerk of her chin and a "Hey, dude." She was dressed in white sweats. A pair of protective goggles dangled around her neck like a necklace, and she wore sweatbands on both wrists. She opened a can of balls and rolled one out into her palm, squeezing it so tightly that her forearm rippled with muscle. When she smacked the ball against the wall so hard that the echo hurt his ears, José realized that he was in trouble. He felt limp as a dead fish.

Estela hit the ball repeatedly. When she noticed that José was just standing there, his racket in one hand and a dog-slobbered tennis ball in the other, she asked, "Aren't you going to practice?"

"I forgot my balls at home," he said.

"Help yourself." She pointed with the racket toward the can.

José took a ball, squeezed it, and bounced it once. He was determined to give Estela a show. He bounced it again, swung with all his might, and hit it out of the court.

"Oops," he said. "I'll go get it, Stinger."

He found the ball in the gutter, splotched with mud that he wiped off on his pants. When he returned to the court Estela had peeled off her sweats and was working a pair of knee pads up her legs. José noticed that her legs were bigger than his, and they quivered like the flanks of a thoroughbred horse.

"You ready?" she asked, adjusting her goggles over her eyes. "I have to leave at five."

"Almost," he said. He took off his shirt, then put it back on when he realized how skinny his chest was. "Yeah, I'm ready. You go first."

Estela, sizing him up, said, "No, you go first."

José decided to accept the offer. He figured he needed all the help he could get. He bounced the ball and served it into the ground twice.

"You're out," she said, scooping the ball up onto her racket and walking briskly to the service box.

José wanted to ask why, but he kept quiet. After all, he thought, I am the winner of several tournaments.

"Zero-zero," Estela said, then served the ball, which ricocheted off the front and side walls. José swung wildly and missed by at least a foot. Then he ran after the ball, which had rolled out of the court onto the grass. He returned it to Estela and said, "Nice, Estela."

"Stinger."

"Yeah, Stinger."

Estela called out, "One-nothing." She wound up again and sizzled the ball right at José's feet. He swung and hit his kneecap with the racket. The pain jolted him like a shock of electricity as he went down, holding his knee

and grimacing. Estela chased the ball for him. "Can you play?" she asked. He nodded as he rose to his feet.

"Two-nothing," she said, again bouncing the ball off the front wall, this time slower so that José swung before the ball reached his racket. He swung again, the racket spinning like a whirlwind. The ball sailed slowly past him, and he had to chase it down again.

"I guess that's three to nothing, right?" José said lamely.

"Right." Estela lobbed the ball. As it came down, José swung hard. His racket slipped from his fingers and flew out of the court.

"Oops," he said. The racket was caught on the top of the chain-link fence surrounding the courts. For a moment José thought of pulling the racket down and running home.

But he had to stick it out. Anyway, he thought, my backpack is at the court. "Four-nothing," Estela called when she saw José running back to the court, his chest heaving. She served again, and José, closing his eyes, connected. The ball hit the wall, and for three seconds they had a rally going. But then Estela moved in and killed the ball with a low corner shot.

"Five-nothing," she said.

83

"It's getting cold. Let me get my sweats back on."

She slipped into her sweats and threw off her sweat-bands. José thought about asking to borrow the sweatbands because he had worked up a lather of sweat. But his pride kept him quiet.

Estela served again and again until the score was seventeen to nothing and José was ragged from running. He wished the game would end. He wished he would score just one point. He took off his shirt and said, "Hey, you're pretty good."

Estela served again, gently this time, and José managed to return the ball to the front wall. Estela didn't go after it, even though she was just a couple of feet from the ball. "Nice corner shot," she lied. "Your serve."

José served the ball and, hunching over with his racket poised, took crab steps to the left, waiting for the ball to bounce off the front wall. Instead he heard a thunderous smack and felt himself leap like a trout. The ball had hit him in the back, and it stung viciously. He ran off the court and threw himself on the grass, grimacing from the pain. It took him two minutes to recover, time enough for Estela to take a healthy swig from the bottle of Gatorade in her sport bag. Finally, through his teeth, he muttered, "Good shot, Stinger."

"Sorry," Estela said. "You moved into my lane. Serve again."

José served and then cowered out of the way, his racket held to his face for protection. She fired the ball back, clean and low, and once again she was standing at the service line calling, "Service."

Uncle Freddie was right. He had lost twenty-one to *nada.* After a bone-jarring handshake and a pat on his aching back from Estela, he hobbled to his uncle's house, feeling miserable. Only three weeks ago he'd been hoping that Estela—Stinger—might like him. Now he hoped she would stay away from him.

Uncle Freddie was in the garage lifting weights. Without greeting him, José hung the racket back on the wall. Uncle Freddie lowered the weights, sat up, and asked, "So how did it go?"

José didn't feel like lying. He lifted his T-shirt and showed his uncle the big red mark the ball had raised on his back. "She's bad."

"It could have been your face," Freddie said as he wiped away sweat and lay back down on his bench. "Too bad."

José sat on a pile of bundled newspapers, hands in his lap. When his uncle finished his "reps," José got up slowly and peeled the weights down to sixty pounds. It was his turn to lift. He needed strength to mend his broken heart and for the slight chance that Stinger might come back, looking for another victory.

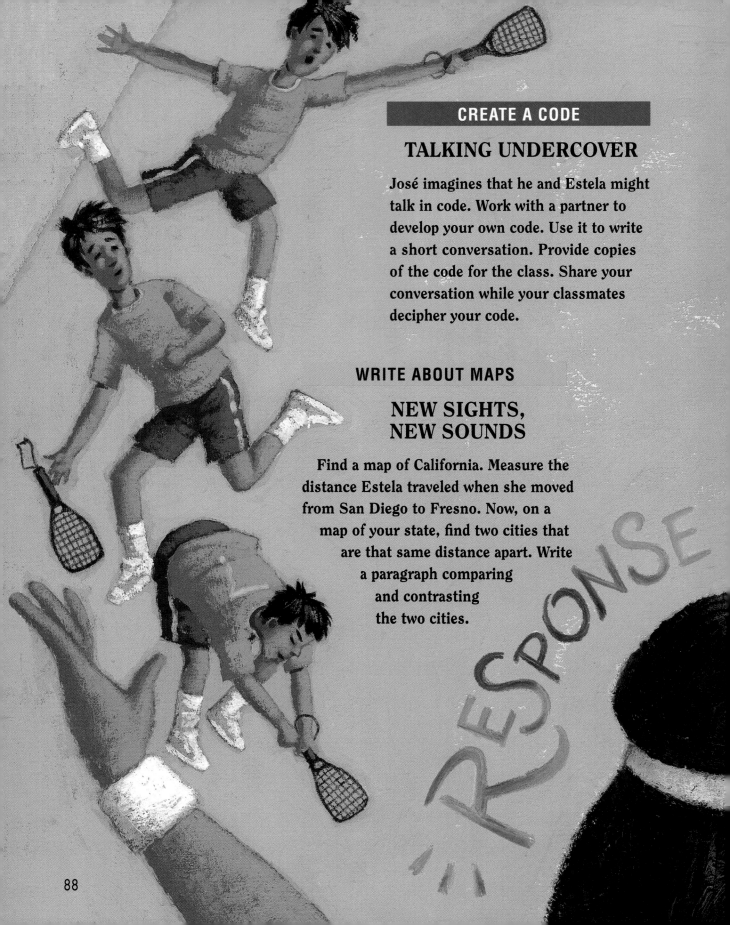

TALKING UNDERCOVER

José imagines that he and Estela might talk in code. Work with a partner to develop your own code. Use it to write a short conversation. Provide copies of the code for the class. Share your conversation while your classmates decipher your code.

WRITE ABOUT MAPS

NEW SIGHTS, NEW SOUNDS

Find a map of California. Measure the distance Estela traveled when she moved from San Diego to Fresno. Now, on a map of your state, find two cities that are that same distance apart. Write a paragraph comparing and contrasting the two cities.

RESPONSE

INTERVIEW A FRIEND

SPORTS REPORT

Interview a friend or family member who plays one sport regularly. Ask how the sport keeps the person physically fit. Record your interview and share your new knowledge with the rest of the class.

WHAT DO YOU THINK?

- What do you think José learns about himself by playing against Estela?

- How do you feel about José's situation? Explain your answer.

- Does José choose the best way to get to know Estela? Explain your answer.

Gary Soto

Gary Soto's youthful outlook on life led him to write stories for children. He likes writing short stories because they are easier to share. And with short stories he doesn't have to keep notes. Instead, he says, "When I get an idea for a story, I pounce on it right away to keep it from disappearing." Gary Soto also writes nonfiction. In "The Inner Tube," he recalls an incident from his childhood.

Gary Soto

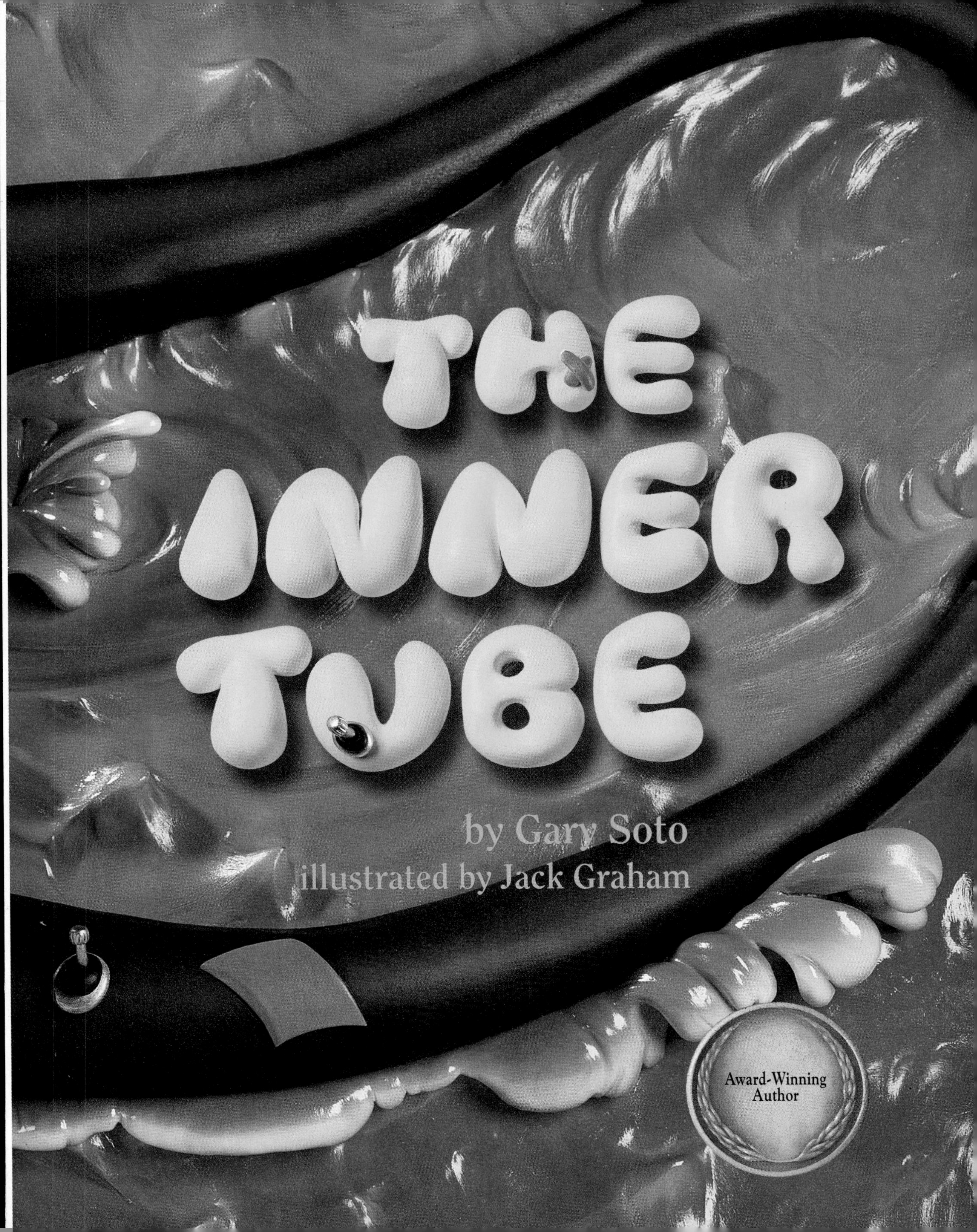

THE INNER TUBE

by Gary Soto

illustrated by Jack Graham

Award-Winning
Author

he tractor inner tube hung in defeat on a nail, accompanied by three flies swinging back and forth, sentries of all that goes unused in a garage. The heat was oppressive for July, especially so for a one-car garage full of the smells of paint remover and open jars of red salmon eggs. I stepped over boxes of old clothes and warped magazines, a lawn mower, and oily engine parts. I kicked over a lamp shade, the bulb bursting its brittle glass, and pushed aside fishing tackle. I reached for the inner tube and touched the rigging of a spider web. I pulled it off quickly and leaped through the debris to the patio. Sweat flooded my face and forked down my arms. I grabbed our hose and washed the inner tube, a slack mouth that I carried over my shoulder to a friend's house.

David had a tire patch kit. He inflated the inner tube with a bicycle pump, and it filled unevenly, one side growing fat like a swollen mouth backhanded by a mean brother. He let the air out, stomped it flat as a shadow, and tried again. Again the air swelled to one side. We stared at the inner tube in confusion.

I asked, "What's wrong with it?"

David didn't say anything. Instead, he jumped up and down on the fat side, but although I joined his weight, laughing as I jumped, the air wouldn't move to the skinny side. After that, we stopped because there was no time to waste. Kathy's pool party was at 1:00, and it was already a quarter after twelve.

We lowered our ears and listened for the hiss of air.

"Put your finger there," David said once we found the puncture. I licked a finger and pressed it into the deflating tube while he squeezed the glue and got the matches ready. But first he scratched the puncture so the patch would stick. I removed my finger, and he buffed the tube back and forth with the rough lid of the tire patch kit. He then smeared the glue and lit the match, the blue flame exciting us for a few seconds. He quickly fit the patch over the puncture and counted to twenty before taking his finger away. We lassoed the inner tube, now nearly deflated, onto the handlebars of my bicycle.

e sat under his cool sycamore waiting for the patch to dry. I asked David what went on at a "pool party," and he said he thought there would be cake and ice cream and races in the pool. I thought about this for a while. The only party that I knew was a birthday party, so when I received an invitation in the mail to a "pool party," I thought it involved the kind of *pool* that my stepfather and uncle shot at Uncle Tom's Tavern. After I caught on, I began to plan what to wear and what to take. I had a snorkel and fins, but my brother had lent the snorkel to his loudmouth friends and it disgusted me that I should fill my mouth with the rubber thing that others had sucked in dirty canals. And the fins were too small; they left painful rings on the insteps of my feet. At the last minute I remembered the inner tube.

David and I got up and poked the patch tenderly, as if it were a wound. The inner tube was healed. He pumped it up until it was huge, and a hollow *thump* resounded when I flicked a finger against the taut skin. I got on my bicycle, and with the

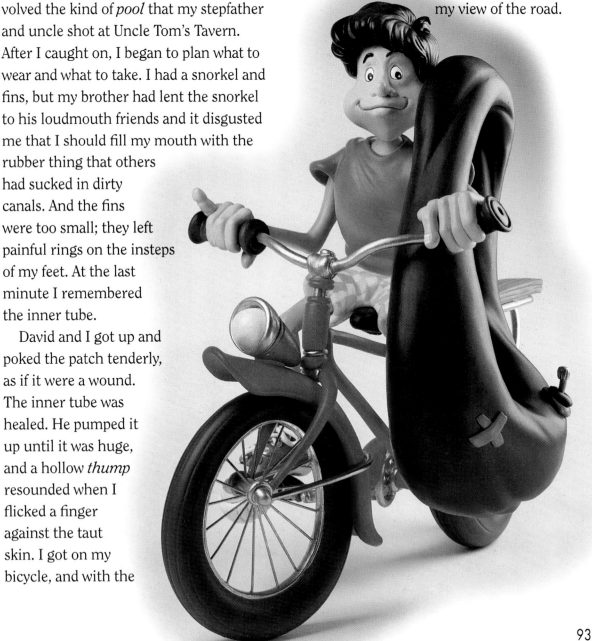

inner tube crossed over my shoulder, David gave me a good push. The bike wobbled, but straightened as my legs strained for speed. I was off to a "pool party."

By the time I arrived I was sweaty and nearly dead from not seeing oncoming cars, because every time I turned left the inner tube blocked my view of the road.

he mother who answered the door clapped her hands and said, "Wow!" When I had difficulty getting the inner tube through the front door, she suggested that I go along the side of the house to the backyard. I rolled and pushed and lugged the inner tube, and when everyone saw me come around a bush, they yelled, "Gary's got a tire." I was more than sweaty. My once clean T-shirt was now smeared black along the front, and my hair, earlier parted on the right side and smelling sweetly of Wildroot hair cream, was flat as a blown-over hut. I licked my lips and tasted the hair cream.

When Kathy said hello, I waved my invitation at her and told her I nearly got killed by three cars. Then I jumped into the pool and stayed under for a long time. I was hot, so oiled up by the two-mile ride with an inner tube over my shoulder. I surfaced, got out, and threw the tube in the water. Someone asked, "How come it's big on one side?"

I shrugged, leaped in, and came up among an armada of pink and yellow air mattresses and an inflated plastic swan with a drooping neck. I tried to climb

onto the swan, but it sank under my weight. I swam over to my tube, which was like a doctor's couch on the water, huge and plush. Two boys joined me, then a girl, and finally, Kathy and her best friend. We floated around the pool, pushing aside the air mattresses and dunking the plastic swan for good. We stood up on the tube, the boys on the fat side, the girls on the skinny side, and bounced up and down, sometimes falling off but quickly climbing back on. We jumped and laughed, until a toe peeled off the patch and our feet began to mash the deflating tube. Stinky bubbles hissed on the water, and we began to sink, very slowly and happily.

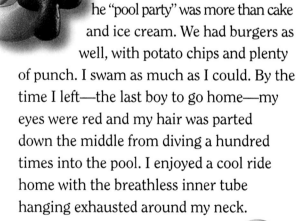

he "pool party" was more than cake and ice cream. We had burgers as well, with potato chips and plenty of punch. I swam as much as I could. By the time I left—the last boy to go home—my eyes were red and my hair was parted down the middle from diving a hundred times into the pool. I enjoyed a cool ride home with the breathless inner tube hanging exhausted around my neck.

Island of the Blue Dolphins

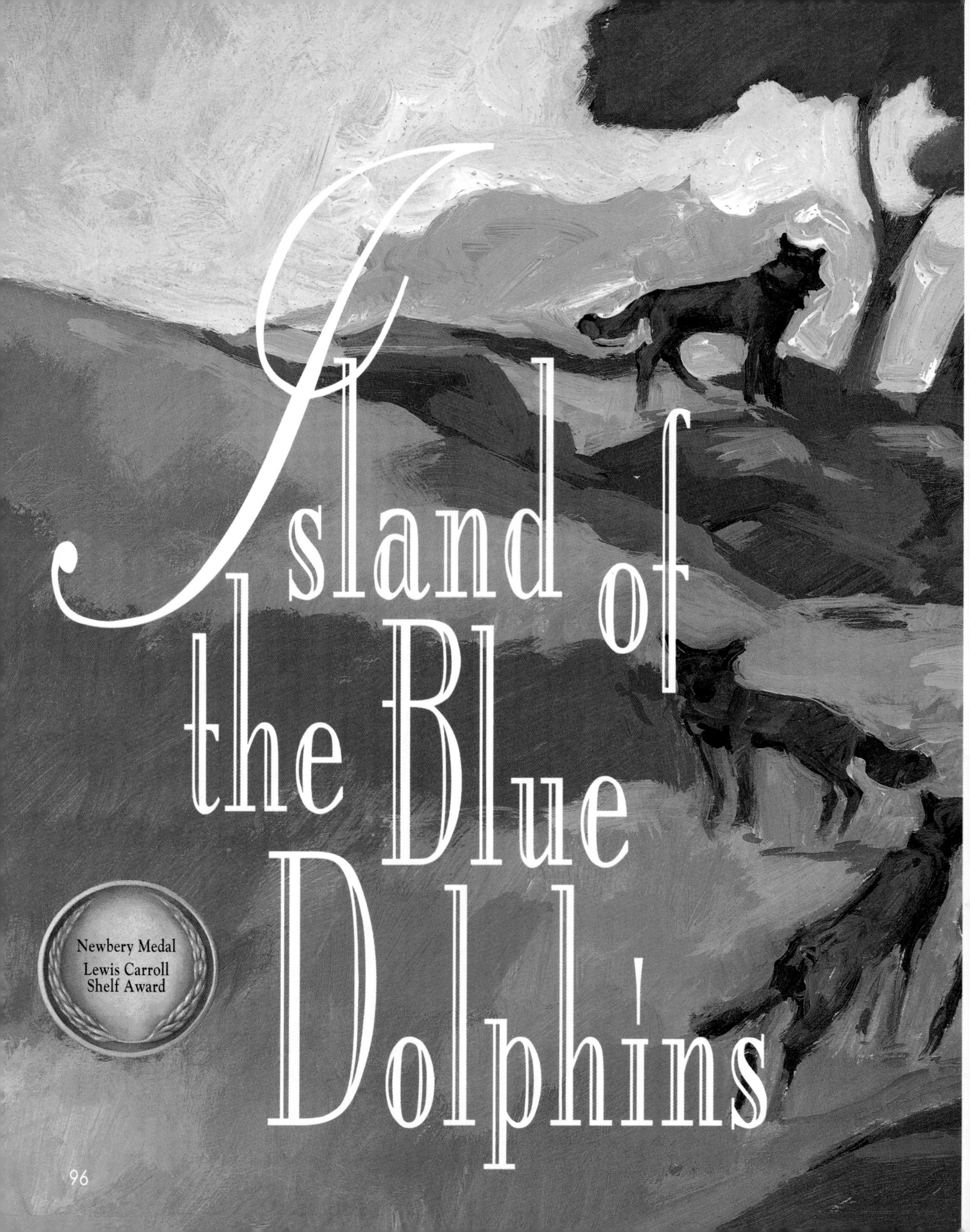

Newbery Medal
Lewis Carroll
Shelf Award

BY SCOTT O'DELL

ILLUSTRATED BY LORI LOHSTOETTER

IN THE EARLY 1800S, KARANA, A NATIVE AMERICAN GIRL, LIVED WITH HER TRIBE ON AN ISLAND OFF THE COAST OF CALIFORNIA. ALEUT HUNTERS ATTACKED THE TRIBE, KILLING MOST OF THE MEN. FEARFUL OF ANOTHER ATTACK, KARANA AND THE OTHER REMAINING VILLAGERS BOARDED A RESCUE SHIP BOUND FOR THE MAINLAND. WHEN KARANA DISCOVERED HER YOUNG BROTHER HAD ACCIDENTALLY BEEN LEFT BEHIND, SHE DOVE OFF THE SHIP AND SWAM BACK TO THE ISLAND. TWO DAYS LATER, KARANA'S BROTHER WAS KILLED BY A PACK OF WILD DOGS, AND SHE WAS LEFT TOTALLY ALONE.

THERE HAD been wild dogs on the Island of the Blue Dolphins as long as I remember, but after the Aleuts had slain most of the men of our tribe and their dogs had left to join the others, the pack became much bolder. It spent the nights running through the village and during the day was never far off. It was then that we made plans to get rid of them, but the ship came and everyone left Ghalas-at.

I am sure that the pack grew bolder because of their leader, the big one with the thick fur around his neck and the yellow eyes.

I had never seen this dog before the Aleuts came and no one else had, so he must have come with them and been left behind when they sailed away. He was a much larger dog than any of ours, which besides have short hair and brown eyes. I was sure that he was an Aleut dog.

Already I had killed five of the pack, but there were many left, more than in the beginning, for some had been born in the meantime. The young dogs were even wilder than the old ones.

I first went to the hill near the cave when the pack was away and collected armloads of brush which I placed near the mouth of their lair. Then I waited until the pack was in the cave. It went there early in the morning to sleep after it had spent the night prowling. I took with me the big bow and five arrows and two of the spears. I went quietly, circling around the mouth of the cave and came up to it from the side. There I left all of my weapons except one spear.

I set fire to the brush and pushed it into the cave. If the wild dogs heard me, there was no sound from them. Nearby was a ledge of rock which I climbed, taking my weapons with me.

The fire burned high. Some of the smoke trailed out over the hill, but much of it stayed in the cave. Soon the pack would have to leave. I did not hope to kill more than five of them because I had only that many arrows, but if the leader was one of the five I would be satisfied. It might be wiser if I waited and saved all my arrows for him, and this I decided to do.

None of the dogs appeared before the fire died. Then three ran out and away. Seven more followed and a long time afterwards a like number. There were many more still left in the cave.

The leader came next. Unlike the others, he did not run away. He jumped over the ashes and stood at the mouth of the cave, sniffing the air. I was so close to him that I could see his nose quivering, but he did not see me until I raised my bow. Fortunately I did not frighten him.

He stood facing me, his front legs spread as if he were ready to spring, his yellow eyes narrowed to slits. The arrow struck him in the chest. He turned away from me, took one step and fell. I sent another arrow toward him which went wide.

At this time three more dogs trotted out of the cave. I used the last of my arrows and killed two of them.

Carrying both of the spears, I climbed down from the ledge and went through the brush to the place where the leader had fallen. He was not there. While I had been shooting at the other dogs, he had gone. He could not have gone far because of his wound, but though I looked everywhere, around the ledge where I had been standing and in front of the cave, I did not find him.

I waited for a long time and then went inside the cave. It was deep, but I could see clearly.

Far back in a corner was the half-eaten carcass of a fox. Beside it was a black dog with four gray pups. One of the pups came slowly toward me, a round ball of fur that I could have held in my hand. I wanted to hold it, but the mother leaped to her feet and bared her teeth. I raised my spear as I backed out of the cave, yet I did not use it. The wounded leader was not there.

Night was coming and I left the cave, going along the foot of the hill that led to the cliff. I had not gone far on this trail that the wild dogs used when I saw the broken shaft of an arrow. It had been gnawed off near the tip and I knew it was from the arrow which had wounded the leader

Farther on I saw his tracks in the dust. They were uneven as if he were traveling slowly. I followed them toward the cliff, but finally lost them in the darkness.

The next day and the next it rained and I did not go to look for him. I spent those days making more arrows, and on the third day, with these arrows and my spear, I went out along the trail the wild dogs had made to and from my house.

There were no tracks after the rain, but I followed the trail to the pile of rocks where I had seen them before. On the far side of the rocks I found the big gray dog. He had the broken arrow in his chest and he was lying with one of his legs under him.

He was about ten paces from me so I could see him clearly. I was sure that he was dead, but I lifted the spear and took good aim at him. Just as I was about to throw the spear, he raised his head a little from the earth and then let it drop.

This surprised me greatly and I stood there for a while not knowing what to do, whether to use the spear or my bow. I was used to animals playing dead until they suddenly turned on you or ran away.

The spear was the better of the two weapons at this distance, but I could not use it as well as the other, so I climbed onto the rocks where I could see him if he ran. I placed my feet carefully. I had a second arrow ready should I need it. I fitted an arrow and pulled back the string, aiming at his head.

Why I did not send the arrow I cannot say. I stood on the rock with the bow pulled back and my hand would not let it go. The big dog lay there and did not move and this may be the reason. If he had gotten up I would have killed him. I stood there for a long time looking down at him and then I climbed off the rocks.

He did not move when I went up to him, nor could I see him breathing until I was very close. The head of the arrow was in his chest and the broken shaft was covered with blood. The thick fur around his neck was matted from the rain.

I do not think that he knew I was picking him up, for his body was limp, as if he were dead. He was very heavy and the only way I could lift him was by kneeling and putting his legs around my shoulders.

In this manner, stopping to rest

when I was tired, I carried him to the headland.

I could not get through the opening under the fence, so I cut the bindings and lifted out two of the whale ribs and thus took him into the house. He did not look at me or raise his head when I laid him on the floor, but his mouth was open and he was breathing.

The arrow had a small point, which was fortunate, and came out easily though it had gone deep. He did not move while I did this, nor afterwards as I cleaned the wound with a peeled stick from a coral bush. This bush has poisonous berries, yet its wood often heals wounds that nothing else will.

I had not gathered food for many days and the baskets were empty, so I left water for the dog and, after mending the fence, went down to the sea. I had no thought that he would live and I did not care.

All day I was among the rocks gathering shellfish and only once did I think of the wounded dog, my enemy, lying there in the house, and then to wonder why I had not killed him.

He was still alive when I got back, though he had not moved from the place where I had left him. Again I cleaned the wound with a coral twig. I then lifted his head and put water in his mouth, which he swallowed. This was the first time that he had looked at me since the time I had found him on the trail. His eyes were sunken and they looked out at me from far back in his head.

Before I went to sleep I gave him more water. In the morning I left food for him when I went down to the sea, and when I came home he had eaten it. He was lying in the corner, watching me. While I made a fire and cooked my supper, he watched me.

His yellow eyes followed me wherever I moved.

That night I slept on the rock, for I was afraid of him, and at dawn as I went out I left the hole under the fence open so he could go. But he was there when I got back, lying in the sun with his head on his paws. I had speared two fish, which I cooked for my supper. Since he was very thin, I gave him one of them, and after he had eaten it he came over and lay down by the fire, watching me with his yellow eyes that were very narrow and slanted up at the corners.

Four nights I slept on the rock, and every morning I left the hole under the fence open so he could leave. Each day I speared a fish for him and when I got home he was always at the fence waiting for it. He would not take the fish from me so I had to put it on the ground. Once I held out my hand to him, but at this he backed away and showed his teeth.

On the fourth day when I came back from the rocks early he was not there at the fence waiting. A strange feeling came over me. Always before when I returned, I had hoped that he would be gone. But now as I crawled under the fence I did not feel the same.

I called out, "Dog, Dog," for I had no other name for him.

I ran toward the house, calling it. He was inside. He was just getting to his feet, stretching himself and yawning. He looked first at the fish I carried and then at me and moved his tail.

That night I stayed in the house. Before I fell asleep I thought of a name for him, for I could not call him Dog. The name I thought of was Rontu, which means in our language Fox Eyes.

Scott O'Dell

Scott O'Dell moved around a lot when he was growing up. There was San Pedro, which is a part of Los Angeles. And there was also Rattlesnake Island, across the bay from San Pedro, where he lived in a house on stilts.

In 1960, when O'Dell began to write *Island of the Blue Dolphins*, his first book for young people, he remembered those early years on Rattlesnake Island. He and other boys his age used logs as canoes and paddled with their hands around the bay, exploring the surrounding islands. Karana, the heroine of the novel, is based on a Mexican girl named Carolina, whose father took care of the small house that O'Dell and his wife rented one summer. His fond memories of Rattlesnake Island and of Carolina were part of what inspired O'Dell to write *Island of the Blue Dolphins*. O'Dell hoped that his book would convey a simple message: "Forgive your enemies and have respect for life—all life."

A SONG
OF GREATNESS

a Chippewa Indian song
(transcribed by M...
illustrated by Rocco Baviera

When I hear the old men
Telling of heroes,
Telling of great deeds
Of ancient days,
When I hear them telling,
Then I think within me
I too am one of these.

When I hear the people
Praising great ones,
Then I know that I too
Shall be esteemed,
I too when my time comes
Shall do mightily.

Response Corner

DESCRIBE A JOB

DOCTOR DOOLITTLE TODAY

Karana takes care of Rontu, the wild dog. Veterinarians take care of exotic creatures, as well as household pets. Work with a partner to find out more about the training and work of a veterinarian. Write a job description.

WRITE A POEM

THROUGH CANINE EYES

Imagine that you are Rontu. Write a poem from his perspective in which you describe how you feel about Karana and her actions. Share your poem with your classmates.

KARANA THE GREAT?

Do you think Karana is a heroine? Can a "song of greatness" be sung about her? Write your thoughts in a paragraph.

What Do You Think?

- How do Karana's feelings toward the dog change during the story?

- Karana makes a choice about the wild dog. Would you make the same choice? Explain your answer.

- Do you think Karana is brave? Explain your answer.

The people in this theme faced challenges in different ways. As they displayed determination, perseverance, courage, and self-reliance, what do you think they learned about themselves?

How did the way Karana handled her challenge differ from the way José handles his? Explain your answer.

Theme Wrap-Up

ACTIVITY CORNER

Is there something that you have been wanting to do but are afraid to try? Describe your challenging goal in a paragraph. Then list the steps you could take to achieve it. Does your goal seem reasonable? If so, take the first step toward it today.

THEME

Ancient Civilizations

What was life like in ancient Egypt and China? Folktales, artifacts, and ruins help us explore the stories and secrets of wealthy kings, clever generals, greedy thieves, and brave heroes.

THEME
Ancient Civilizations

CONTENTS

Tales of a Dead King
by Walter Dean Myers

John Robie and Karen Lacey travel to Egypt to investigate secrets of the pharaohs, but first they must unravel a modern-day mystery.

AWARD-WINNING AUTHOR

SIGNATURES LIBRARY

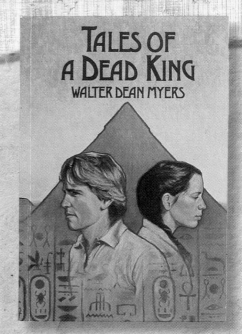

Bookshelf

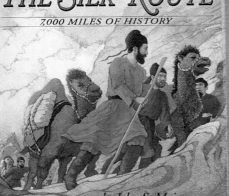

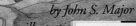

The Silk Route
by John S. Major
illustrated by Stephen Fieser

Vivid illustrations bring to life the difficult journey made by Chinese silk merchants along a 7,000-mile trail that came to be known as the Silk Route.

SIGNATURES LIBRARY

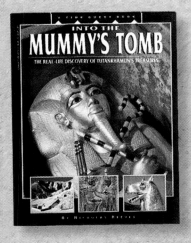

Into the Mummy's Tomb: The Real-Life Discovery of Tutankhamun's Treasures
by Nicholas Reeves

Read about one of history's greatest archaeological finds in this fast-paced account of Howard Carter's famous discovery.

TEACHER'S CHOICE, *SLJ* BEST BOOKS, NOTABLE TRADE BOOK IN SOCIAL STUDIES

Aïda
told by Leontyne Price
illustrated by Leo Dillon and Diane Dillon

Aïda, an Ethiopian princess, must make a difficult decision when she falls in love with an officer of the Egyptian army.

ALA NOTABLE BOOK, CORETTA SCOTT KING AWARD

Growing Up in Ancient China
by Ken Teague

People in China developed their own arts, philosophy, and science about 2,000 years ago. Find out what everyday life was like in this ancient civilization.

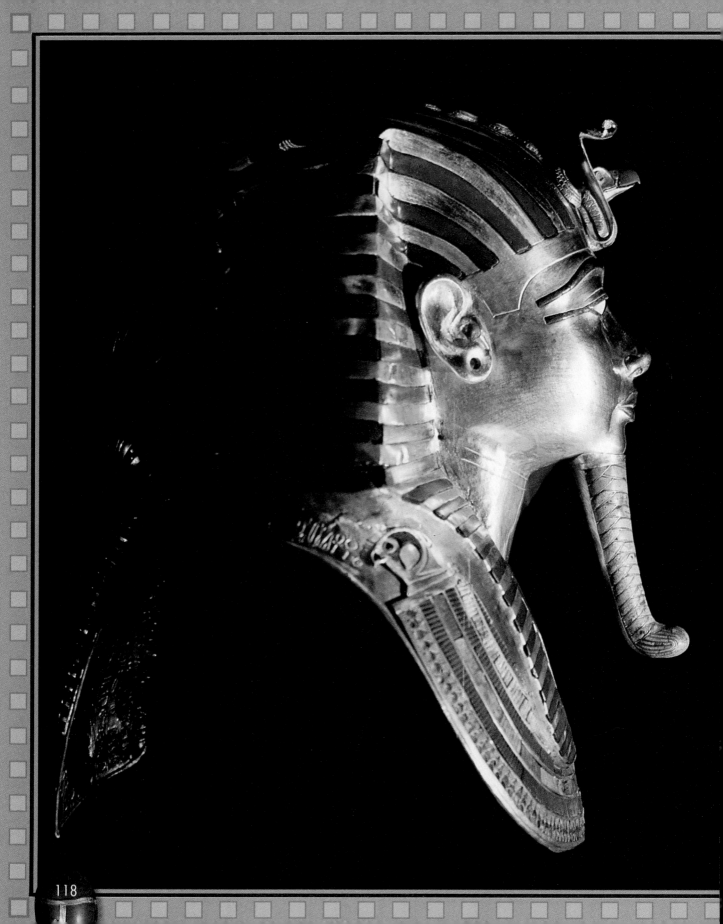

ALA Notable
Book

BEHIND
THE
SEALED DOOR

BY IRENE AND LAURENCE SWINBURNE

The great kings of Egypt built large tombs and piled them high with treasures. Jewels, precious oils, gold chairs and thrones, bracelets, rings, statues—all this and much more was stored in these final resting places. Why did the kings hoard so much wealth in their tombs? It was because of their religion. Someday, they firmly believed, the gods would raise them from the dead. Also, they believed that they themselves were gods and would be welcomed into the land of the dead by their fellow gods. When that happened, they would need the things they had used in this world.

Scarab bracelet from King Tut's tomb

But, in fact, the kings would be very poor indeed when they arrived in the other world. Through the centuries, grave thieves upset the royal plans and made off with the valuables buried in the tombs.

The thieves had no respect for the dead kings. They did not care if the rulers got to the land of the gods or not. They only cared about looting the riches in the tombs.

To get to the treasures, they had to dig through rock, break down huge doors, puzzle out mazes of passages that were found in the pyramids, and avoid traps that had been made to catch them. Often they bribed the guards to look the other way. The robbers did all this knowing that if they were caught, they would be horribly tortured and then put to death. Because of their greed, many priceless objects have been lost forever—golden statues melted down and sold, jewels removed from their settings, works of art destroyed.

Earring from King Tut's tomb

Between the years 2600 and 1529 B.C., the kings built enormous pyramids for their tombs. When a king died, his body would be carried into the tomb as high priests wailed funeral chants. But the dead king would not rest in peace for long. In a few years or even months, thieves would find their way to the heart of the pyramid where the king lay and carry off anything they could get their hands on. Even though probably many of the robbers were caught, just the

Queen Hatshepsot's Temple in the Valley of the Kings

sight of those massive tombs would remind others of the riches that lay within them, and a new gang would try its luck.

Finally, Tuthmosis I, who ruled from 1505 to 1493 B.C., realized a new way must be found to keep the royal graves from being looted. He decided to break with that long tradition and be buried in the valley that would be known as the Valley of the Kings. From this time on, the kings would be buried in tombs cut out of the rocky soil of the Valley.

You might think that the Valley would be a beautiful area, with shady trees, sparkling brooks, and flowers of every color. But you would be wrong. The Valley of the Kings is one of the most deserted and uninviting places in the world. Its landscape consists of brown rocks and brown sand. It has no trees, no streams, and no flowers. Few birds fly into this forbidding cemetery. However, it was much easier to protect than the pyramids.

Statue of King Tut

Hundreds lived or worked in the Valley. There were men who did the heavy work of digging into the rock. There were craftsmen who performed such jobs as painting the walls of the tombs. There were the priests who were in charge of all activity in the Valley. And, of course, there were the soldiers, whose duty it was to keep out the thieves. The most important work was that of the mummifiers, people who made the kings' bodies into mummies. Mummifying is a process that can preserve bodies for hundreds, sometimes even thousands, of years.

The ancient Egyptian skill of mummifying has fascinated people up to our time. After the body had been specially treated, it was dried, a process that took seventy days. Then it was washed with special sweet-smelling oils. The body was carefully wrapped in linen. The linen had been soaked in gum, a sticky substance that came from a gum tree. Metal charms and special prayers on papyrus were enfolded in the wrappings. There was plenty of room for these items, for the linen was wound around the body many times.

The exact location of a king's tomb was usually kept a secret—though, of course, some people had to know about it. Tuthmosis I assigned a trusted official, Ineni, to prepare his tomb. Ineni carried out his duty faithfully. As he wrote later, "I alone supervised the construction of His Majesty's cliff tomb. No one saw it, no one heard it."

Sarcophagus of King Tut

But nothing stopped the tomb robbers. In fact, the thieves became so successful that sometimes the priests, hoping to fool them, would have the royal mummies moved from cave to cave. Several mummies might be stored in one tomb for a time while other tombs were empty. This created puzzles for archaeologists much later, who might find the tomb of one king occupied by a different king's mummy.

The ancient Egyptian civilization lasted for over 3,000 years. Yet finally it too came to an end. At various times after that, other nations conquered the country, but the work of the tomb robbers continued as before. It was as if they had discovered an unending goldmine in the Valley of the Kings, and through the centuries they searched for undiscovered graves of kings.

By the late 1800s the Valley had been gone over carefully, and many archaeologists believed that nothing more would be found. However, in 1871 they were surprised to learn that objects of great value were being sold by people who lived on a hill near the Valley of the Kings. Experts agreed that these objects could only have come from the tombs of kings.

After some very clever detective work, it was found that most of the objects had been sold by a man named Abdel-Rasul.

Artifacts from King Tut's Tomb

Abd-el-Rasul was arrested, and he confessed that he had been the seller of the valuable relics. Even more amazing was his statement that for years the entire income of the village of Qurna had been derived from selling such relics. What's more, his family had been in this business for six centuries!

Recently his people had found a tomb high on the face of a cliff. It could be entered only through a small hole, into which a thin man could squeeze. Hoping to please the officials and avoid a long jail sentence, he offered to lead the way to the grave.

Forty mummies were found in the small tomb! The mummies were taken to the Cairo Museum. As the boat carrying the remains of the kings passed down the Nile, hundreds of thousands of Egyptians lined the banks of the great river. They threw dust upon themselves, a sign of mourning. People fired rifles in the air in salute. All this was done to honor these dead kings who had ruled some 3,000 years before.

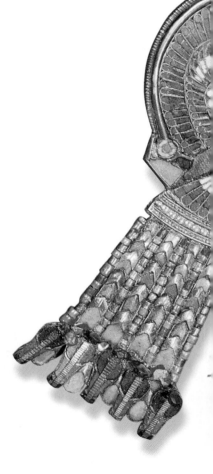

Detail of Sarcophagus of King Tut

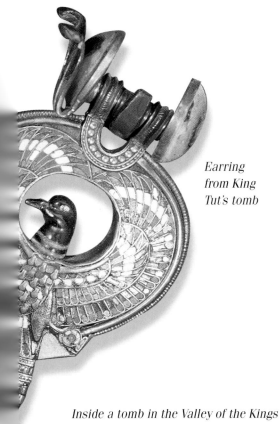

Earring from King Tut's tomb

IRENE & LAURENCE
SWINBURNE

*I*rene and Laurence Swinburne have been a writing team since they were married in 1947. When they work on a writing project, Irene usually does the research and Laurence does the writing, but sometimes Irene helps with the writing as well. *Behind the Sealed Door* is one book the couple wrote together.

Laurence remembers wanting to be a writer all his life. He first saw his work in print when he was on the staff of his college literary magazine. After college, however, he began a career as a textbook salesman and educational editor. He didn't start writing stories for children until 1964.

The Swinburnes believe that kids are the best audience a writer could have, and the authors often go directly to young people to get the ideas for their books. Over the years, Laurence Swinburne has given talks to thousands of children in the New York area. "Children ask a lot of good questions about the writing craft," he says, "and they also tell me what they would like to read." Much can be gained, he believes, from taking the time to ask children what they think.

Inside a tomb in the Valley of the Kings

Hierog

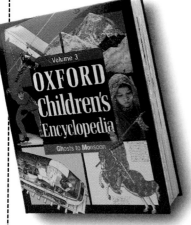

Volume 3
OXFORD
Children's
Encyclopedia
Ghosts to Monsoon

HIEROGLYPHICS is the word we use for a form of writing which uses pictures instead of words. The best-known hieroglyphics are those invented by the Egyptians, but other peoples used them as well. At first each picture represented an object—water, for example—but later some pictures also stood for particular sounds.

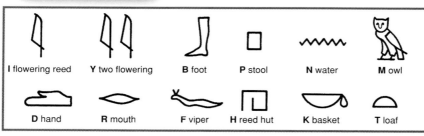

I flowering reed	Y two flowering	B foot	P stool	N water	M owl
D hand	R mouth	F viper	H reed hut	K basket	T loaf

Here are some of the signs used by the Egyptians. Each sign represented an object but also a sound, and so can be "translated" into letters we use today.

Egyptian

The Egyptians were not the first people to invent a written language (the Sumerians did this), but they did use their hieroglyphics for nearly 3,500 years, from about 3100 B.C. to the end of the 4th century A.D.

The names of pharaohs were written in oval frames called cartouches. This is how Queen Cleopatra's name was written.

The language started in a very simple way with pictures for objects such as the sun or a flower. The Egyptians found it difficult to explain complicated ideas with these, and so pictures were used to represent groups of things or ideas. For example, a soldier with a bow and arrow came to mean a whole army. The Egyptians needed a large number of pictures or signs to make up their written language. Over 700 different signs were used. They are found on stone-carved inscriptions (on temples, for example), painted on the wooden cases of buried mummies, and drawn on papyrus.

Eagle *Cuauhtli*	Crocodile *Cipacti*	Wind *Ehecatl*	House *Calli*	Lizard *Cuetzpellin*	Rain *Auiahuitl*
Flint knife *Tecpatl*	Serpent *Coatl*	Deer *Mazatl*	Rabbit *Tochtli*	Water *Atl*	Flower *Xochitl*
	Dog *Itzcuintli*	Monkey *Ozomatli*	Grass *Malinalli*	Reed *Acatl*	

The Aztecs, like the Maya people, used a form of writing in which ideas and objects were shown as pictures (pictograms) or symbols. These are some of the signs for days. The Aztecs used a 365-day calendar divided into 18 months with 20 days each.

The hieroglyphics shown at left represent particular sounds. To make a word the Egyptians used these signs and some of the other 700 pictures. It was a complicated way of writing.

Maya writing

The Maya people of Central America used hieroglyphs for writing. They are preserved on a type of document, called a codex, made of folded strips of deerskin or bark of trees. These records tell us what they knew about the stars, about their religious ceremonies, and about their calendar.

Hieroglyphics rediscovered

By the end of the 3rd century A.D. there were many Greeks in Egypt and the Greek language was much used. Egyptian Christians called Copts began to write their own language in a form of the Greek alphabet. Soon people forgot what the hieroglyphic signs meant. It was rediscovered after 1799, when a large inscription was found in Egypt. This was on the Rosetta Stone, as it was called (now in the British Museum), and was an inscription written in two languages, Egyptian and Greek. Because Greek could be understood, the ancient hieroglyphic writing was rediscovered.

Courtesy of British Museum

The Rosetta Stone

See Also

Egyptian ancient history
Symbols
Writing systems

PYRAMID PUZZLE

Draw a large pyramid shape on a sheet of paper. Inside the pyramid, draw a maze with many pathways. Make sure that only one pathway connects the beginning to the end of the maze. Decorate your maze with pictures of wall paintings and other artifacts. Exchange mazes with a partner. See who can pass through the pyramid first.

RESPONSE

TIME CAPSULE

The artifacts found in the Egyptian pyramids give us a glimpse of life in ancient Egypt. If you created a time capsule of your life today, what things would you include? Write a list of ten things and a brief reason for including each. Compare your list with a classmate's.

WHAT DO YOU THINK?

- Why do you think people's attitudes toward the tombs of the ancient Egyptian kings has changed from one of disrespect to one of respect?

- If you were an archaeologist who found Egyptian treasures, what would you do with them? Explain your answer.

- What facts could you tell a friend about Egyptian tombs and tomb robbers?

CORNER

WRITE A DESCRIPTION

IMAGINE SUCH TREASURES!

Imagine that you are an archaeologist working alone at a dig site. You come upon a fantastic artifact and you want to report back to your coworkers about it. Write a brief, vivid description of your remarkable find. Read your description to the class.

the GOLDEN GOBLET

BY ELOISE JARVIS MCGRAW

ILLUSTRATED BY OREN SHERMAN

Newbery Honor

Ranofer lives in ancient Egypt with his guardian, Gebu. One day, he finds a beautiful golden goblet in Gebu's room, and he begins to suspect that Gebu is a tomb robber. Early one morning, Ranofer secretly follows Gebu and his partner, Wenamon, to the Valley of the Tombs.

It stretched before him, a wasteland of glaring red hills rising from a giant's block pile of tumbled boulders—desolate, barren and ominously still. Nowhere was there a single sprig of green.

The sun had cleared the horizon now. By the time he reached the Valley floor it was beating fiercely upon his naked shoulders, reheating rocks and sands not yet cooled from yesterday, wrapping the whole Valley of the Tombs in shimmering, burning heat. Ranofer, threading his way among the scorching rocks, wondered in panic if he would ever be able to find his way out again. Every pile of boulders looked like every other; the cool, flooding Nile and the familiar streets of Thebes seemed as far away as stars. High above him in the brazen sky a lone falcon wheeled; far ahead the figures of Gebu and Wenamon were dwarfed by their surroundings to mere swatches of black and white. Two thieves, a falcon, and himself. Except for these not a living thing stirred in all this burning, silent world.

Licking his parched lips, Ranofer tiptoed nervously across the sands, wondering if even now he was treading over the hidden chambers of some long-dead pharaoh and rousing his outraged *ba.*[*] He jumped as he heard the faint, seven-noted cry of the falcon and stood with pounding heart, watching it soar away toward the south. When he turned back, the two figures ahead of him had vanished without a trace.

---

[*] ba: spirit of a dead person in ancient Egyptian beliefs

In consternation he scanned the cluster of rocks where he had seen them only a moment before, then broke into a run. Even their dubious company was preferable to the death-haunted emptiness which surrounded him now.

Apprehensive and breathless, he arrived at the rock pile, stopped short, and sprang back behind it. Not three paces away on the other side of the rocks were the two he followed, working busily at something he had not time to make out. He stood flattened against a hot boulder, trying to control his jerky breathing. He could hear crunching and scraping, an occasional guttural curse. Then the noises stopped and all was still.

Moments later he dared peer out around the boulder. What he saw was an irregular black crevice in the rocks ahead, and a scattering of small stones around a large one which had evidently been rolled aside. Was this the entrance to the tomb, then? It looked barely large enough to admit a man's body, much less the huge coffin that must lie somewhere below. Ranofer crept out of hiding and stood peering fearfully into the crevice. It did not look like any tomb entrance he had ever seen or heard of. Casting a nervous glance over his shoulder at the desolate Valley, in which he was now utterly alone, he lay down flat on the hot sand and lowered his head into the dark, irregular hole. He could see nothing for a moment; then a dimly glimpsed surface made him stretch an arm down to explore it. It was a narrow projection. Perhaps a step? Wriggling forward, he eased more of himself over the edge until he was hanging head-downward into the hole with the edge cutting his waist. His groping hand touched a second projection not quite an arm's length below the first. Another step. It was certainly an entrance of some sort. This flight of crude and uneven steps, hacked out of the rock and earth, led down the shaft. At the bottom a passage must tunnel away toward the tomb.

Ranofer wriggled backward again and got to his feet, threw another uneasy glance around him and turned back to the crevice. He could not make it out. Never could a huge coffin have been carried down that shaft. It must be a second entrance to the tomb, a secret one.

A secret one, of course! He stood transfixed by a flash of understanding. The whole of Gebu's plot was suddenly clear to him. He had heard tales of such tunnels, dug out during the construction of a tomb by scheming workers. They would hack through the wall of a tomb chamber secretly, and tunnel as far as time allowed toward the surface of the earth, adding the rock chips to the other debris from the excavation of the tomb. The hole in the chamber wall would then be plastered over like the other walls, so that no passage showed at all. A few years, or perhaps months, later, when the funerary visits of the surviving family became infrequent, they had only to dig a shaft down from the surface to meet their tunnel. When this was done they could enter the tomb at their leisure and cart away the gold, undetected by the guards at the real entrance, which might be a quarter of a league away and out of sight behind some rocky hillock.

Gebu was a stonecutter, Wenamon a mason. They had done this thing. It would be easy for them to arrange it. Ranofer caught his breath as another realization struck him. The little room in the tomb drawing, the one for Pharaoh's Master of Storehouses. It was no room at all. It was a passage like this, disguised so that the workmen could hack it out without knowing it was anything but another storage chamber.

A sudden queer noise made him swing around. What was it? He saw no one, nothing, only the same glaring, lifeless wasteland with its tumbled piles of boulders stretching all around him. His eyes went slowly to the rock pile near at hand, behind which he had hidden a few moments ago. Was Something Else hidden there now?

He edged closer to the crevice, still staring at the rock pile. Once more, even Gebu and Wenamon seemed companions fervently to be desired. At least they were human, they were alive.

But I do not want to go into a tomb! Ranofer thought desperately. I do not want to follow them clear into that dark and awful place. Surely it is enough that I know they are there. I can run now and give the alarm.

Run past that ominous rock pile? Through all that terrible, empty Valley again, alone? His flesh crawled, he shrank another step toward the crevice, and as he did so he heard the sound again, eerily distinct and close. It was the dry rustling of wings. A cold moisture chilled Ranofer's forehead, as if an icy hand had been laid there. At that moment a gust of wind swept across the sands, there was a loud clapping and beating, and from behind the rock pile a huge black form with outstretched wings rose cumbersomely, tilting and flapping directly toward him.

With a cry, Ranofer leaped for the crevice and slid feet-first into the dark.

Ranofer's plunge into the crevice sent him half falling, half jumping, from one to another of the crude, wide-spaced steps. After a moment he missed one altogether and simply tumbled, striking his knees and wildly waving arms on every rough projection he passed. He landed at the bottom feeling bruised, dazed, and as terrified of the inky blackness around him now as he was of the great winged thing from which he had fled. He got to his feet and stumbled about blindly, hands out-stretched, until he located the opening of the passage he had guessed was there. It sloped gently downward as it led away into the unknown dark. As he hesitated, eyes stretched wide in a futile effort to see something, anything, a dim glow of light shone far ahead of him. Gebu and Wenamon must have kindled a torch; that glow was its faint reflection on some distant curve of the passage wall.

Ranofer fixed his gaze on it, licking his trembling lips. He could not stay here shivering and dreading, he must follow—or else climb back to the surface and be carried off to some unthinkable Land of Khefts by that great winged thing. He was still weighing bad against worse when the dim glow ahead faded and disappeared.

Setting his teeth hard, Ranofer started along the passage.

It sloped gently at first, then more steeply, leading ever deeper into the earth, growing blacker and still blacker until Ranofer was seized by the conviction that he was moving along a slim bridge over vast empty space, and repeatedly clutched in panic at the walls while his bare toe fearfully explored the step ahead. The floor was strewn with sharp fragments that hurt his feet. The air was hot and close, and so dry it seemed to shrivel his very flesh. It *was* shriveling, he was sure of it. Was it from the breath of that great black creature, still after him, or the deathly, withering wind of its wings? He moved faster, scrambling blindly forward, longing for another glimpse of that light. Once his head struck sharply against something hard and rough-edged, and he sank into a terrified heap. He was too weak to run, too frightened to stay where he was. Stumbling to his feet, arms locked about his head, he bumped the same hard thing again and realized it was the ceiling of the passage, pressing so low that from here on he would have to crawl.

He crawled, his teeth chattering and his whole body shaking so uncontrollably that it felt as if it belonged to someone else. He had never felt so small, so alone, so outnumbered, as in this terrible black place haunted by Beings he could not see or hear or feel but only knew were there. Worse, every inch he moved forward took him nearer to an even more terrible place, the citadel of death itself, the dwelling of the outraged Departed One whose mere sentries these other creatures were. Now and then he caught sight of the torch glow ahead and flung himself recklessly toward it, though the faint, far-off gleam only intensified the blackness that enclosed him. Any living human—thieves and murderers included, Gebu included—would seem a friend and rescuer now.

After what seemed an eternity he realized that the blackness around him was no longer entirely black; it had turned to the lesser dark of night. Presently it became almost grayish, so that he could see faintly the hacked-out walls on either side. Obviously the torch had stopped moving, and he was drawing closer to the light.

There was a sudden sound of chipping, followed by the noise of falling plaster. Ranofer halted, his desire for Gebu's companionship abruptly vanishing. Even the fear of bodiless devils gave way before the sudden clear picture of this all-too-solid one up ahead. Gebu was still Gebu, human or not; and he was at this moment breaking through the plastered wall of a tomb. Ranofer waited until all sounds had ceased and the torch glow moved on before he cautiously crept ahead. Around a bend in the passage he was suddenly dazzled by a patch of golden light. He flung up his hand, blinking until his eyes grew accustomed to what seemed a brilliant glare, though it was only the torchlight, shining directly through an irregular hole in the wall. Even as his vision adjusted, the glare dimmed; the torch was being carried farther into the interior of the tomb. He could see now that, as he had expected, the opening ahead of him was jagged with broken plaster.

He eyed it fearfully, rubbing his cold hands against his thighs. For the first time he wondered who the man had been that now lay buried here. Some Great One, for the tomb was large. The torch had receded into what was apparently a second chamber, and the thieves' footsteps came echoing back to Ranofer eerily, as though in a vast space. His flesh crawled and the little hairs prickled on the back of his neck as he edged slowly toward the hole in the wall.

Shivering, he rose to his feet before it, peered fearfully in, and found himself staring into a pair of strange, glazed eyes not two paces from his own.

With a gasp he flung himself backward, eyes tight shut against the horror that was sure to strike him dead. At the same moment, a voice growled, "What was that?"

There was a silence that seemed as long as time itself to Ranofer, who lay in a tight ball, dizzy with fright, on the floor of the passage. Then he heard Gebu's voice in the second room, sounding unconcerned as ever.

"It was nothing, son of the jackal, son of a pig! You're afraid of your own shadow."

"I tell you I heard a sound," the voice of Wenamon insisted.

"There is no one here but us and the dead. Make haste with those boxes, now."

Slowly, uncertainly, Ranofer rose to his knees, then stood. No one here? But what was that face he had seen? Trembling, he peered again through the opening, and met the same pair of eyes. This time, though he shrank back involuntarily, he realized that they did not move, did not live. They were the inlaid glass eyes of a life-sized wooden statue, and he saw now that they had been partially smashed, as if from the blow of a dagger hilt. Gebu and Wenamon had wanted no gaze upon them as they went about their evil work, especially the gaze of this watchful *ushabti* placed here as servant and guardian of the dead.

Nervously Ranofer examined the figure more closely, and his fear of its vengeance changed to an unexpected pity. It was the statue of a slim and lovely servant girl, wearing a painted white dress and a painted gilt necklace, steadying a box on one shoulder and carrying a painted wooden duck by its feet in her other hand. Her expression was one of serenity and joy, and the sculptor who carved her had been a master. Now her clear, wide eyes were cloudy and blinded by the blow that had splintered them; her beauty was marred and her usefulness as a watchful guardian ended. It was like seeing some innocent, happy creature lying murdered, victim of Gebu's callous greed.

Ranofer's gaze turned from her to move in wonder about the rest of the chamber, which was dimly illumined by the glow of the torch from the next room. As he looked a strange emotion took possession of him. Beyond and around the graceful statue were articles of household furniture, arranged as in a beautiful home. There were armchairs and beds of carved wood decorated with gold, there were alabaster honey jars, painted boxes resting on delicately wrought ivory legs. There was a wicker trunk ventilated by little slatted openings, through which the fragrance of the perfumed garments within escaped into the room. There were winecups

arranged on shelves, there were scent jars and jeweled collars and arm bands. Everywhere was the gleam of gold.

It was not the gold, however, that held Ranofer's gaze and drew him slowly through the jagged entrance to stand, silent and awed, within the Precious Habitation. It was the garlands of flowers, only a little withered, as if placed here in love and grief only yesterday, and the sight of a worn oaken staff leaning against the wall, of two pairs of sandals, a new and an old, of favorite joints of meat placed neatly in boxes as if for a journey. Whatever he had expected, it was not this intimate look of home, of a well-loved room to which

its owner might at any moment return. Whatever horrors haunted the passage, they were not here, in this quiet sanctuary.

Who was the owner? Ranofer's eyes searched farther, and halted in surprise. There were two owners. Slowly, soundlessly, he crossed the chamber to the pair of silver-inlaid coffins, on the lids of which were sculptured in gold the figures of their occupants, a man and a woman. They lay as if sleeping, side by side, their folded hands eloquent of the same defenseless trust that had caused them to order a sweet-faced servant girl as their only guardian. As Ranofer looked into their quiet golden faces the stealthy sounds of plundering in the next room became horrible to him. For the first time he fully understood this crime.

He straightened, all his fear gone and in its place hot fury. Those merciless and wicked ones!—to break into this sacred place and steal the treasures meant to comfort this old couple through their Three Thousand Years! Whether rich gold or worn-out sandals, these things belonged to them, no living human had a right to set foot in this chamber, not even the son of Thutra, who meant no harm. Almost, he could hear the helpless fluttering of these Old Ones' frightened *bas*. So

strong was the sensation that he dropped to his knees in profound apology for his own intrusion. As he did so he saw something else, a stack of wine jars just beyond one of the coffins. They were capped with linen and sealed with clay, and pressed into the clay was a mark as well known to Ranofer as it was to everyone else in Egypt. It was the personal seal of the great noble, Huaa, only two years dead, the beloved father of Queen Tiy.

Shocked to his very toes, Ranofer scrambled up and retreated a few respectful steps, involuntarily stretching out his hands toward the coffins in the gesture of homage. Here lay Huaa and his cherished wife Tuaa, the parents of the queen of Egypt. And here he stood, an insignificant nobody, daring to gaze into their faces! He was acutely, desperately embarrassed; he felt like a dusty urchin trespassing in a palace, which he was. Worse, at any moment those thieves would be in here to wreck and pillage, to tear the gold trim from chairs and chests, to snatch the jewel boxes, to break open the beautiful coffins and even strip the wrappings from the royal mummies themselves in search of golden amulets. It must not happen. These Old Ones should have someone grand and fierce to protect them.

They have only me, Ranofer thought. I must do something—anything—go fetch help—

He turned and started swiftly toward the entrance hole, too swiftly, for his elbow grazed a little inlaid table and tilted the alabaster vase upon it. He clutched at it wildly but it fell, shattering on the stone floor with a crash that echoed like the very sound of doom.

The small noises in the chamber beyond ceased instantly. Ranofer breathed a prayer to Osiris and flung himself behind the coffins, which was all he had time to do before the torch and Gebu's murderous face appeared in the doorway.

"Ast!" came Wenamon's hiss. "I told you we were not alone!"

"We will be soon," Gebu answered in tones that turned Ranofer cold. He could see their two shadows on the wall, black and clear-cut: Gebu's bulky one, Wenamon's, thin and vulture-shaped, behind it. The shadows moved, rippled in deadly silence along the wall, leaped crazily to the rough ceiling and down again as the two began methodically to search the room. The dancing black shapes advanced relentlessly toward the coffins, looming huge as giants as they came nearer. Ranofer's hand groped out blindly and closed on a small heavy object that felt like a jewel box. At that instant Gebu's rage-distorted face was thrust over the coffin.

Ranofer lunged to his feet and hurled the box with all his strength.

There was a glittering shower of gems as the box struck Gebu full in the eyes, jarring the torch from his hand. He gave a hoarse cry and staggered backward into Wenamon, who began to scream and curse as he fought the flame that was licking upwards into his cloak. In that one instant of confusion Ranofer saw his chance. He seized the nearest wine jar and aimed it straight at the blaze. There was a splattering crash and the torch hissed out, plunging the chamber into darkness. With the reek of wine and scorched cloth rising strong about him, Ranofer leaped for the far wall, feeling frantically along it for the entrance hole. Behind him the dark was hideous with yells and curses, with the sounds of splintering wood and jewelry crushed under foot as the two thieves plunged this way and that over the wine-slippery floor in search of him.

Where, in the name of all the gods, was the hole?

His fingers met a jagged bit of plaster and, beside it, empty space. In an instant he was through the hole and stumbling along the black passage, bent double under its crowding roof, banging and bumping into its roughhewn walls, but running, flying away from the death behind him. The sounds of rage faded as he ran, grew fainter with every bend, then suddenly grew louder. The thieves had found the wall opening, too, and were after him, in the passage. He scrambled around a curve, almost fell, dashed on again and brought up with a stunning impact against solid wall. Walls on three sides of him? Was he trapped? He wasted precious moments seeking a way around the obstruction; then his hand touched a rough shelf of stone. A step! He had reached the bottom of the entrance shaft much sooner than he had expected, for his headlong flight back had consumed far less time than his first cautious, crawling journey.

He clawed at the wall, found step after narrow step and hoisted his trembling body up them one by one. As he put his weight on the last one it crumbled under him. In a panic he flung both arms over the top of the shaft and for a terrible moment hung there, then wriggling, straining, pushing, he was over the top and through the crevice in the rocks.

The sunlight hit him like a blow. Half blind and shaking all over, he could think only of that last crumbled step and what it could mean to him. The thieves might climb past by jumping and then wriggling as he had done,

but they could not get out if the top of the shaft were solidly blocked. They would have nothing to stand on to shove away the stones. He could hear stumbling, rapid footsteps approaching the bottom of the shaft, and Gebu's enraged voice bellowing his name; but already he was grabbing up rocks as fast as he could move, his eyes squinted tight against the glare of day. He hurled a few into the shaft and felt a fierce joy at the roar of pain below, and the thud of someone falling. Quickly he wedged some larger stones into the crevice, then began to shove and strain at the biggest, a boulder three times the size of his head, which had originally blocked the entrance.

It would not budge. He put his shoulder to it, dug his toes into the hot sands, and shoved with all his strength. It stirred a little, tilted. He heard more scrambling sounds below and gave one last desperate thrust. The boulder tipped and rolled across the opening.

Later, the thieves were captured, and Ranofer was recognized by the queen for his courage.

ELOISE JARVIS McGRAW

"Writing," says Eloise Jarvis McGraw, "is as necessary to my well-being as breathing or eating." Although McGraw has a wide range of artistic talents—she is a painter, a sculptor, a printmaker, and a dancer—writing is her favorite creative outlet.

McGraw was born in Houston, Texas, in 1915. She wrote her first story when she was eight years old but spent her early years exploring the visual arts, studying painting and sculpture in college. As an artist, she tried to capture the essence of a person in a picture. This approach influenced the way she writes. She says, "For me a story always starts with a character. I may have a small ember of a plot idea, but until I have the character, the fire won't start."

Here's how she explains the way she writes: "When a book idea comes to me, it is usually something I can put in one sentence. I write that sentence on a file card and put it in a box. As questions about the idea arise in my mind, I write them on other cards and add the answers when I have them. I note down other ideas that seem to want to join up with the first one. The book grows in this way while I may be doing other things."

THE
PYRAMIDS
OF EGYPT
FROM *KIDS DISCOVER MAGAZINE*

Egypt's pyramids are the oldest stone buildings in the world. They were built nearly five thousand years ago. These ancient tombs are also among the world's largest structures. The biggest is taller than a *40-story* building and covers an area greater than that of *ten* football fields. Men built these huge structures without the help of equipment that we have today, such as cranes and bulldozers. Sometimes up to 100,000 men worked for 20 seasons on one pyramid.

More than 80 pyramids still stand today. Inside their once-smooth white limestone surfaces there are secret passageways, hidden rooms, ramps, bridges, and shafts. Most had concealed entrances and false doors. What fun it would be to explore one!

However, the pyramids were not built for exploring. They served a very serious purpose. Ancient Egyptians had a strong belief in life after death. The kings, called pharaohs, wanted their bodies to last forever, so they had pyramids built to protect their bodies after death. Each pyramid housed a pharaoh's preserved body. It also held the goods he would need in the next life to continue living as he had when he was alive.

The pyramids of Egypt are massive monuments to the pharaohs' power. Today they are reminders of a resourceful and creative ancient civilization.

HOW TO BUILD A PYRAMID

Follow these directions to make a scale model of the Great Pyramid at Giza. The real pyramid is almost 2,000 times larger than your model! Thin cardboard or construction paper is the best to work with.

Cut a sheet of paper so that it is $8\frac{1}{2}$ inches square.

Mark the midpoint on each side. Draw a line (black) connecting opposite center points.

Measure $3\frac{1}{4}$ inches out from the center on each of the four lines. Draw a line (red) from each corner of the paper to each point you just marked. Cut along these lines to see what to throw away. Draw lines (blue) as shown at right.

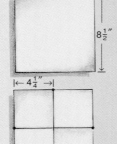

Fold along the lines. Tape the edges together.

Congratulations! You now have a pyramid that is a scale model of the Great Pyramid of Giza.

THE OUTSKIRTS of modern-day Cairo, the capital of Egypt, with the Pyramids of Giza in the background. The Giza Pyramids are the only one of the Seven Wonders of the Ancient World still standing.

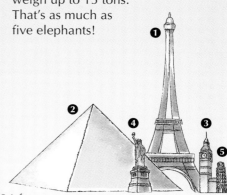

HOW HEAVY?

The average weight of one of a pyramid's stone blocks is two and a half tons. That's the weight of two medium-sized cars. Some blocks, however, weigh up to 15 tons. That's as much as five elephants!

HOW TALL?

1. Eiffel Tower, 984 feet
2. **Great Pyramid at Giza, 480 feet**
3. Big Ben (Westminster Palace), 316 feet
4. Statue of Liberty, 305 feet
5. Leaning Tower of Pisa, 179 feet

JUST THE FACTS, PLEASE

Suppose Ranofer went straight to the local police station after discovering the crime. Create a form on which a police officer might write Ranofer's information. Fill in the form, using details from the story. Share your police report with a partner.

HAIL THE HERO!

Work with a small group to honor Ranofer for his detective work. Take the roles of Ranofer, Queen Tiy, and the people of Thebes. Design an award for Ranofer. Have Queen Tiy and others make short speeches to praise Ranofer.

STATUE NO MORE

Reread the description of the statue of the servant girl who guarded the tomb. Use the details in the story to draw a picture of how the girl might have looked.

RESPONSE CORNER

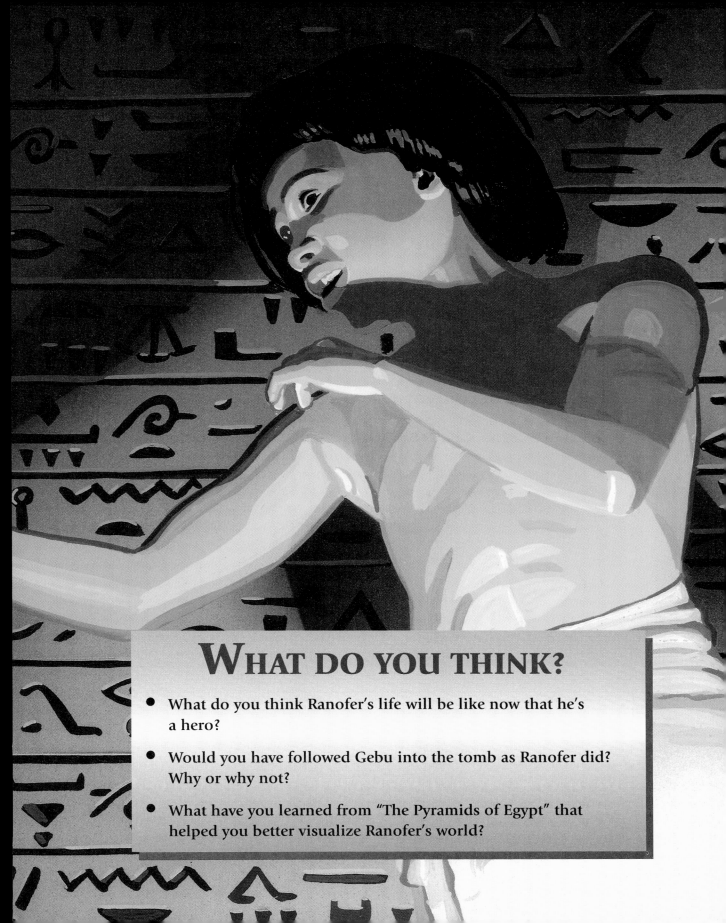

WHAT DO YOU THINK?

- What do you think Ranofer's life will be like now that he's a hero?

- Would you have followed Gebu into the tomb as Ranofer did? Why or why not?

- What have you learned from "The Pyramids of Egypt" that helped you better visualize Ranofer's world?

Art & Literature

One way to learn about ancient civilizations is to study what they have left behind. Look at this picture of the carved back of a chair. What does it tell you about life in ancient Egypt? From your readings and this picture, what can you figure out about artists and craftspeople in ancient Egypt?

Detail of Cedarwood Chair

This picture shows the back panel of a chair found in King Tutankhamun's tomb. The chair was carved about 3,400 years ago from cedarwood. Imagine how much time and skill were required to do such detailed work. The king's names are carved into the two panels attached to the top of the chair. Many of the animals and designs decorating the chair have symbolic meanings. Can you guess which animals were important to ancient Egyptians?

Newbery
Medal

Four

FROM *SHEN OF THE SEA*

BY Arthur Bowie Chrisman

ILLUSTRATED BY

Heidi Stevens

Shen of the Sea
Chinese Stories for Children
By Arthur Bowie Chrisman
Illustrated by Else Hasselriis

Generals

Prince Chang petitioned his father, the King: "My honored parent, give me permission to make a journey throughout the kingdom. I would learn how the people live, and note wherein they are contented and discontented. Thus I shall be prepared against the time when I ascend the throne."

The King nodded approval. "Your plan is good, my son. I shall immediately order that new gold tires be put upon the royal carriage, and summon ten troops of cavalry to guard you."

But the prince would not listen to such arrangements. "Oh, no, sire, I mean to go alone and in disguise. Instead of the carriage, a stick will serve for my vehicle. Instead of the troops, that selfsame stick will guard me."

Whereat, the King was greatly troubled, and the prince was put to much argument before he won his point. "Then do as you wish, my only and much beloved son," said the King, grudgingly. "But it behooves you to observe extreme care. Disorder is rife in all the provinces. Go, and may your stick be as strong as the magic mace of Sun How Erh."

"Farewell, my royal father."

"Farewell, my noble son."

Now, it must be remembered that Prince Chang was no graybeard. In years he was nearing thirteen. Is it, after all, such a great wonder that homesickness caused his heels to drag, and his eyes to need the kerchief? He had walked all of twenty *li.*[1] That, he began to imagine, was journey enough for the present. To the edge of Hu Pei[2] Forest he continued. At the edge of the forest he stopped. The woodland was so dark . . . so dark. The wolves howled "Oo-o-o-o-o-wh." (We starve.) And such a futile little stick with which to enter the forest of Hu Pei. "Oo-o-o-o-o-wh." What wolves . . .

The prince had turned his face toward home when a merry voice hailed him. "Ho. Brother, I'm glad you are come. Tell me if my fiddle be in tune."

A comical fellow hopped down from a stump and chinned his fiddle while Prince Chang stared. "Eek. Eek. Eeek." "How does it sound, little Brother?"

---

[1] li (lē): about one-third of a mile

[2] Hu Pei (hoō´pā´)

"I dare say it—"

But the fiddler was not waiting for an answer. His bow arm fell to sawing while his legs and voice joined in the tune—"A beggar asked the King to dine." And that's a foolish song. Prince Chang thought he had never before heard or seen anything so funny by half. The more he laughed, the greater his need for laughter. Such a comical beggar, and how he could play and sing!

From one end of Hu Pei Forest to the other, Prince Chang laughed while the beggar capered and fiddled. No wolves at all appeared. Homesickness was a thing of the past—forgotten. "Let me give you a copper cash, merry stranger," said Chang, when they came to a Y of the road.

> Such a comical beggar,
> and how he could
> play and sing!

"Not now," said he of the fiddle and bow. "I judge you are poorer than I."

"Indeed?" laughed the prince. "When I am King (he forgot himself there), I shall reward you handsomely."

"Ho. Ho," shrieked the beggar. "When you are King. When you are King, I'll accept a reward. Make me a general in your army."

"It shall be done," said Chang. "What is your very nice name?"

"My pitiful name is Tang—Tang the fiddler. Farewell, my little King, who rides a bamboo horse." So they parted, both merry.

Sad to relate, Prince Chang's merriment was to be of brief duration. A band of robbers sprang up from the roadside and surrounded him, pummeling him without mercy—all striking at one time. They took his stick and his clothing and the little bag of coins that hung from his neck. They left him in the road for dead. A sorry ending, that, to his journey . . .

Shortly, another traveler chanced by, and he was a man of warm heart. He revived Prince Chang and took him on his shoulder, carrying him to a village. There he set out food and clothing and bade the prince ask for what more he desired. Chang was deeply thankful. "How can I ever repay you?"

"*Ya ya pei*"[3] (Pish, tush), said the man. "It is nothing. What is a bit of food? And what is a gift of clothing? Besides, you must know that I am a tailor and will charge my next customer double. 'A tailor—a rogue,' says the proverb."

---

[3] Ya ya pei (yä·yä·pā´)

"I do not believe it," exclaimed Chang, "and when I become King—" (There he forgot himself again.)

"Ho. Ho. Ho," roared the tailor. "When you become King. Ho. Ho. When you are King, you may reward me. You may make me a general in your army."

"It shall be done," declared Chang. "What is your honorable name?"

"Wang is my miserable name. Wang the tailor. Farewell, and good luck be with you, my future King." So they parted, merrily enough—each laughing at the excellent jest.

Prince Chang continued his journey. For three days he saw no man of flesh and bone, nor came upon a dwelling. At the end of the third day he was weak and unsteady from hunger. His stick broke beneath his weight, and he lay beside the road, waiting for death to come. Instead of death, there came a shepherd with sheep and goats. The shepherd picked up Chang and saw that the boy was far spent. It was quite plain that hunger had used him evilly. Promptly the quick-witted fellow slung Chang on his shoulder and carried him off to a cave. Milk in bottles of leather hung on the cavern walls. Also, there were cheeses. Chang was made to drink of the milk—a little at first—only enough to moisten his throat. With the return of strength, he drank greedily, completely emptying a goatskin. And the emptier the bottle grew, the more he thanked the shepherd. "You have done me a great service," said Chang. "If I had money I—"

"Ya ya pei" (Pish, tush), said the shepherd. "It is nothing. I fed you with no thought of reward."

"Nevertheless," declared Chang, "when I am made King I—"

The shepherd was like to strain his throat with guffawing. "Ho. Ho. Ho. When you are made King. What a merry chap you seem to be! Very well, when you are King you may reward me. Make me a general in your army. Ho. Ho. Ho."

"I shall. I shall." The prince was emphatic. "What is your honorable name?"

"My paltry name? Most folk call me Mang—Mang the shepherd. And here, you must carry some food with you, for the nearest house is thirty *li* distant. Take this cheese—and may good luck be your companion, my King of the wandering road."

Burdened as he was, Prince Chang made slow work of getting over the mountain. He had begun to think seriously of dropping the cheese when a troop of soldiers clattered up the road behind him. "How fortunate!" said Chang. "Here are my father's soldiers. They will take me on their horses to the next village."

But the soldiers halted with a "Who are you, and what brings you here?" queried most fiercely and with scowls. The prince stammered that he was sometimes called Chun—a most unfortunate invention, for Chun was the name of a local bandit. The soldiers' frowns turned to pleased smiles (there was a reward offered), and the captain said: "So you are Chun, and you have just robbed some poor person of a new suit and a cheese. Off with his head, my braves."

Chang now saw that he was indeed in a tangle. A bold face seemed the only escape. He put on a stern look, saying: "How dare you execute men without a trial? Do you not know that I am Prince Chang, son of your noble King?"

The captain bowed in mock humility. "Your Highness seems large for such a tender age. I happen to know that King Yen Chi's eldest son is only two years old. Let your swords drink, men."

The terrible truth was made plain to Chang. He had wandered across the border of his father's kingdom. He was in a neighboring and hostile country. . . .

> The terrible truth was made plain to Chang.

The swords were lifted to strike, when—swish—came an arrow. After it, quickly, another, and another. Each found its mark. For each arrow a soldier crumpled. The others dug heels in their horses, galloping pell-mell for their lives.

A stalwart youth stepped out from a pine. "You had better go quickly," he said to Chang. "The border of our own country lies a full mile back."

"I thank you with all my heart," declared Prince Chang, "and shall reward you fittingly when—"

"When you are King?" finished the other. "I heard what you said to the soldiers, and wondered at your daring. Very well. Make me a general when you become King, and that will be ample reward."

"It shall be done," vowed the prince. "What brave name do you bear?"

"Name? Oh, you may call me Lang. Lang the very indifferent archer. And now you must go, for more soldiers will come, and my arrows are few."

Prince Chang was not long returned from his journey when the King passed away in an illness. Immediately the crown was placed on Chang's brow, and all the people burned much incense of *la ka* wood, crying, "Hail!" And almost with their next breath they shouted *"Kou chou!"*[4] (The enemy!) An enemy was marching upon Ku Hsueh.[5] The new King had barely seated himself upon the heighty throne before he found it necessary to see about raising an army. There were two great troubles with the old army. It was dwarfish small, and it boasted more generals than bowmen. Of course, the generals never fought. They did nothing but plan—usually what they'd have for dinner, and which sword they'd wear to the King's next reception. Yet, King Chang added more generals to the army.

The first complaint raised against King Chang by his people was that he had added four more generals to the army. His new generals were named Tang, Wang, Mang, and Lang—though doubtless such information is hardly necessary. They were old friends of the King. The four arrived at the capital in time to see a huge army of hostiles encamp on the far side of the river that bordered the city. By great good fortune, the river was past fording, so holding the enemy in check. The King and his generals gazed across the river. Said he: "It is easily seen that the enemy has twenty men for every one we muster. What are your plans?"

Of all his generals, only Wang seemed to have so much as the shadow of a plan. Wang said, "Give me all the tailors in the city, and all the cloth stored in the royal godowns.[6]"

"Take them," said King Chang. "If you don't, the enemy will."

Throughout the night General Wang and his tailors slaved with needle and thread. The click of thimbles made a continuous humming sound. The hostiles on the farther shore heard, and wondered what strange warlike engines King Chang might be preparing.

---

[4] Kou chou (kō´jō´)

[5] Ku Hsueh (gōō´shyōō´)

[6] warehouses

With day's coming, Chang moved all his troops—he had only a thousand. The thousand men marched in parade along the river's brim. The uniforms were old and dowdy. The words, "We are brave," that adorned their tattered jackets seemed a poor and weak boast. They were ragamuffins. They marched as if weary. The enemy jeered.

But, lo. The first thousand had no sooner disappeared than another thousand circled past the river—stepping smartly, smartly uniformed in cloth of gold, the words "Very brave" embroi-

dered upon their fronts. The enemy was not so quick to jeer.

Following the second thousand came a thousand men in trig[7] red uniforms. Upon their breasts were broidered the words "Extremely brave." They stepped it briskly, shouting dares across the river. The enemy replied with very little heart.

Another thousand followed. Jade-green uniforms clothed them. Rumble-dumblededum sang their drums, and their steps kept perfect time. Upon their breasts were the words "Still braver," and upon their lips great threats. The enemy said little.

Now came men in crow's-wing black. Upon their breasts were the words

---

[7] stylishly trim

"Braver by far." Their taunts were hard to bear. Yet, the enemy remained silent.

A thousand men in pink, the same number in blue. Came white-clad men and orange-clad men. Violet uniforms replaced uniforms of brown. . . . The enemy thought it hardly fair. King Chang, evidently, had a million soldiers. . . . How could they fight against a million? The tents came down, and the enemy vanished.

General Wang continued to sew until the last hostile disappeared. He and his tailors were terribly tired. But the thousand soldiers were even more tired. All day long they had marched and changed uniforms, then marched again. They had changed from red to green, to black, to every color in the spectrum. They were color blind and weary. But King Chang merried much, and blessed the day that had sent him General Wang, the tailor.

In a month or so King Chang's happiness turned to gloom. The enemy had learned of Wang's clever trick, and resolved to march again. The army of Chang was scarcely larger than before.

To come off victorious each man would have to whip a dozen of the enemy. There was no time to increase the royal army. And the enemy lay on the other side of Ku Hsueh River, waiting for the waters to lower.

King Chang rode with his generals to the river. Said he: "There lies the enemy. The depth of the river lessens with each minute. Who has a plan?" Some of the generals stroked their beards. Others twisted their mustachios. All wrinkled their brows. Not one of them parted his lips. "Come. Come, my doughty generals. Have you no plan? General Tang?"

Tang bowed his head the three times required by law and courtesy. "Sire, with your permission, I have a small scheme that may serve."

"*Chen hao*[8] (Very good); spare no expense. Draw on the treasury for whatever you may desire—silk, tailors, fans, or false faces—anything except more soldiers, for soldiers we have not."

> How could they fight against a million?

---

[8] Chen hao (chən´hou´)

"Then, please, Your Majesty," said Tang, "may I ask you to sign an order on the treasury for one ounce of pine resin?" Then the King thought Tang jesting. His first impulse was to strike off his head. Instead of doing so, however, he signed the order for two cents' worth of resin.

At night General Tang sat upon a crag that towered above the river. He fondled his precious violin. A little breeze sprang up at his back. Tang the general was no more, but Tang the musician lived and thrilled. Bow swept strings with a magic sweetly sad. The breeze caught up the melody. The river was its sounding board. The soldiers on the farther shore turned in their blankets to listen. Than home there is no spot dearer—and the violin sang of home. More and more sad came the music. The musician wept. Across the river ten thousand eyes grew moist. The soldiers wept and were unashamed. Why had they left their warm hearthstones—to die in an alien land? Fierce resolve faded, and a longing took its stead, a longing for home and the loved ones it sheltered.

Morning saw the hostile camp deserted. Soldier after soldier had stolen away in the darkness, thinking only of home. Not one remained to threaten Ku Hsueh City.

King Chang assembled his generals, and spoke high praise of Tang. Then he discussed the need of preparation for the future. He knew very well that the enemy would return. "Have any of you, my trusty generals, a plan for humbling the enemy in his next invasion?"

General Mang, the former shepherd, voiced a plan. "I would suggest that all horses be replaced by lean sheep of the mountain."

General Lang, the archer, said, "I would suggest that all cases at law be settled by trial with bow and arrow."

"So be it," said the King. "I grant both requests."

The enemy soon marched upon Ku Hsueh in greater numbers than before. Grasshoppers in the August fields were never thicker. It was plain that only a miracle could save the city. All eyes were turned to General Mang, turned beseechingly, and rather doubtfully. Could a mountain shepherd save Ku Hsueh?

That night the question was answered. Mang herded his sheep in a tremendous body toward the enemy camp. At the proper moment he raised a great din and startled the animals into flight. Through the camp of the enemy they rushed, and instantly the camp was confusion. The soldiers had fared none too well on their march. They were hungry. And here was good food to be had for the catching. Away went sheep. Away went soldiers. Thoroughly frightened, the lean-limbed sheep sped their fastest. Thoroughly desirous, the hungry soldiers followed at their fastest.

While the camp was empty, Mang and a score of daring men darted from tent to tent. In their hands were torches. Behind them rose a flare of ever-spreading flame. "To roast their meat when they catch it," said Mang. The wind was a helpful friend, scattering brands with a will. The destruction was soon finished. What had been a white encampment became a red and rolling flame. The tents were burned, and the spears and the bows. Nothing was spared. A thoroughly discomfited enemy stole away from Ku Hsueh that night.

So far, General Lang had done nothing of a warlike nature—nothing at all—unless stepping upon the toes of a citizen be considered warlike. Lang had done that. Naturally, the citizen was incensed. He wished to see justice done, and went to a court of law. The judge said: "Take this bow and shoot five arrows in yonder target. He who shoots best has the right on his side." The young citizen shot first, and his marksmanship was poor, to say the least. Whereupon, Lang drew the bow. Oddly enough, his aim was no better than that of the citizen. With that the judge declared the suit undecided and set a future date for its retrial. General Lang left court well pleased. The young citizen went home to spend many hours in practice with bow and arrow.

Thereafter the courts were flooded with lawsuits. From morn till night the bowstrings twanged. It appeared that all the men of Ku Hsueh had grievances to be settled. And they who were wise spent much time in archery practice ere they went to court. Many became quite expert with the bow and arrow. . . .

King Chang impressed all of them into his army. At last he had a large force, a force that would give pause to any foe. Long the King waited for his enemy's return. But he waited in vain. Spies had watched the men of Ku Hsueh at practice with the bow. They sent messages that Ku Hsueh was prepared. So the country was troubled no more by alarms of hostile armies.

Thus, without loss of a man, was the kingdom saved for Chang, by Wang, Tang, Mang, and Lang—a thousand years ago all this, but very learned men still dispute as to which was the greatest, Lang, Mang, Tang, or Wang—which of the four generals.

Arthur Bowie Chrisman

Arthur Bowie Chrisman was born in 1889 at Westbrook, his family's farm in Virginia. His birthplace was part of a very rural community, and, as a young boy, Chrisman went to school at a one-room schoolhouse. His favorite place, though, was Westbrook's old abandoned slave quarters. He spent hours on end there playing with the hundreds of toys that he made for himself. He never liked toys bought from the store, he claimed, not even when his family could afford them.

When he got older, Chrisman worked as a farmer and a school teacher, and even tried his hand at movie acting. Then he decided to become a writer. "I never have written with the idea of making a fortune," he once said. "I merely decided to write and let fate take care of all subsequent happenings."

View from the Cliffs

I climb the cold mountain by

A steep path through the rocks,

To my little cabin in

The place where the clouds are born.

I halt my cart and look out

Over the forest of maples

In the sunset. The frosted

Leaves are more brilliant than

Any flowers of Spring.

by Tu Mu

Response

WRITE PARAGRAPHS

Imagine that Prince Chang meets a fifth general-to-be on his journey. What special talent does this person have? Give the fifth general a name, and write a few paragraphs about how he or she helps Prince Chang.

PANTOMIME CHARACTERS

Work with a small group to pantomime the characters in the story. Each of you should portray one general. Perform your pantomimes for the rest of the class. Have your classmates guess the names of each general during the performance.

Corner

WRITE DIARY ENTRIES

Imagine that Prince Chang carries a diary with him on his journey. What does he write about each one of the men he meets? Write a diary entry for each of the four men, explaining why they make good generals.

What do you think?

- If this folktale had a moral, what would it be? Explain your answer.

- If you could be one of the four generals, which one would you be? Why?

- If the narrator of the poem were another of Prince Chang's generals, what do you think his or her special talent would be?

Golden Kite Award

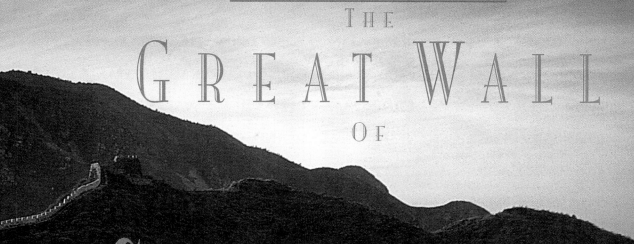

THE
GREAT WALL
OF
CHINA

BY JAMES CROSS GIBLIN

FROM WALLS: DEFENSES
THROUGHOUT HISTORY

THROUGHOUT HISTORY AND IN ALL PARTS OF THE WORLD PEOPLE HAVE BUILT WALLS FOR DEFENSE. ICE AGE PEOPLE BUILT WALLS OF MAMMOTH BONES. IN EUROPE MANY CITIES BUILT WALLS TO DEFEND THEMSELVES AGAINST ENEMIES. IN ENGLAND, IN 122 A.D., THE ROMAN EMPEROR HADRIAN ORDERED A WALL BUILT TO DEFEND THE COUNTRY TO THE SOUTH FROM INVADERS FROM THE NORTH. AND THEN THERE IS THE GREAT WALL OF CHINA.

When Hadrian's Wall was new, another wall already stretched across a vast country on the other side of the world. This rampart is the longest structure ever built. It contains enough building materials to circle the entire globe at the equator with a wall eight feet high and three feet thick. It is the only man-made structure on earth that can be seen with the naked eye from the moon. It is the Great Wall of China.

The Great Wall extends across northern and central China from the Yellow Sea in the east to a point deep in central Asia. There are different estimates of its overall length. Those who count only its distance east to west say it is approximately sixteen hundred miles long. Others claim that, with all of its loops and offshoots included, the wall is more than thirty-six hundred miles long. If straightened, they say, it would cross the United States from New York City to San Francisco, and there would be enough left over to wind back to Salt Lake City.

Construction of the wall spread over almost two thousand years, from 400 B.C., when the first sections were erected, until the 1600s A.D., when it was rebuilt and extended. But most of the wall was built in the ten years between 224 and 214 B.C. by Emperor Shih Huang-ti.[1]

So that people and goods could travel easily from one part of China to another, Shih embarked on a vast road- and canal-building program. And to protect his new nation from northern invaders, Shih launched his most ambitious project—the linking of many smaller, older walls into one great defensive wall.

---

[1] shē wang·tē

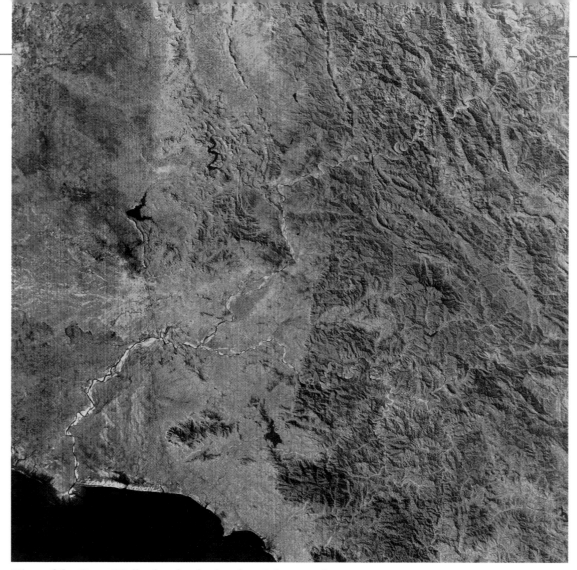

View of the Great Wall taken by the Landsat 2 Spacecraft

Such a wall was badly needed. For years the Tartars and other nomadic tribes had swept across the loosely defended border and attacked Chinese living in settled communities. The nomads looted Chinese homes, shops, and temples, burned the settlements to the ground, killed most of the men and children, and carried off some of the women as slaves.

The nomads laid siege to larger cities, too. Sometimes the inhabitants managed to hold out for a few weeks behind their city's walls. But unless an army garrison came to relieve them, the city dwellers were usually forced by hunger and disease to surrender. Then the looting, burning, and killing began all over again.

To prevent such terrible raids and bring hope to Chinese living on the border, Emperor Shih made construction of the Great Wall his first priority. He assigned an army of three hundred thousand men under one of his best generals, Meng Tien, to work on the project. Local laborers were recruited to assist the soldiers. Among them were thousands of women, who were hired to weave tents and help to carry loads.

Some of the hardest jobs were given to prisoners who were sent to the construction sites under armed guard. Besides common criminals, these prisoners included many people who had been captured in war or arrested for political reasons.

Historians estimate that all told more than a million people worked on the Great Wall. They labored from dawn to dusk, in freezing winter blizzards and blinding summer sandstorms. Clay for bricks was carried in baskets at the ends of shoulder poles. Building stones often had to be transported for long distances on crude sledges or wagons. In mountainous areas, the stones were sometimes raised into position by teams of specially trained goats.

Most of the workers suffered under harsh living conditions. Food rations frequently ran short and wells dried up. Flimsy tents offered little protection from blazing summer heat or sub-zero winter temperatures. Another problem was surprise attacks by nomadic enemy tribes. Often the soldiers in General Meng's army had to stop work in order to protect the other laborers.

As a result of all this, according to some Chinese historians, more than four hundred thousand men and women died while working on the wall. That was almost half the total work force. Many of the dead were buried within the wall, causing some people to call it "the longest cemetery in the world."

At last, after more than ten years, the Great Wall was completed. Its thirty-six-hundred-mile route ran across plains and deserts, bridged ravines and rivers, and climbed over mountains as high as six thousand feet above sea level.

The wall was generally twenty-five feet wide at the base, slanting to seventeen feet at the top. It was between twenty-five and thirty feet high. In eastern China, where rocks were plentiful, the sides were faced with large stones or granite boulders, and the top was paved with bricks. The interior was

Soldier in traditional uniform standing on the ancient brick road atop the wall

composed of small stones and earth, cemented with a mortar so hard that nails couldn't be driven into it.

Five-foot-high stone parapets rose on both sides of the wall's flat top. The parapets had openings at regular intervals through which arrows could be shot at attackers. The top itself served as a road, wide enough for eight people to walk abreast, or two horse-drawn chariots to pass each other.

Farther west, the wall crossed barren deserts where stones were scarce. In those sectors it was constructed of earth alone. The builders moistened the earth with water carried from distant wells, and pounded it to make it solid.

Every few hundred yards along the wall, a watchtower rose about twelve feet above the walkway. These towers were manned by small groups of soldiers and served as lookout posts. If the soldiers saw a hostile band approaching the wall, they sent up a signal—smoke during the day, colored lights at night. The lights came from blazing logs that were coated with metal oxides to produce different colors. A red light meant danger, a blue one signified that all was quiet.

There were also many larger *garrison towers,* or forts, along the wall. Each of these could hold between one hundred and two hundred soldiers with their weapons, ammunition, and provisions. When a danger signal sent from a watchtower was seen at one of the garrison towers, the soldiers stationed there raced along the top of the wall to the spot that was threatened.

The entire wall was probably not garrisoned at any given time; that would have required many millions of soldiers. But historians estimate that in the days of Shih Huang-ti an army of perhaps a million men guarded the rampart.

For centuries the Great Wall protected northern China against small-scale attacks. But gradually the number of troops manning it was reduced, and large sections fell into ruin. In 1211 A.D. it proved no barrier to the Mongol leader Genghis Khan. He and his horse soldiers broke through the wall's defenses and conquered much of China.

The Mongols were driven out of China in the late 1300s and the wall was rebuilt. Frontier defense forces patrolled its fortifications from Manchuria in the east to Kansu in the west, and kept China largely free of Mongol raiders.

The Great Wall winding through the mountains

As the military threat from the north lessened, much of the wall was abandoned again. People living nearby started chipping away at it and removing stones to use in building houses and temples. Over time, long stretches of the wall—especially those made of earth—simply crumbled into dust. Other sections remained intact, however. During the war with Japan in the 1930s, Chinese soldiers marched to the northern front along the ancient brick road atop the wall.

After the Chinese Communists took power in 1949, several sections of the wall were restored once more—not as a military fortification but as a historical monument. The restored section north of Peking has become a major tourist attraction, visited each year by thousands of people from all over the world.

It takes two hours to reach this restored section by train or bus. Suddenly, craggy mountains loom into view above the plain, and then the wall itself appears, curving over and around the mountains like a giant stone snake.

From the parking lot, steep inclines lead up to watchtowers at both ends of the restored section. It's a hard climb, but the view from the towers is worth the effort. Gazing out at the wall as it winds away across the mountains, one can't help but be amazed at the simple fact that it's there.

Besides its appeal as a tourist attraction, the wall is being used in other ways today. Scientists study it to learn the effects of earthquakes that occurred in the past. Archaeologists dig in and around it in search of tools and other objects from the time when it was built.

And previously unknown sections are still being discovered. In 1983 archaeologists unearthed a sixty-two-mile segment, thus adding to the already incredible length of the Great Wall of China—truly one of the wonders of the world.

Parapets along the Great Wall

JAMES CROSS GIBLIN

James Cross Giblin, author of *The Riddle of the Rosetta Stone* and *Walls: Defenses Throughout History,* writes with a fast-paced style that creates a vivid picture of great historical events. Here, writer Ilene Cooper and James Giblin discuss his writing.

Ms. Cooper: You've chosen such unusual subjects for your books, everything from chairs to the Rosetta Stone. How do you decide what you're going to write about?

Mr. Giblin: The subject has to be something that interests me. My interest in the Great Wall came from personal experience. In 1975, I was part of a cultural delegation that toured China, and I was the only person in publishing.

Ms. Cooper: That was before China hosted many foreign tourists, wasn't it?

Mr. Giblin: One of the tour guides told me they were very excited because they were expecting a thousand tourists that year, so, yes, that was very much before the days of McDonald's in China.

Ms. Cooper: Did you take a tour of the Great Wall?

Mr. Giblin: We went out to the Great Wall on a bus. It's very impressive. When the book describes the feeling of looking out from the wall, that's something I experienced myself.

Ms. Cooper: Do most of your books come from your travels?

Mr. Giblin: Almost everything in *Walls* comes from the traveling I did in the 1960s and 1970s. I had been to the Berlin Wall and I also visited walled cities, and that, along with my visit to the Great Wall, made me want to write the book.

Ms. Cooper: You started out doing a completely different kind of writing than you do now.

Mr. Giblin: Yes, as a young man, I was a playwright. I was a movie-crazy kid, and that led to my interest in theater, which I studied in college. Eventually, I gave up the theater and moved into the publishing world, where I worked as an editor. My writing career in children's books started slowly, but eventually I had to decide if I wanted to be an editor or a writer. I still do some editing, but now, I've made my choice. I'm a writer.

夜上受降城聞笛　李益

回樂峯前沙似雪

受降城外月如霜

不知何處吹蘆管

一夜征人盡望鄉

ON HEARING A FLUTE AT NIGHT FROM THE WALL OF SHOU-HSIANG

by Li Yi

The sand below the border-mountain lies like snow,
And the moon like frost beyond the city-wall,
And someone somewhere, playing a flute,
Has made the soldiers homesick all night long.

translated by Witter Bynner
illustrated by Peter Siu

STAGE A DEBATE

ROYAL DEBATE

With a partner, take the roles of two of the emperor's advisors who hold opposing views: one in favor of building the Great Wall and the other opposed to its construction. Look for details from the selection to support your opinion. Allow enough time to prepare a convincing argument before you stage your debate.

MEASURE DISTANCES

FROM HERE TO THERE

With a partner, find a globe and some string. Then reread the second paragraph of the selection. Using the details given there and the globe, cut the string to match the length of the Great Wall. Stretch the string across the United States and then across another section of the globe. Name several pairs of cities or land forms that fit within the length of the Great Wall.

WRITE A POEM

VIEW FROM THE WALL

Imagine standing on top of the Great Wall. What do you see, hear, and smell? Write a short poem describing your feelings. Share your poem with the class.

RESPONSE CORNER

WHAT DO YOU THINK?

- Much human toil and suffering went into the building of the Great Wall of China. Do you think building it was worth that price? Explain your answer.

- What is the most surprising fact that you learned about the Great Wall of China?

- Why do you think so many people want to visit the Great Wall?

Theme Wrap-Up

Some remnants of the ancient civilizations of Egypt and China can still be seen; others must be re-created in our imaginations. Which of these civilizations is more fascinating to you? Why?

The rulers of ancient China and ancient Egypt left behind huge works, such as the Great Wall and the pyramids. Do you think it was worth the effort to build them? Explain your answer.

ACTIVITY CORNER

Think about the civilizations you have read about. Use your imagination to write a folktale set in one of them. Illustrate your folktales and share it with your classmates.

Celebrating Differences

Sometimes people fear what they do not understand about one another. When they communicate, however, they find that they have a lot in common, and their differences become something to celebrate.

Celebrating Differences

CONTENTS

Bookshelf

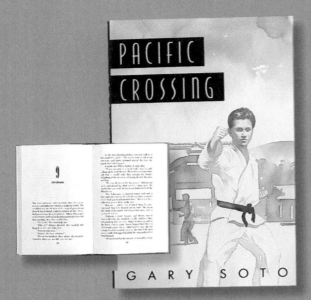

Pacific Crossing
by Gary Soto

In this sequel to *Taking Sides*, Linc and his friend Tony leave their native California far behind while they spend three months studying *kempo* in Japan.

AWARD-WINNING AUTHOR
SIGNATURES LIBRARY

A Jar of Dreams
by Yoshiko Uchida

When Rinko is snubbed at school and in the street, she almost wishes she were not Japanese. Then Aunt Waka visits from Japan, and the whole family finds new strength.

NOTABLE TRADE BOOK IN SOCIAL STUDIES
SIGNATURES LIBRARY

Anne Frank: Beyond the Diary

by *Ruud van der Rol and Rian Verhoeven*

Anne Frank's diary remains a classic of hope and
courage, and this book helps readers understand
the events that shaped her tragically short life.

ALA NOTABLE BOOK

NOTABLE TRADE BOOK IN SOCIAL STUDIES

TEACHERS' CHOICE

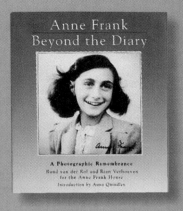

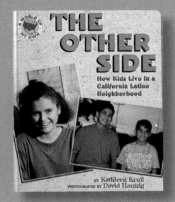

The Other Side: How Kids Live in a California Latino Neighborhood

by *Kathleen Krull*

In this photo essay, three young people talk about their
lives growing up in a close-knit Latino neighborhood.

NOTABLE TRADE BOOK IN SOCIAL STUDIES

It's Our World, Too! Stories of Young People Who Are Making a Difference

by *Phillip Hoose*

Through their inspiring stories, these determined
young people teach practical lessons about
how to create positive change in the world.

ALA NOTABLE BOOK

NOTABLE TRADE BOOK IN SOCIAL STUDIES

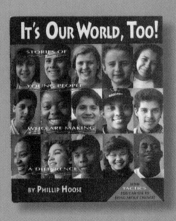

The Vietnamese in AMERICA

BY PAUL RUTLEDGE

Immigrants have been coming to the United States since early in its history. Among the most recent groups of immigrants are people from Vietnam, a country in Southeast Asia.

Almost every aspect of daily life changes for Vietnamese refugees who settle in the United States. Attitudes toward the family, methods of education, language, even as common a matter as shopping for food—all these can be sources of culture shock for the Vietnamese. Their backgrounds, habits, and ways of everyday life are sometimes the opposite of American customs, and trying to blend the old ways with the new may cause the refugees bewilderment, pain, and conflict.

FAMILY

The Vietnamese family is under a great deal of pressure in trying to adjust to the American way of life. In the United States, a family usually consists of father, mother, and children. In Vietnam, a family is an extended one that includes the parents and the younger children, grandparents, married children, aunts, uncles, and a variety of other relatives. In some cases, all the members of an extended family live in the same house.

The family is the center of Vietnamese society, and it is the responsibility of every member to help the family survive. But the size of an extended Vietnamese family can make it difficult to find housing in America. Families want to establish themselves as close units but often cannot find adjacent housing large enough to accommodate 20 or 30 relatives.

In the Vietnamese culture, the older a person is, the more he or she is respected. Young people are always expected to seek the advice of older persons within the family. Children are taught to listen to and accept the decisions of their elders. In the traditional American family, however, individual members are more independent. In the United States, children are taught and advised by their parents in a less structured way.

When young Vietnamese refugees become friends with young Americans and see the more informal relationships between them and their families, the Vietnamese are likely to want the same kind of independence—something their Vietnamese parents find difficult to accept.

EDUCATION

The Vietnamese culture places a high value on education. As persons of knowledge, teachers are considered some of the most important members of society.

Before the Europeans entered Vietnam, the Confucian system of education dominated the country. This system was based on memorization.

People could memorize large amounts of material and then take exams in which they quoted the memorized material. If they passed, they could improve their employment and social standing. Anyone—farmer or aristocrat—could take the exams.

During the French colonial period[1] in Vietnam, public schools were built, and education was emphasized. Teachers in these schools were considered role models as well as instructors, and children were reluctant to question their statements. Discipline was an important part of the educational system.

When they attend American schools, refugee children may find a conflict between Vietnamese methods of education and those used in the United States. In Vietnam, children listen to, and learn from, the teacher, who is always correct. In America, students learn from the teacher but are also taught to think for themselves. Many Vietnamese children find this difficult to do. They will always agree with everything the teacher says because to do otherwise would show great disrespect.

Some other aspects of U.S. education are unfamiliar to Vietnamese students. Activities such as individual research, classroom debates, learning by doing, and group projects are new and strange to them. Despite these differences, many young Vietnamese have adapted well to American education and are making good grades.

LANGUAGE

One of the most necessary, but also one of the hardest, tasks for a new refugee is learning the English language. The Vietnamese language contains six basic tones, and the sound of each word is part of the meaning of the word. English, which is not tonal, uses one word to mean many things. For the non-English speaker, this can be very confusing and a source of difficulty in attempting to learn English.

Even the way names are written is different in the two languages. In Vietnam, the family name is always written first in order to emphasize the importance of the family and of one's inheritance. In the United States, the family name is usually written last. For instance, an American man would write his name John Michael Doe, but in Vietnam, the correct form would be Doe John Michael. (To avoid confusion, some Vietnamese in the United States have adopted the American system and put their family names last instead of first.) There are only about 30 family names for all Vietnamese. The most common one is Nguyen, which is used by almost half the population.

[1] French colonial period: the period during which Vietnam was governed by France—from 1883 to 1945

When a Vietnamese woman marries, she keeps her maiden name and also uses her husband's name. For example, if Le Thi Ba married Nguyen Pham Binh, she would be called Le Thi Ba in informal situations, but on formal occasions, such as during a ceremony, she would be called Mrs. Nguyen Pham Binh.

CUSTOMS

The basic customs of Vietnamese life have been handed down from generation to generation just as American customs have been. There are many differences between the habits and attitudes of the two cultures.

Respect is very important to Vietnamese people. When greeting others, the Vietnamese bow their heads to show respect and honor. It takes some time for newly arrived refugees to get used to a casual "Hi" or "Hello" from people they pass on the street. In Vietnam, it is polite to look away when speaking to someone and rude to look directly at the person. This is exactly the opposite of behavior in the United States and often causes misunderstandings. Refugees are accused of being rude and unfriendly because they apparently ignore those speaking directly to them.

Even something as simple as color can be the source of conflict for the refugees. In Vietnam, the color white represents death. For the Vietnamese who enter an American hospital for the first time, seeing the white sheets and doctors and nurses dressed in white may convince them they are going to die.

Many of the practical aspects of life in the United States demand an adjustment by Vietnamese people. For example, the American transportation system presents a challenge, particularly for those used to living in farming areas. In Vietnam, walking and riding a bike were the most common forms of travel. Certainly not every family had a car. In the United States, the Vietnamese must cope with buses, subways, trains, airplanes, and especially cars.

Learning to drive is very difficult for older refugees, who are fearful of the heavy traffic and fast speeds in large U.S. cities. The younger generation, however, has fallen in love with

American cars, and this causes some conflict in Vietnamese families. The parents feel that the car is breaking up the family, that the teenagers are always driving off by themselves or with friends when they should be spending time with relatives.

The ways in which food is prepared and even packaged can be confusing to recent arrivals. Fast-food hamburgers, pizza, and fried chicken are new to the refugees. In fact, the Vietnamese are not used to eating such greasily prepared items and usually do not like fried food at first.

Even the cans, boxes, and jars in American supermarkets can cause misunderstanding. One Vietnamese family in a large city spent several hours in a grocery looking at all the items. They were confused because they thought that the picture on each can and box showed what was inside the container. The family's young daughter was understandably frightened by a box of cereal with a monster pictured on it. These people would buy nothing but the fresh vegetables they could see and touch. Experience eventually made them more comfortable shopping for food American style.

Although Vietnamese immigrants want to learn as much as possible about American culture and to adapt to American life, most of them also want to keep the customs and language of their homeland alive. Like many earlier groups of immigrants, their goal is to become Americans without losing their ethnic identity.

Hello, My Name Is Scrambled Eggs

by Jamie Gilson

illustrated by Hui Han Liu

Harvey and Julia Trumble's family is hosting a family of Vietnamese refugees who have just arrived in America. Harvey knows it will be tough for the Nguyens to feel at home in their new country. So he takes on the responsibility of teaching young Tuan Nguyen everything he needs to know about American life. Harvey also wants to help Tuan make friends with the right people—and to keep him away from people like Quint Calkins, the class know-it-all. Right away, Harvey realizes that learning a new language is likely to be Tuan's biggest obstacle.

Award-Winning
Author

"Harvey, come look!" Julia called from the top of the third-floor steps. "They sleep funny."

"Quiet," I whispered and leaped the stairs two at a time to shush her. "Quiet, or they won't sleep at all." Still, it was the middle of Sunday afternoon, and they'd been up there almost twenty-four hours. The trip must really have zonked them out.

"Look at *that*," she whispered back and pointed into Pete's room.

The door was open and I could see inside. It wasn't true they slept funny. They were sleeping like people do, all curled up. It was *where* they were sleeping that was funny. They were all in Pete's bedroom, but they weren't in bed. They'd taken the bedspreads off and put them on the floor, and that's where they were sleeping. I'd only slept on the floor at sleepovers, but it never worked out too good. When I woke up in the morning, I always had a crick in my neck.

"Julia!" I pulled her away from the door. "Don't be nosy." And I headed her back down the steps. On the way, though, I coughed a little, hoping to wake the kid up. We had work to do.

When Tuan came downstairs about an hour later, he was a lot hungrier for food than for facts. He ate two apples from the bushel in the kitchen, some of the big bowl of rice Mom had made special, and a whole lot of beef stew. I would never have thought that using a fork could be so hard. Just watching him made me nervous. And I wondered how anybody could possibly eat all those slippery little grains of rice with sticks.

Right after he ate, I steered him down to the basement to meet Felix, our trusty computer. I'd decided it was time for Felix to teach him some new words. The first one would be *marble*. My dad had dug out a wrinkled leather pouch of his old marbles and given them to me so I'd have something in common with the kid. I mean, it wasn't as though I could shoot marbles or anything like that. My dad said it was an old American sport, but since I wasn't an old American, I didn't play it. Anyway, I opened the bag and dug out a big yellow one with tiny bubbles in it and gave it to the kid. He looked it over but didn't remember what it was called.

"Marble," I said, and typed it out on Felix. "What is it called in Vietnamese?"

He typed DANH-BI. "Need mark through *d* and over *n*," he told me, but the computer couldn't handle that. "Say, '*danh-bi*.'"

It was hard to say. It didn't fit my mouth, and so I only tried once. He started to hand the marble back. "Keep it," I said, holding my hands behind my back. "Keep it." He put it on the workbench.

Pete's bike was leaning up against the wall, in storage till he came home.

BICYCLE, I typed out on Felix and, giving the handlebars a pat, said it out loud.

So did the kid. "Bi-cyc-le."

"Close," I told him.

XE-DAP, he typed. "And mark through . . ." He pointed at the d. "*Bicycle* is *xe-dap*."

"Shut up?" I asked. That's sure what it sounded like.

"Close," he said.

"Do you know what *shut up* means?"

"*Shut up*? No. What means *shut up*?"

"It means 'be quiet.'" I put my finger in front of my lips and said, "Shhhhhhhhhh." He nodded. "Shut up!" I yelled.

"You talk loud to ask be quiet?"

"Right. *Shut up*! That's the way to say it," I shouted.

"*Shut up*!" he yelled back, laughing.

"You boys all right down there?" Mom called down the steps.

"Fine," I told her. "We're OK."

"What means OK?" he asked.

"OK means 'good,' 'terrific.' OK is basic. OK is the best. We'll have Felix tell you 'OK' every time you get a word right, OK?"

"OK."

We sat there for a long time with me teaching him words like *follow*. First I marched around behind him. "I *follow* you." Then I got in front of him and made him say, "I *follow* you." I was the leader. He was my follower. We did verbs like *throw* and *hide* and *laugh* and *vomit*. After we'd both acted them out, I'd write them into the computer. And Tuan would write in the Vietnamese word so he'd remember what the English one meant. Input, output. Input, output. It was terrific. We were working on *hiccup* when Mom called down the steps again.

"Harvey, you've got company. It's almost ten o'clock, though, just about time for bed."

"Tuan just barely got up," I told her, "and he's got lots of work to do. Who's there?"

"Quint the Quintessential," he called down grandly.

Big deal, I thought. "Enter," I said, though, since nothing was likely to stop him. He took the steps slow and heavy, waving and grinning. I turned back to the computer.

"Hi, there, Zilch," he said. "Having a good time with your new toy?"

"The computer's not all that new," I told him, punching a few keys casually.

"I wasn't talking about the computer." He grinned, and leaning with his mouth close to my ear, he whispered, "Uncovering the mysteries of the Orient?"

"No!" I pushed him away with my shoulder. "I'm teaching Tuan English."

He gave the kid a big hello like he was his biggest admirer and then circled around behind him and rolled his eyes at me. "So, why bother?" he asked.

"He's got to learn it. He starts school Friday, the end of this week. With us."

"You're kidding. Our *class*?"

"Why not? He's twelve. Mom says it's fixed so he can be with me."

Quint laughed through his nose. "He doesn't know his elbow from an escalator and he's going to be in the same class with *me*? Gifted old me? He ought to be in Julia's room."

Tuan was working on the words we'd programmed. OK, Felix printed, turning on his computer charm. OK, TUAN. The kid glanced at Quint, who clapped his hands, yelled, "OK!" and nodded as if the kid had just won the Nobel Peace Prize.

Tuan turned back to the computer, smiling. Quint rolled his eyes again.

"You *are* good," he said to Tuan, as Felix went OK once again.

The kid beamed back.

"Will you teach me marbles?" Quint asked him.

"Teach?" He turned away from the computer. "*Teach* you?"

"Right." Quint picked up my yellow marble from the counter. "Will you teach me how?"

"Yes." Tuan grinned at him. "OK."

"Tomorrow?" Quint was trying to take my kid away from me. That's what he was trying to do. He handed Tuan the marble I'*d* given him just ten minutes before. "My uncle wants to ask the kid some questions," he whispered to me, like we were both in on some big joke. "Wayne knows a lot of words in Vietnamese. He wants to look him over."

"Sorry. Tuan's busy with important stuff tomorrow and Tuesday and Wednesday and Thursday, and he starts school Friday."

"After school Friday it is, then. You come to my house Friday," Quint told the kid. "OK?"

"I've got to work after school Friday," I told him.

"I didn't ask you," Quint explained like I was a little kid who'd begged to tag along to a party. "OK?" he said to Tuan again.

"OK! Marbles." You'd have thought the president had invited him to breakfast at the White House, he was so pleased.

"See you around." Quint took the stairs two a time, slamming the basement door so we'd have something to remember him by.

When the place had stopped shaking, I said to the kid, patiently and slowly, "You don't want to go to Quint's."

"Yes," he said, smiling broadly, "I go to him house."

"H*is* house."

"His house. He is . . . Quint?"

"Yes, he's Quint, all right."

"Quint is OK. Right way to use OK?"

"Right," I said. But I sure didn't mean it.

"Hello, my name is Jelly," Julia said, staring at the name tag stuck to a jar on the kitchen table. She'd guessed wrong. It said, HELLO, MY NAME IS JAM. Tossing her stuffed owl Zachary onto her chair, Julia climbed on top of him, leaned back, and stared up.

"Hello, my name is Ceiling. Is that right?" I nodded. "I can read *ceiling*! Maybe they'll let me skip first grade." She craned her neck to look at the sign again. "Are you sure that says *ceiling*? Mrs. Broderick says the snake sound, Sssssssssssssssss, is S. Silly Sally Ceiling. See, it's got to be wrong."

"Ceiling," Tuan said automatically, copying it into a small notebook I'd given him. NEW WORDS, I'd printed on the cover. He was eating breakfast and hadn't noticed that one yet.

"Remember 'I before E except after C,'" I told him as he wrote. He blinked at me.

I'd got the name tags from this huge stack left over from a party of Mom's where nobody wore them. The tags had little red wavy borders with HELLO, MY NAME IS printed on the front and sticky stuff on the back. I'd written about a hundred names of things on them. Then I'd matched them up, sticking them on the sugar bowl, the doors, floors, apples, toilet, computer, boot box. Every day after I came home from school, I'd take the kid around naming things for him. The house was beginning to look like a first-grade workbook.

"Hello, my name is Butter Dish," Julia said. "Harvey, make one for Zachary. He's jealous."

"That tag better not leave a mark on the ceiling," Dad told me, wiping his mouth with his napkin. "And the day you lay one on my scrambled eggs, you've had it."

Actually, I *had* made a Scrambled Eggs label, but I'd decided it would slide off, and so I'd just stuck it in my back pocket.

"Your father is absolutely right," Mom said. "If there's anything that flusters me, it's eggs that try to get too friendly. More toast, Tuan?"

He shook his head and leaned over his scrambled eggs with a fork, watching me closely as I ate. He waited a long time before picking up the bacon with his fingers as I did, making sure that's how Dad ate his, too. His grandmother sat by herself at the end of the table. He called her Ba Noi, which means, he said, "your father's mother." A white wool shawl Mom had found for her was tucked tightly around her like a cocoon. She was not having scrambled eggs for breakfast, but broth with noodles in it, first drinking the broth and then eating the noodles with chopsticks she'd brought with her.

"Get Tuan to school on time, now," Dad called, barreling out the back door. Then Ba Noi spoke. She said something to Tuan—low, fast, and kind

212

of sharp. Tuan answered her quietly, glancing around at us and then down at his feet.

"Is something wrong?" Mom asked him. "May we help?"

The kid shook his head and took a deep breath. I wondered if he was trying to think what to say or how to say it. "Ba Noi say I not . . . look good for school," he whispered.

He looked good to me. I'd told him what to wear—faded jeans, a striped T-shirt, and the red, white, and blue tennis shoes Mom had bought him the day before. Perfect.

"Tell her I say it's *very* American."

"She want me *very* Vietnamese . . . blue pants. . . ." He sliced across his leg with his hand to show he meant the short ones he'd worn when he arrived.

I laughed. "You dress like that and everybody'll think you're weird. Besides, in this weather you'd die of terminal goose bumps." I knew he hadn't understood that. "Cold," I said, shaking myself with a shiver. "Short pants are for summer."

"Hello, my name is Clock," Julia announced. "We're going to be late."

Tuan spoke again to his grandmother. She still did not look pleased. But we waved good-bye to her and to Mom and hurried off. Tuan was smiling as if he liked looking very American.

On the way, we worked on tree names and street names. I named. He repeated. Once we got to school, I showed him the water fountain, the john, and the trophy case. People kept saying, "Hi," and so I taught him a few of the kids' names, too. It was an educational experience.

Finally, I got him to the principal's office. Mr. Saine was on the phone when I poked my head in. ". . . will deal with that matter immediately," he told the phone, motioning us to come on in.

Mr. Saine stood up, way up. I mean, he must be six-five. Tuan came about to his belt.

"Hi," Tuan said, holding out his hand when Mr. Saine came over to greet us.

"Why, hello, young man." Mr. Saine shook his hand, looking pleased by good manners and all that. "I've been expecting you. How's his English?" he asked me, his voice lowered.

"I'm teaching him," I said.

"Good, fine." He sat back in his chair and started looking through some papers. "First you take him to homeroom. And after that we'll line up some diagnostic tests to see where square one should be, since there aren't any transcripts. Understood?"

I nodded. The kid smiled, understanding nothing. I could read the look by now. Mr. Saine shuffled through a stack of papers on his desk. "Reverend Zito tells me your name is . . ." He clamped his hands together, took a deep breath, and pronounced it all wrong.

And that was when I got the idea. If the kid really did want to be an American and to be one fast, the name Tuan Nguyen wouldn't do. It wouldn't do any more than short pants on a cold day. You put that name in lights or across a headline and people would get it wrong almost every time.

"He's just decided to change it. The name you've got isn't right. It *used* to be Tuan Nguyen. But now he's going to be . . ." I tossed the sounds around in my head a few times until his name turned, without any problem at all, into . . . "Tom. His first name is Tom." Mr. Saine glanced at Tuan/Tom, who smiled and nodded, but clearly understood not a word. Mr. Saine wrote down Thomas. I took a breath, and before I let it out, had the whole thing. From Nguyen to Gwen to Win, easy as that. "Win. His full American name is Tom Win. W-I-N." I felt like an artist painting a brand-new picture.

"*And a fine name it is, too,*" Mr. Saine said loudly to the kid, who was still staring blankly into our fog of too-fast words. "*Welcome to Pittsfield and Pittsfield Junior High School, Tom Win!*" His voice made the trophies on the shelf vibrate.

"Thank you." Tuan smiled politely. "Shut up," he said, a little louder.

Mr. Saine's jaw dropped open. So did mine. The room turned suddenly still, as if somebody had vacuumed out all the sound. My knees felt like rubber bands. Mr. Saine's face was gray.

Tuan kept smiling, though he did look uneasy.

"I . . . I . . . I . . ." I stuttered, my voice turned high like I'd just swallowed a balloonful of helium. "I think . . . I think . . . See, I told him, I taught him, that 'shut up' means 'be quiet.' I think"—I swallowed hard because my throat had become a desert—"he means you don't have to shout. A lot of people have been shouting at him, thinking it will help him understand. And it *doesn't* help, really. I taught him 'shut up' because it sounds a lot like Vietnamese bicycles." Mr. Saine's frown deepened. "He means to be polite. He learns fast. I even *told* him to say it loud, I —"

"All right, Harvey," Mr. Saine interrupted me, still looking grim. His face was flushed. "I'll accept that." He said it, but I wasn't sure he meant it. "It's late," he said, using his normal voice. "Give these papers to your home-room teacher, and, Harvey"—he took a deep breath—"*re*-explain 'shut up.'"

"Good night," the kid said, beaming.

We hurried out of the office toward homeroom, Tuan looking so cheerful I started to laugh out loud. He was positively the only kid in the whole school, in the whole world, maybe, who could get away with saying "shut up" to Mr. Saine. I was laughing, but my knees wobbled as I walked.

"Oh, by the way," I told Tuan as we reached the homeroom door, "your new American name is Tom." I stopped, opened my notebook, and wrote it down. "Tom," I repeated. "You."

"Tuan," he said. "Me."

"You have a new name, Tom Win. It's a terrific name. I made it up myself. I wish it was mine. I mean, like, it goes more with jeans and tennis shoes than the old one did. When you hit a homer at the bottom of the ninth with the bases loaded, they'll say, 'Win wins!' Tom Win," I repeated slowly. "The American you."

He stopped and thought about it. "Ba Noi say no. Father say no." The last bell rang.

"Do you want to be American or don't you?"

He nodded. "But Ba Noi say . . ."

"OK, then, just at school. Tom Win at school. Tuan Nguyen in the privacy of your own home. Ba Noi won't have to know. To her and your dad you'll stay Tuan. No kidding, could I be Vietnamese and have a name like Harvey Trumble?"

He laughed and shook his head. "OK," he said. "Tom Win is me."

I rushed him into homeroom, a new kid.

The class, most all of them in their seats by now, looked up from what they were doing and stared at us.

"Uh, Miss Schwalbach," I said, handing her the papers Mr. Saine had given me, "this is the new Vietnamese boy we've been talking about, only he's changed his name. It's . . . uh . . . Tom Win. Mr. Saine says after homeroom he's supposed to go to the office for tests."

"Of course." She beamed at him. "So it's to be Tom Win?"

He glanced at me. "Yes," he told her. He held his hand out, and she shook it.

"We're glad you're here, Tom. People," she told the class, "I want you to be sure to welcome Tom Win cordially."

"That's not what I heard him called." Quint tilted back in his chair.

"Goes to show you don't know everything," I said very casual, like of course I did. "He's called Tom Win," I announced to the class. My kid, named by me.

Miss Schwalbach motioned to an empty place in the front row. "Sit here, Tom."

He sat. Tom Win sat. He could host a game show with a name like that.

When the bell rang for first period, I delivered the kid to the office. Even though I said good-bye and wished him good luck, I was certain they'd be calling me out of science or language arts to help him with the tests. The morning went by without a messenger, though, and I guessed they'd given up on him or something. So I was really surprised when I got to the cafeteria at lunch and there he was, still smiling, sitting with Suzanna, eating a hamburger layered with pickles, mustard, and catsup.

"I just explained that hamburger isn't made out of ham." Suzanna popped a french fry in her mouth.

"It is cow," Tom told me. "It is good." He took another bite.

"Did the whole family change their names?" She drew a smiley face in a pool of catsup with her last fry.

"Not yet." That might take some doing. We'd break it to them slowly. It was going to be some trick keeping the Tom/Tuans straight. The kid had this double identity like a spy. If only I could change my name, too. Tom Win would have suited me fine. "How'd it go?" I asked him. "Were the tests hard?"

He took a gulp of chocolate milk and blinked at the taste, licking his upper lip. "Words hard, Harvey. Numbers . . . weird."

That was a word I'd taught him by making faces. *Weird*. He liked it, but I guess it was like *shut up*. He didn't know what it meant. Numbers are a lot of things—like impossible. Weird, though, they're not.

But Mr. Tandy, our math teacher, sounded like he thought so, too. "A little strange," he said when class started. He smiled at Tom, who had finished his tests in time to come to the last class of the day. "Yes, class, you'd think that math was math the whole world over, but there are differences. I talked to our remarkable new student, Tom Win, this morning as he was taking some tests, and he suggested that some of our ways with numbers were unusual. I thought I'd check it out with the rest of you."

The kid looked at the floor, embarrassed.

"Tom, go to the chalkboard. And Quint, you too, just to demonstrate the differences."

Quint, wearing his fabulous-me face, brought the kid with him to the board. They both took pieces of chalk and, when Mr. Tandy told them to, wrote down 675 divided by 15. Quint's problem looked normal: $15\overline{)675}$. When he finished doing the problem, he looked over at the kid, who already had the answer. "Bizarre," he said. Mr. Tandy grinned. The kid had written, very neatly:

$$
\begin{array}{c|c}
675 & 15 \\
075 & 45 \\
\end{array}
$$

"Why'd he do it like that?" Quint asked, cocking his head. He shrugged. "I could have done it in my head."

"I expect he could have too, but that, of course, is not the point." Mr. Tandy was annoyed with him. "Now, both of you, write down twenty-five dollars."

Quint scribbled out $25.00 as fast as he could. Nobody was going to outrace him.

Carefully, the kid wrote: 25$00.

"More bizarre," Quint said, and everybody had to agree.

"You boys can sit down." I never saw Mr. Tandy quite so pleased. He

grinned like everybody had gotten the extra-credit question right, or something equally miraculous. "And in Vietnam, when two thousand is written down it's . . ." Glancing first to the ceiling, where he always looks for approval, he wrote on the board 2.000. "There's a point after the thousand. On the other hand, they use a decimal *comma*. Thusly." He wrote 1,52. "Anybody think of a reason why one system is any better than the other, aside from the fact that you're used to it?"

Nobody raised a hand. He chuckled. "Neither can I. Isn't that fascinating!"

Quint rolled his eyes. "Knocks me out," he said sarcastically. A few kids giggled. Mr. Tandy laughed mildly, too. He knows not everybody is as crazy about math as he is. But he could afford to laugh. He was passing out a pop quiz. Aaarg.

"So, will this test count?" Caroline asked.

"Pieces of paper can't count. But I certainly hope you can. Any other questions?"

"Yes." Caroline sighed. "Do we have to take it?"

"You're wasting our time, Caroline."

All the time in the world wouldn't help. I knew I should have studied the night before instead of helping the kid learn English. We'd fooled around at Felix for a couple of hours, watched a little TV, sung with the commercials. I scratched on.

When Mr. Tandy said, "Exchange papers, please," a mass groan swelled out over the desks. I wasn't finished. A lot of kids weren't. The story problem was quicksand sucking me under.

Quint had already turned his paper over on his desk so no one could cheat from it. He was cleaning his fingernails with a toothpick.

Suzanna grabbed the kid's paper quick before I could. How she thought she was going to read it, I couldn't imagine. "What do I do about the commas and points?" she asked.

"If everything else is OK, grade them right. He'll get the knack of the mechanics soon enough."

"That's not fair," Quint complained.

Mr. Tandy started down the row, asking kids for answers and talking about problems.

"So, what do I do when Quint's decimal point's wrong?" Caroline asked. "Because one *is*."

"Mark it wrong. He knows better." Quint leaned over to look, not believing it.

When we got to the last problem, Suzanna raised her hand excitedly and said, "Tuan . . . or Tom, whatever, got them all right. He did most of the marks our way. But he skipped the story problem."

"Terrific! Tom? The story problem?" Mr. Tandy pointed to it.

"I cannot read it."

Mr. Tandy looked at the ceiling again with a smile. He'd found another math person. Big deal. "I think it's *remarkable* that he's adjusted so quickly. Suzanna, mark the paper one hundred percent. And a big A. It ought to give him a real boost. He'll be able to read the story problems as well as you can before long."

"That isn't fair," I said. "If it's wrong, it's wrong. He's got to learn that." I'd gotten it wrong. And half the other problems too. There's such a thing as being too nice. I didn't want my kid spoiled. Besides, he'd kept me from studying. And he'd had all day Wednesday and Thursday to look at the books I'd brought him from school. He couldn't read most of the stuff, and so he'd probably spent all his time on the math I'd told him we were doing. He'd been *studying*. Hours probably. He didn't have anything else to do with me gone. "No fair," I said again.

Quint, who'd been looking pretty mad himself, suddenly crossed his arms and tilted his chair back. "Oh, forget it. He's no real hotshot," he said to me. "But he's no Zilch either." Then he looked at me funny. "*You* didn't teach him that stuff, did you?"

I smiled, genius in disguise.

"Your problem," Mr. Tandy said to the class, "is that you're not reading carefully enough. You're not following directions. I want you all to read that story problem over tonight and then to work it correctly."

Caroline opened her assignment notebook. It was plastered with puffy and smelly stickers. "Tonight's Friday," she said. "That's T.G.I.F."

"As good a night as any. Do this as part of your weekend homework. You *must* learn to follow directions." He chopped the air with his hand to pound out every single syllable. "Fol-low the di-rec-tions!"

Tom Win stood up at once. All heads turned to him. He turned his to me. What did he think he was doing? "Harvey?" he asked me.

I shrugged and stared down at the field of initials scratched on my desk. I didn't know what he was getting at. He was embarrassing me, standing there all by himself saying, "Harvey?"

"Where," he asked Mr. Tandy, "where is . . . Directions . . . so I can follow him?"

The bell rang, but even though it was Friday, the kids stayed in their seats and laughed out loud. He was a big joke to them. A hundred percent in math, and he thought it was time for Follow the Leader. And they weren't just laughing at *him*. I could feel it in the hairs on the back of my neck. They knew he was mine. They were laughing at me, too.

But when I looked up again, Quint had already gathered the kid up and was heading him out the door.

"Marbles," Tom Win called, holding up his bag of them. "Good night."

Quint waved. "This foreign person may be more interesting than I thought. I'll find out if my uncle is right. Anyway, your clone," he said, "has flown."

I couldn't possibly have followed them, even though *follow* seemed to be the word of the day. I'd have been late for work. But, I decided, the kid seems to be pretty smart. He'll figure Quint out in a hurry. It'll be good for him. I headed off, whistling.

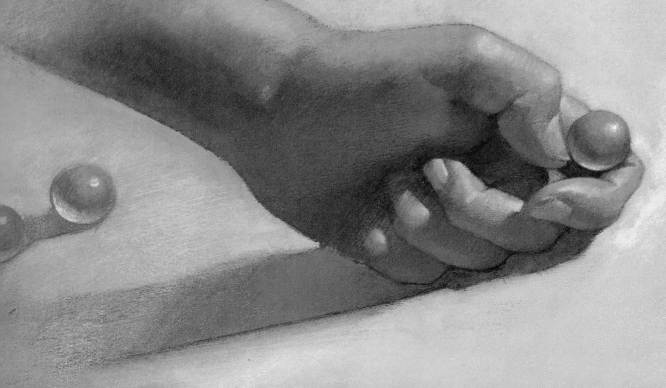

Jamie Gilson

Jamie Gilson is the author of several books, including *Do Bananas Chew Gum?*, *Thirteen Ways to Sink a Sub*, and *Hobie Hanson, You're Weird*. She taught junior high school students and wrote for radio stations before she began writing books for young people.

"My novels have all been contemporary adventures with boy narrators, and they have been great fun to research and write. I research my books closely, not only for details about such things as lice and skunks, which have played important parts in my stories, but about the children, too."

Jamie Gilson

Hui Han Lui

Hui Han Lui (hwē hän loo), the illustrator of "Hello, My Name Is Scrambled Eggs," came to the United States from China to study at the Academy of Art in San Francisco. Although he had studied English in China, he did not use the language everyday. When he came to America, Hui Han had trouble with questions that could not be answered simply "yes" or "no." He had a roommate at the Academy who spoke both Chinese and English. They decided to declare an "English Only Day" once a week for several months. Hui Han is pleased to say his English is much better now.

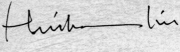

Foreign Student

by Barbara B. Robinson

In September she appeared
   row three, seat seven,
   heavy pleated skirt,
   plastic purse, tidy notepad,
there she sat,
silent,
straight from Taipei,
and she bowed
when I entered the room.
A model student
I noticed,
   though she walked
   alone through the halls,
every assignment neat,
on time, complete,
and she'd listen
when I talked.

But now it's May
and Si Lan
is called Lani.
She strides in with Noriyo and
Lynne
and Natividad.
She wears slacks.
Her gear is crammed
into a macrame
shoulder sack.
And she chatters with Pete
during class
and
I'm glad.

Response Corner

WRITE A LETTER

GREETINGS FROM THE U.S.

Imagine that you are Tuan and you want to write a letter to send to your family and friends back home in Vietnam. What kinds of things would you include about your new life in the United States? Write a letter telling about you new experiences.

WRITE A PLAN

TEACH AN EXPRESSION

Harvey uses a computer, name tags, and a small notebook to help Tuan learn English. Write a plan to explain how you might teach Tuan a new word or expression, using different methods and materials from those that Harvey uses.

FIRST IMPRESSIONS

Draw a picture that might depict Tuan's or Si Lan's impressions of one of the following: their first day in America, their first day at school, or their first hamburger. Or choose your own events to record.

What Do You Think?

★ Besides a new language, what other things does Tuan have to learn?

★ Do you think you would enjoy hosting a family from another country like the Trumbles do? Explain your answer.

★ What similarities are there between Tuan and Si Lan, the girl in the poem?

227

NUMBER THE STARS

BY LOIS LOWRY

By 1943, German troops had occupied Denmark for about a year. Annemarie Johansen; her little sister, Kirsti; and her best friend, Ellen, could remember when the tall German soldier, "the Giraffe," and his partner didn't stand watch on the street corner near the school. As the Germans began to "relocate" all the Jews in Denmark, the Johansens had to act heroically during a time of terror and war.

ILLUSTRATED BY ROBERTA LUDL

Alone in the apartment while Mama was out shopping with Kirsti, Annemarie and Ellen were sprawled on the living room floor playing with paper dolls. They had cut the dolls from Mama's magazines, old ones she had saved from past years. The paper ladies had old-fashioned hair styles and clothes, and the girls had given them names from Mama's very favorite book. Mama had told Annemarie and Ellen the entire story of *Gone With the Wind*, and the girls thought it much more interesting and romantic than the king-and-queen tales that Kirsti loved.

"Come, Melanie," Annemarie said, walking her doll across the edge of the rug. "Let's dress for the ball."

"All right, Scarlett, I'm coming," Ellen replied in a sophisticated voice. She was a talented performer; she often played the leading roles in school dramatics. Games of the imagination were always fun when Ellen played.

The door opened and Kirsti stomped in, her face tear-stained and glowering. Mama followed her with an exasperated look and set a package down on the table.

"I won't!" Kirsti sputtered. "I won't ever, *ever* wear them! Not if you chain me in a prison and beat me with sticks!"

Annemarie giggled and looked questioningly at her mother. Mrs. Johansen sighed. "I bought Kirsti some new shoes," she explained. "She's outgrown her old ones."

"Goodness, Kirsti," Ellen said, "I wish my mother would get *me* some new shoes. I love new things, and it's so hard to find them in the stores."

"Not if you go to a *fish* store!" Kirsti bellowed. "But most mothers wouldn't make their daughters wear ugly *fish* shoes!"

"Kirsten," Mama said soothingly, "you know it wasn't a fish store. And we were lucky to find shoes at all."

Kirsti sniffed. "Show them," she commanded. "Show Annemarie and Ellen how ugly they are."

Mama opened the package and took out a pair of little girl's shoes. She held them up, and Kirsti looked away in disgust.

"You know there's no leather anymore," Mama explained. "But they've found a way to make shoes out of fish skin. I don't think these are too ugly."

Annemarie and Ellen looked at the fish skin shoes. Annemarie took one in her hand and examined it. It was odd-looking; the fish scales were visible. But it was a shoe, and her sister needed shoes.

"It's not so bad, Kirsti," she said, lying a little.

Ellen turned the other one over in her hand. "You know," she said, "it's only the color that's ugly."

"Green!" Kirsti wailed. "I will never, *ever* wear green shoes!"

"In our apartment," Ellen told her, "my father has a jar of black, black ink. Would you like these shoes better if they were black?"

Kirsti frowned. "Maybe I would," she said, finally.

"Well, then," Ellen told her, "tonight, if your mama doesn't mind, I'll take the shoes home and ask my father to make them black for you, with his ink."

Mama laughed. "I think that would be a fine improvement. What do you think, Kirsti?"

Kirsti pondered. "Could he make them shiny?" she asked. "I want them shiny."

Ellen nodded. "I think he could. I think they'll be quite pretty, black and shiny."

Kirsti nodded. "All right, then," she said. "But you mustn't tell anyone that they're *fish*. I don't want anyone to know." She took her new shoes, holding them disdainfully, and put them on a chair. Then she looked with interest at the paper dolls.

"Can I play, too?" Kirsti asked. "Can I have a doll?" She squatted beside Annemarie and Ellen on the floor.

Sometimes, Annemarie thought, Kirsti was such a pest, always butting in. But the apartment was small. There was no other place for Kirsti to play. And if they told her to go away, Mama would scold.

"Here," Annemarie said, and handed her sister a cut-out little girl

doll. "We're playing *Gone With the Wind*. Melanie and Scarlett are going to a ball. You can be Bonnie. She's Scarlett's daughter."

Kirsti danced her doll up and down happily. "I'm going to the ball!" she announced in a high, pretend voice.

Ellen giggled. "A little girl wouldn't go to a ball. Let's make them go someplace else. Let's make them go to Tivoli!"

"Tivoli!" Annemarie began to laugh. "That's in Copenhagen! *Gone With the Wind* is in America!"

"Tivoli, Tivoli, Tivoli," little Kirsti sang, twirling her doll in a circle.

"It doesn't matter, because it's only a game anyway," Ellen pointed out. "Tivoli can be over there, by that chair. 'Come, Scarlett,'" she said, using her doll voice, "'we shall go to Tivoli to dance and watch the fireworks, and maybe there will be some handsome men there! Bring your silly daughter Bonnie, and she can ride on the carousel.'"

Annemarie grinned and walked her Scarlett toward the chair that Ellen had designated as Tivoli. She loved Tivoli Gardens, in the heart of Copenhagen; her parents had taken her there, often, when she was a little girl. She remembered the music and the brightly colored lights, the carousel and ice cream and especially the magnificent fireworks in the evenings: the huge colored splashes and bursts of lights in the evening sky.

"I remember the fireworks best of all," she commented to Ellen.

"Me too," Kirsti said. "I remember the fireworks."

"Silly," Annemarie scoffed. "You never saw the fireworks." Tivoli

Gardens was closed now. The German occupation forces had burned part of it, perhaps as a way of punishing the fun-loving Danes for their lighthearted pleasures.

Kirsti drew herself up, her small shoulders stiff. "I did too," she said belligerently. "It was my birthday. I woke up in the night and I could hear the booms. And there were lights in the sky. Mama said it was fireworks for my birthday!"

Then Annemarie remembered. Kirsti's birthday was late in August. And that night, only a month before, she, too, had been awakened and frightened by the sound of explosions. Kirsti was right—the sky in the southeast had been ablaze, and Mama had comforted her by calling it a birthday celebration. "Imagine, such fireworks for a little girl five years old!" Mama had said, sitting on their bed, holding the dark curtain aside to look through the window at the lighted sky.

The next evening's newspaper had told the sad truth. The Danes had destroyed their own naval fleet, blowing up the vessels one by one, as the Germans approached to take over the ships for their own use.

"How sad the king must be," Annemarie had heard Mama say to Papa when they read the news.

"How proud," Papa had replied.

It had made Annemarie feel sad and proud, too, to picture the tall, aging king, perhaps with tears in his blue eyes, as he looked at the remains of his small navy, which now lay submerged and broken in the harbor.

"I don't want to play anymore, Ellen," she said suddenly, and put her paper doll on the table.

"I have to go home, anyway," Ellen said. "I have to help Mama with the housecleaning. Thursday is our New Year. Did you know that?"

"Why is it yours?" asked Kirsti. "Isn't it our New Year, too?"

"No. It's the Jewish New Year. That's just for us. But if you want, Kirsti, you can come that night and watch Mama light the candles."

Annemarie and Kirsti had often been invited to watch Mrs. Rosen light the Sabbath candles on Friday evenings. She covered her head with a cloth and said a special prayer in Hebrew as she did so. Annemarie always stood very quietly, awed, to watch; even Kirsti, usually such a chatterbox, was always still at that time. They didn't understand the words or the meaning, but they could feel what a special time it was for the Rosens.

"Yes," Kirsti agreed happily. "I'll come and watch your mama light the candles, and I'll wear my new black shoes."

But this time was to be different. Leaving for school on Thursday with her sister, Annemarie saw the Rosens walking to the synagogue early in the morning, dressed in their best clothes. She waved to Ellen, who waved happily back.

"Lucky Ellen," Annemarie said to Kirsti. "She doesn't have to go to school today."

"But she probably has to sit very, very still, like we do in church," Kirsti pointed out. "*That's* no fun."

That afternoon, Mrs. Rosen knocked at their door but didn't come inside. Instead, she spoke for a long time in a hurried, tense voice to Annemarie's mother in the hall. When Mama returned, her face was worried, but her voice was cheerful.

"Girls," she said, "we have a nice surprise. Tonight Ellen will be coming to stay overnight and to be our guest for a few days! It isn't often we have a visitor."

Kirsti clapped her hands in delight.

"But, Mama," Annemarie said, in dismay, "it's their New Year. They were going to have a celebration at home! Ellen told me that her mother managed to get a chicken someplace, and she was going to roast it—their first roast chicken in a year or more!"

"Their plans have changed," Mama said briskly. "Mr. and Mrs. Rosen have been called away to visit some relatives. So Ellen will stay with us. Now, let's get busy and put clean sheets on your bed. Kirsti, you may sleep with Mama and Papa tonight, and we'll let the big girls giggle together by themselves."

Kirsti pouted, and it was clear that she was about to argue. "Mama will tell you a special story tonight," her mother said. "One just for you."

"About a king?" Kirsti asked dubiously.

"About a king, if you wish," Mama replied.

"All right, then. But there must be a queen, too," Kirsti said.

Though Mrs. Rosen had sent her chicken to the Johansens, and Mama made a lovely dinner large enough for second helpings all around, it was not an evening of laughter and talk. Ellen was silent at dinner. She looked frightened. Mama and Papa tried to speak of cheerful things, but it was clear that they were worried, and it made Annemarie worry, too. Only Kirsti was unaware of the quiet tension in the room. Swinging her feet in their newly blackened and shiny shoes, she chattered and giggled during dinner.

"Early bedtime tonight, little one," Mama announced after the dishes were washed. "We need extra time for the long story I promised, about the king and queen." She disappeared with Kirsti into the bedroom.

"What's happening?" Annemarie asked when she and Ellen were

alone with Papa in the living room. "Something's wrong. What is it?"

Papa's face was troubled. "I wish that I could protect you children from this knowledge," he said quietly. "Ellen, you already know. Now we must tell Annemarie."

He turned to her and stroked her hair with his gentle hand. "This morning, at the synagogue, the rabbi told his congregation that the Nazis have taken the synagogue lists of all the Jews. Where they live, what their names are. Of course the Rosens were on that list, along with many others."

"Why? Why did they want those names?"

"They plan to arrest all the Danish Jews. They plan to take them away. And we have been told that they may come tonight."

"I don't understand! Take them where?"

Her father shook his head. "We don't know where, and we don't really know why. They call it 'relocation.' We don't even know what that means. We only know that it is wrong, and it is dangerous, and we must help."

Annemarie was stunned. She looked at Ellen and saw that her best friend was crying silently.

"Where are Ellen's parents? We must help them, too!"

"We couldn't take all three of them. If the Germans came to search our apartment, it would be clear that the Rosens were here. One person we can hide. Not three. So Peter has helped Ellen's parents to go elsewhere. We don't know where. Ellen doesn't know either. But they are safe."

Ellen sobbed aloud, and put her face in her hands. Papa put his arm around her. "They are safe, Ellen. I promise you that. You will see them again quite soon. Can you try hard to believe my promise?"

Ellen hesitated, nodded, and wiped her eyes with her hand.

"But, Papa," Annemarie said, looking around the small apartment, with its few pieces of furniture: the fat stuffed sofa, the table and chairs, the small bookcase against the wall. "You said that we would hide her. How can we do that? Where can she hide?"

Papa smiled. "That part is easy. It will be as your mama said: you two will sleep together in your bed, and you may giggle and talk and tell secrets to each other. And if anyone comes—"

Ellen interrupted him. "Who might come? Will it be soldiers? Like the ones on the corners?" Annemarie remembered how terrified Ellen had looked the day when the soldier had questioned them on the corner.

"I really don't think anyone will. But it never hurts to be prepared. If anyone should come, even soldiers, you two will be sisters. You are together so much, it will be easy for you to pretend that you are sisters."

He rose and walked to the window. He pulled the lace curtain aside and looked down into the street. Outside, it was beginning to grow dark. Soon they would have to draw the black curtains that all Danes had on their windows; the entire city had to be completely darkened at night. In a nearby tree, a bird was singing; otherwise it was quiet. It was the last night of September.

"Go, now, and get into your nightgowns. It will be a long night."

Annemarie and Ellen got to their feet. Papa suddenly crossed the room and put his arms around them both. He kissed the top of each head: Annemarie's blond one, which reached to his shoulder, and Ellen's dark hair, the thick curls braided as always into pigtails.

"Don't be frightened," he said to them softly. "Once I had three daughters. Tonight I am proud to have three daughters again."

"Do you really think anyone will come?" Ellen asked nervously, turning to Annemarie in the bedroom. "Your father doesn't think so."

"Of course not. They're always threatening stuff. They just like to scare people." Annemarie took her nightgown from a hook in the closet.

"Anyway, if they did, it would give me a chance to practice acting. I'd just pretend to be Lise. I wish I were taller, though." Ellen stood on tiptoe, trying to make herself tall. She laughed at herself, and her voice was more relaxed.

"You were great as the Dark Queen in the school play last year," Annemarie told her. "You should be an actress when you grow up."

"My father wants me to be a teacher. He wants *everyone* to be a teacher, like him. But maybe I could convince him that I should go to acting school." Ellen stood on tiptoe again, and made an imperious

gesture with her arm. "I am the Dark Queen," she intoned dramatically. "I have come to command the night!"

"You should try saying, 'I am Lise Johansen!'" Annemarie said, grinning. "If you told the Nazis that you were the Dark Queen, they'd haul you off to a mental institution."

Ellen dropped her actress pose and sat down, with her legs curled under her, on the bed. "They won't really come here, do you think?" she asked again.

Annemarie shook her head. "Not in a million years." She picked up her hairbrush.

The girls found themselves whispering as they got ready for bed. There was no need, really, to whisper; they were, after all, supposed to be normal sisters, and Papa had said they could giggle and talk. The bedroom door was closed.

But the night did seem, somehow, different from a normal night. And so they whispered.

"How did your sister die, Annemarie?" Ellen asked suddenly. "I remember when it happened. And I remember the funeral—it was the only time I have ever been in a Lutheran church. But I never knew just what happened."

"I don't know *exactly*," Annemarie confessed. "She and Peter were out somewhere together, and then there was a telephone call, that there had been an accident. Mama and Papa rushed to the hospital—remember, your mother came and stayed with me and Kirsti? Kirsti was already asleep and she slept right through everything, she was so little then. But I stayed up, and I was with your mother in the living room when my parents came home in the middle of the night. And they told me Lise had died."

"I remember it was raining," Ellen said sadly. "It was still raining the next morning when Mama told me. Mama was crying, and the rain made it seem as if the whole *world* was crying."

Annemarie finished brushing her long hair and handed her hairbrush to her best friend. Ellen undid her braids, lifted her dark hair away from the thin gold chain she wore around her neck—the chain that held the Star of David—and began to brush her thick curls.

"I think it was partly because of the rain. They said she was hit by a car. I suppose the streets were slippery, and it was getting dark, and maybe the driver just couldn't see," Annemarie went on, remembering. "Papa looked so angry. He made one hand into a fist, and he kept pounding it into the other hand. I remember the noise of it: slam, slam, slam."

Together they got into the wide bed and pulled up the covers. Annemarie blew out the candle and drew the dark curtains aside so that the open window near the bed let in some air. "See that blue trunk in the corner?" she said, pointing through the darkness. "Lots of Lise's things are in there. Even her wedding dress. Mama and Papa have never looked at those things, not since the day they packed them away."

Ellen sighed. "She would have looked so beautiful in her wedding dress. She had such a pretty smile. I used to pretend that she was *my* sister, too."

"She would have liked that," Annemarie told her. "She loved you."

"That's the worst thing in the world," Ellen whispered. "To be dead so young. I wouldn't want the Germans to take my family away—to make us live someplace else. But still, it wouldn't be as bad as being dead."

Annemarie leaned over and hugged her. "They won't take you away," she said. "Not your parents, either. Papa promised that they were safe, and he always keeps his promises. And you are quite safe, here with us."

For a while they continued to murmur in the dark, but the murmurs were interrupted by yawns. Then Ellen's voice stopped, she turned over, and in a minute her breathing was quiet and slow.

Annemarie stared at the window where the sky was outlined and a tree branch moved slightly in the breeze. Everything seemed very familiar, very comforting. Dangers were no more than odd imaginings, like ghost stories that children made up to frighten one another: things that couldn't possibly happen. Annemarie felt completely safe here in her own home, with her parents in the next room and her best friend asleep beside her. She yawned contentedly and closed her eyes.

It was hours later, but still dark, when she was awakened abruptly by the pounding on the apartment door.

Annemarie eased the bedroom door open quietly, only a crack, and peeked out. Behind her, Ellen was sitting up, her eyes wide.

She could see Mama and Papa in their nightclothes, moving about. Mama held a lighted candle, but as Annemarie watched, she went to a lamp and switched it on. It was so long a time since they had dared to use the strictly rationed electricity after dark that the light in the room seemed startling to Annemarie, watching through the slightly opened bedroom door. She saw her mother look automatically to the blackout curtains, making certain that they were tightly drawn.

Papa opened the front door to the soldiers.

"This is the Johansen apartment?" A deep voice asked the question loudly, in terribly accented Danish.

"Our name is on the door, and I see you have a flashlight," Papa

answered. "What do you want? Is something wrong?"

"I understand you are a friend of your neighbors the Rosens, Mrs. Johansen," the soldier said angrily.

"Sophy Rosen is my friend, that is true," Mama said quietly. "Please, could you speak more softly? My children are asleep."

"Then you will be so kind as to tell me where the Rosens are." He made no effort to lower his voice.

"I assume they are at home, sleeping. It is four in the morning, after all," Mama said.

Annemarie heard the soldier stalk across the living room toward the kitchen. From her hiding place in the narrow sliver of open doorway, she could see the heavy uniformed man, a holstered pistol at his waist, in the entrance to the kitchen, peering in toward the sink.

Another German voice said, "The Rosens' apartment is empty. We are wondering if they might be visiting their good friends the Johansens."

"Well," said Papa, moving slightly so that he was standing in front of Annemarie's bedroom door, and she could see nothing except the dark blur of his back, "as you see, you are mistaken. There is no one here but my family."

"You will not object if we look around." The voice was harsh, and it was not a question.

"It seems we have no choice," Papa replied.

"Please don't wake my children," Mama requested again. "There is no need to frighten little ones."

The heavy, booted feet moved across the floor again and into the other bedroom. A closet door opened and closed with a bang.

Annemarie eased her bedroom door closed silently. She stumbled through the darkness to the bed.

"Ellen," she whispered urgently, "take your necklace off!"

Ellen's hands flew to her neck. Desperately she began trying to unhook the tiny clasp. Outside the bedroom door, the harsh voices and heavy footsteps continued.

"I can't get it open!" Ellen said frantically. "I never take it off—I can't even remember how to open it!"

Annemarie heard a voice just outside the door. "What is here?"

"Shhh," her mother replied. "My daughters' bedroom. They are sound asleep."

"Hold still," Annemarie commanded. "This will hurt." She grabbed the little gold chain, yanked with all her strength, and broke it. As the

door opened and light flooded into the bedroom, she crumpled it into her hand and closed her fingers tightly.

Terrified, both girls looked up at the three Nazi officers who entered the room.

One of the men aimed a flashlight around the bedroom. He went to the closet and looked inside. Then with a sweep of his gloved hand he pushed to the floor several coats and a bathrobe that hung from pegs on the wall.

There was nothing else in the room except a chest of drawers, the blue decorated trunk in the corner, and a heap of Kirsti's dolls piled in a

small rocking chair. The flashlight beam touched each thing in turn. Angrily the officer turned toward the bed.

"Get up!" he ordered. "Come out here!"

Trembling, the two girls rose from the bed and followed him, brushing past the two remaining officers in the doorway, to the living room.

Annemarie looked around. These three uniformed men were different from the ones on the street corners. The street soldiers were often young, sometimes ill at ease, and Annemarie remembered how the Giraffe had, for a moment, let his harsh pose slip and had smiled at Kirsti.

But these men were older and their faces were set with anger.

Her parents were standing beside each other, their faces tense, but Kirsti was nowhere in sight. Thank goodness that Kirsti slept through almost everything. If they had wakened her, she would be wailing—or worse, she would be angry, and her fists would fly.

"Your names?" the officer barked.

"Annemarie Johansen. And this is my sister—"

"Quiet! Let her speak for herself. Your name?" He was glaring at Ellen.

Ellen swallowed. "Lise," she said, and cleared her throat. "Lise Johansen."

The officer stared at them grimly.

"Now," Mama said in a strong voice, "you have seen that we are not hiding anything. May my children go back to bed?"

The officer ignored her. Suddenly he grabbed a handful of Ellen's hair. Ellen winced.

He laughed scornfully. "You have a blond child sleeping in the other room. And you have this blond daughter—" He gestured towards Annemarie with his head. "Where did you get the dark-haired one?" He twisted the lock of Ellen's hair. "From a different father? From the milkman?"

Papa stepped forward. "Don't speak to my wife in such a way. Let go of my daughter or I will report you for such treatment."

"Or maybe you got her someplace else?" the officer continued with a sneer. "From the Rosens?"

For a moment no one spoke. Then Annemarie, watching in panic, saw her father move swiftly to the small bookcase and take out a book. She saw that he was holding the family photograph album. Very quickly he searched through its pages, found what he was looking for, and tore out three pictures from three separate pages.

He handed them to the German officer, who released Ellen's hair.

"You will see each of my daughters, each with her name written on the photograph," Papa said.

Annemarie knew instantly which photographs he had chosen. The album had many snapshots—all the poorly focused pictures of school events and birthday parties. But it also contained a portrait, taken by a photographer, of each girl as a tiny infant. Mama had written, in her delicate handwriting, the name of each baby daughter across the bottom of those photographs.

She realized too, with an icy feeling, why Papa had torn them from the book. At the bottom of each page, below the photograph itself, was written the date. And the real Lise Johansen had been born twenty-one years earlier.

"Kirsten Elisabeth," the officer read, looking at Kirsti's baby picture. He let the photograph fall to the floor.

"Annemarie," he read next, glanced at her, and dropped the second photograph.

"Lise Margrete," he read finally, and stared at Ellen for a long, unwavering moment. In her mind, Annemarie pictured the photograph that he held: the baby, wide-eyed, propped against a pillow, her tiny hand holding a silver teething ring, her bare feet visible against the hem of an embroidered dress. The wispy curls. Dark.

The officer tore the photograph in half and dropped the pieces on the floor. Then he turned, the heels of his shiny boots grinding into the pictures, and left the apartment. Without a word, the other two officers followed. Papa stepped forward and closed the door behind him.

Annemarie relaxed the clenched fingers of her right hand, which still clutched Ellen's necklace. She looked down, and saw that she had imprinted the Star of David into her palm.

LOIS LOWRY

W riter Ilene Cooper spoke with Lois Lowry about how she came to write her Newbery Award-winning novel, *Number the Stars*.

Many people, children and adults, who read Number the Stars *come away from it wondering if they could be heroes. What do you think makes a hero?*

Although we can't pick the circumstances in which we find ourselves, we can and do choose the way we respond to situations. In my opinion, those who turn out to be heroes are people who respond in particular ways to their circumstances. They respond in a way that may put them at personal risk or call upon them to make sacrifices, without any idea of personal gain. There is great courage in placing human values above personal popularity.

How did you come to write Number the Stars?

I went on vacation with a Danish friend of mine. We were in Bermuda for a week, and we talked about her childhood. Very often what interests me about people is their childhood, because childhood is what I spend my time thinking and writing about. As we talked, I began to get an idea of what it was like for her during the war years. Although the actual incident in the story did not happen to her, she was able to tell me what it felt like when people in her neighborhood started disappearing. Soon it was clear to them that it was the Jewish families that were disappearing.

The Danes were very good about protecting Jewish people from the Nazis.

Yes. Like all Danes, my friend is so proud of her country and its role in World War II. For instance, the Danish doctors began putting Jewish people in hospitals, pretending they were patients. In order to save these people, the doctors had to fill out necessary medical papers, and for all of them, as a sort of bitter joke, they put down German measles as a diagnosis. As my friend told me these stories, I began to see quite clearly that the heroism they reflect would make a wonderful children's book. After I started writing, I saw that I would need to do a great deal of research on the story, and

I eventually went to Denmark. I spoke to people who had been alive during the war. I went to the Holocaust Museum, which is dedicated to the role of Denmark during the Holocaust. That was where I saw the shoes of fish skin that I used in my story.

You've won the Newbery Medal for Number the Stars *and* The Giver. *How did you feel each time?*
I guess I felt the same both times I won, immensely gratified and very surprised.

FREEDOM
RIGHTS
FOR
ALL!

I Have a Dream

by Martin Luther King, Jr.

Excerpt from the speech given in Washington, D.C. on August 28, 1963

Illustrated by Guy Porfirio

. . . I say to you today, my friends, so even though we face the difficulties of today and tomorrow, I still have a dream. It is a dream deeply rooted in the American dream.

I have a dream that one day this nation will rise up and live out the true meaning of its creed: "We hold these truths to be self-evident; that all men are created equal."

I have a dream that one day, on the red hills of Georgia, sons of former slaves and the sons of former slaveowners will be able to sit down together at the table of brotherhood.

I have a dream that one day even the state of Mississippi, a state sweltering with the heat of injustice, sweltering with the heat of oppression, will be transformed into an oasis of freedom and justice.

I have a dream that my four little children will one day live in a nation where they will not be judged by the color of their skin but by the content of their character.

I have a dream today.

I have a dream that one day, down in Alabama, . . . right there in Alabama, little black boys and black girls will be able to join hands with little white boys and white girls and walk together as sisters and brothers.

I have a dream today.

I have a dream that one day "every valley shall be exalted, every hill and mountain shall be made low, the rough places will be made plains, and the crooked places will be made straight, and the glory of the Lord shall be revealed, and all flesh shall see it together."

This is our hope. This is the faith that I go back to the South with. With this faith we will be able to hew out of the mountain of despair a stone of hope. With this faith we will be able to transform the jangling discords of our nation into a beautiful symphony of brotherhood. With this faith we will be able to work together, to pray together, to struggle together, to stand up for freedom together, knowing that we will be free one day.

And this will be the day. This will be the day when all of God's children will be able to sing with new meaning "My country 'tis of thee, sweet land of liberty, of thee I sing. Land where my fathers died, land of the pilgrim's pride, from every mountainside, let freedom ring."

And if America is to be a great nation this must become true. So let freedom ring from the prodigious hilltops of New Hampshire. Let freedom ring from the mighty mountains of New York. Let freedom ring from the heightening Alleghenies of Pennsylvania!

Let freedom ring from the snowcapped Rockies of Colorado!

Let freedom ring from the curvaceous slopes of California!

But not only that; let freedom ring from Stone Mountain of Georgia! Let freedom ring from Lookout Mountain of Tennessee.

Let freedom ring from every hill and molehill of Mississippi. From every mountainside, let freedom ring.

And when this happens, and when we allow freedom to ring, when we let it ring from every village and every hamlet, from every state and every city, we will be able to speed up that day when all of God's children, black men and white men, Jews and Gentiles, Protestants and Catholics, will be able to join hands and sing in the words of that old Negro spiritual, "Free at last! Free at last! Thank God almighty, we are free at last!"

RESPONSE CORNER

MEDAL FOR BRAVERY

The characters in the story show great courage in standing up to the Nazi threat. Design a special medal of courage to be presented to Annemarie, Ellen, and their families. Write a short proclamation acknowledging their bravery. Display your medal and read your proclamation to the class.

CREATE A CLASS BOOKLET

HAPPY NEW YEAR!

Interview a partner about how he or she celebrates the new year. Write a paragraph and draw an illustration about those celebrations. Add your creation to the class booklet called "New Year's Celebrations."

WRITE A POEM

SEEING POETRY

Personification means giving objects human characteristics. Lois Lowry uses personification to create powerful images in the story. For instance, Ellen says, "The rain made it seem as if the whole world was crying," as she recalls when Lise died. Write a poem, using personification. Share your poem with classmates.

What Do You Think?

- Why do the Johansens help the Rosens by hiding Ellen?

- How do you feel about Annemarie, her family, and Ellen? Explain why you feel as you do.

- Have you ever known anyone who acted as bravely as the Johansens to protect another person? Explain what happened.

Art and Literature

Look at *The Library*, by Jacob Lawrence. What kinds of books might these people be reading? What reasons might they have for reading the books? How does a painting of a library illustrate the theme Celebrating Differences?

The Library (1960)
by Jacob Lawrence

Jacob Lawrence was born in New Jersey in 1917. He studied art in New York City and worked there as an artist. In many of his paintings, Lawrence illustrates scenes of everyday life in the African American community. He uses strong shapes and bold colors to show, in his words, "the vital, strong, pulsating beat that has always been humanity." Why do you think Lawrence chose people in a library as one way to illustrate strength and energy?

Emmy Award

THE MONSTERS

WELCOME TO MAPLE
STREET, A FRIENDLY,
TREE-LINED, AMERICAN
STREET. A STREET AS
NORMAL AND QUIET AS
ANY YOU CAN IMAGINE.
UNTIL IT ENTERS THE
TWILIGHT ZONE.

THE MONSTERS ARE DUE ON MAPLE STREET

BY ROD SERLING
ILLUSTRATED BY JOHN NICKLE

CHARACTERS

Narrator

Tommy

Steve Brand

Don Martin

Myra Brand, *Steve's wife*

Woman

Voice One

Voice Two

Voice Three

Voice Four

Voice Five

Pete Van Horn

Sally, *Tommy's mother*

Charlie

Man One

Les Goodman

Ethel Goodman, *Les's wife*

Man Two

Figure One

Figure Two

Ice-cream vendor

Second Boy buying
    ice cream

Charlie's wife

Other Residents of
    Maple Street

ACT ONE

(Fade in on a shot of the night sky . . . the various heavenly bodies stand out in sharp, sparkling relief.)

Narrator: There is a fifth dimension beyond that which is known to man. It is a dimension as vast as space, and as timeless as infinity. It is the middle ground between light and shadow—between science and superstition. And it lies between the pit of a man's fears and the summit of his knowledge. It is the dimension of imagination. It is an area which we call The Twilight Zone.

(The camera moves slowly across the heavens until it passes the horizon and stops on a sign that reads "Maple Street." It is a tree-lined, quiet small-town American street. The houses have front porches on which people sit and swing on gliders, conversing across from house to house. Steve Brand polishes his car parked in front of his house. His neighbor, Don Martin, leans against the fender watching him. A Good Humor man rides a bicycle and is just in the process of stopping to sell some ice cream to a couple of kids. Two women gossip on the front lawn. Another man waters his lawn.)

Narrator: Maple Street, U.S.A., late summer. A tree-lined little world of front-porch gliders, hopscotch, the laughter of children, and the bell of an ice-cream vendor.

(There is a pause, and the camera moves over to a shot of the Good Humor man and two small boys who are standing alongside, just buying ice cream.)

Narrator: At the sound of the roar and the flash of the light, it will be precisely six-forty-three P.M. on Maple Street.

(At this moment one of the little boys, Tommy, looks up to listen to a sound of a tremendous screeching roar from overhead. A flash of light plays on both boys' faces and then moves down the street past lawns and porches and rooftops and then disappears.
Various people leave their porches and stop what they are doing to stare up at the sky.
Steve Brand, the man who has been polishing his car, stands there transfixed, staring upwards. He looks at Don Martin, his neighbor from across the street.)

Steve: What was that? A meteor?

Don *(nods):* That's what it looked like.

I didn't hear any crash, though, did you?

Steve *(shakes his head):* Nope. I didn't hear anything except a roar.

Myra *(from her porch):* Steve? What was that?

Steve *(raising his voice and looking toward the porch):* Guess it was a meteor, honey. Came awful close, didn't it?

Myra: Too close for my money! Much too close.

(The camera moves slowly across the various porches to people who stand there watching and talking in low conversing tones.)

Narrator: Maple Street. Six-forty-four P.M., on a late September evening. *(a pause)* Maple Street in the last calm and reflective moment . . . before the monsters came!

(The camera takes us across the porches again. A man is replacing a light bulb on a front porch. He gets down off his stool to flick the switch and finds that nothing happens.
Another man is working on an electric power mower. He plugs in the

plug, flicks the switch of the power mower off and on, but nothing happens.

Through a window we see a woman pushing her finger up and down on the dial hook of a telephone. Her voice sounds far away.)

Woman: Operator, operator, something's wrong on the phone, operator! (Myra Brand comes out on the porch and calls to Steve.)

Myra (calling): Steve, the power's off. I had the soup on the stove, and the stove just stopped working.

Woman: Same thing over here. I can't get anybody on the phone either. The phone seems to be dead.

(We look down the street. Small, mildly disturbed voices are heard coming from below.)

Voice One: Electricity's off.

Voice Two: Phone won't work.

Voice Three: Can't get a thing on the radio.

Voice Four: My power mower won't move, won't work at all.

Voice Five: Radio's gone dead.

(Pete Van Horn, *a tall, thin man, is seen standing in front of his house.*)

Pete: I'll cut through the back yard. . . . See if the power's still on on Floral Street. I'll be right back.

(*He walks past the side of his house and disappears into the back yard.*

The camera pans down slowly until we are looking at ten or eleven people standing around the street and overflowing to the curb and sidewalk. In the background is Steve Brand*'s car.*)

Steve: Doesn't make sense. Why should the power go off all of a sudden, and the phone line?

Don: Maybe some kind of an electrical storm or something.

Charlie: That don't seem likely. Sky's just as blue as anything. Not a cloud. No lightning. No thunder. No nothing. How could it be a storm?

Woman: I can't get a thing on the radio. Not even the portable.

(*The people again begin to murmur softly in wonderment and question.*)

Charlie: Well, why don't you go downtown and check with the police, though they'll probably think we're crazy or something. A little power failure and right away we get all flustered and everything—

Steve: It isn't just the power failure, Charlie. If it was, we'd still be able to get a broadcast on the portable.

(*There is a murmur of reaction to this. Steve looks from face to face and then over to his car.*)

Steve: I'll run downtown. We'll get this all straightened out.

(*He walks over to the car, gets in it, and turns the key.*

Looking through the open car door, we see the crowd watching him from the other side. Steve starts the engine. It turns over sluggishly and then just stops dead. He tries it again, and this time he can't get it to turn over. Then, very slowly and reflectively, he turns the key back to "off" and gets out of the car.

The people stare at Steve. He stands for a moment by the car and then walks toward the group.)

Steve: I don't understand it. It was working fine before . . .

Don: Out of gas?

Steve *(shakes his head):* I just had it filled up.

Woman: What's it mean?

Charlie: It's just as if . . . as if everything had stopped. . . . *(Then he turns toward Steve.)* We'd better walk downtown.

(Another murmur of assent at this.)

Steve: The two of us can go, Charlie. *(He turns to look back at the car.)* It couldn't be the meteor. A meteor couldn't do *this.*

(He and Charlie exchange a look. Then they start to walk away from the group.)

Tommy, *a serious-faced young boy in spectacles, stands halfway between the group and the two men, who start to walk down the sidewalk.)*

Tommy: Mr. Brand—you'd better not!

Steve: Why not?

Tommy: They don't want you to.

(Steve and Charlie exchange a grin, and Steve looks back toward the boy.)

Steve: *Who* doesn't want us to?

Tommy *(jerks his head in the general direction of the distant horizon):* Them!

Steve: Them?

Charlie: Who are them?

Tommy *(intently):* Whoever was in that thing that came by overhead.

(Steve knits his brows for a moment, cocking his head questioningly. His voice is intense.)

Steve: What?

Tommy: Whoever was in that thing

that came over. I don't think they want us to leave here.

(Steve leaves Charlie, walks over to the boy. He forces his voice to remain gentle.)

Steve: What do you mean? What are you talking about?

Tommy: They don't want us to leave. That's why they shut everything off.

Steve: What makes you say that? Whatever gave you that idea?

Woman *(from the crowd)*: Now isn't that the craziest thing you ever heard?

Tommy *(persistently, but a little intimidated by the crowd)*: It's always that way, in every story I ever read about a ship landing from outer space.

Woman *(to the boy's mother, Sally, who stands on the fringe of the crowd)*: From outer space, yet! Sally, you better get that boy of yours up to bed. He's been reading too many comic books or seeing too many movies or something!

Sally: Tommy, come over here and stop that kind of talk.

Steve: Go ahead, Tommy. We'll be right back. And you'll see. That wasn't any ship or anything like it. That was just a . . . a meteor or something. Likely as not—*(He turns to the group, now trying to weight his words with an optimism he obviously doesn't feel but is desperately trying to instill in himself as well as the others.)* No doubt it did have something to do with all this power failure and the rest of it. Meteors can do some crazy things. Like sunspots.

Don *(picking up the cue):* Sure. That's the kind of thing—like sunspots. They raise Cain with radio reception all over the world. And this thing being so close—why, there's no telling the sort of stuff it can do. *(He wets his lips and smiles nervously.)* Go ahead, Charlie. You and Steve go into town and see if that isn't what's causing it all.

(Steve and Charlie walk away from the group down the sidewalk as the people watch silently.
Tommy *stares at them, biting his lips, and finally calls out again.)*

Tommy: Mr. Brand!

(The two men stop. Tommy takes a step toward them.)

Tommy: Mr. Brand . . . please don't leave here.

(Steve and Charlie stop once again and turn toward the boy. There is a murmur in the crowd, a murmur of irritation and concern, as if the boy were bringing up fears that shouldn't be brought up; words which carried with them a strange kind of truth that came without logic. Again comes a murmur of reaction from the crowd.
Tommy *is partly frightened and partly defiant as well.)*

Tommy: You might not even be able to get to town. It was that way in the story. Nobody could leave. Nobody except—

Steve: Except who?

Tommy: Except the people they'd sent down ahead of them. They looked just like humans. And it wasn't until the ship landed that—*(The boy suddenly stops, conscious of the parents staring at them and the sudden hush of the crowd.)*

Sally *(in a whisper, sensing the antagonism of the crowd):* Tommy, please son . . . honey, don't talk that way—

Man One: That kid shouldn't talk that

way . . . and we shouldn't stand here listening to him. Why this is the craziest thing I ever heard of. The kid tells us a comic book plot, and here we stand listening—

(Steve *walks toward the camera and stops beside the boy.*)

Steve: Go ahead, Tommy. What kind of story was this? What about the people they sent out ahead?

Tommy: That was the way they prepared things for the landing. They sent four people. A mother and a father and two kids who looked just like humans . . . but they weren't.

(*There is another silence as* Steve *looks toward the crowd and then toward* Tommy. *He wears a tight grin.*)

Steve: Well, I guess what we'd better do then is to run a check on the neighborhood and see which ones of us are really human.

(*There is laughter at this, but it's a laughter that comes from a desperate attempt to lighten the atmosphere. The people look at one another in the middle of their laughter.*)

Charlie: There must be something bet-ter to do than stand around makin' bum jokes about it. (*rubs his jaw nervously*) I wonder if Floral Street's got the same deal we got. (*He looks past the houses.*) Where is Pete Van Horn anyway? Didn't he get back yet?

(*Suddenly there is the sound of a car's engine starting to turn over.*

We look across the street toward the driveway of Les Goodman*'s house. He is at the wheel trying to start the car.*)

Sally: Can you get it started, Les?

(*Les Goodman gets out of the car, shaking his head.*)

Les: No dice.

(*He walks toward the group. He stops suddenly as, behind him, inexplicably and with a noise that inserts itself into the silence, the car engine starts up all by itself.* Les *whirls around to stare toward it.*

The car idles roughly, smoke coming from the exhaust, the frame shaking gently.

Les's eyes go wide, and he runs over to his car.

The people stare toward the car.)

Man One: He got the car started somehow. He got *his* car started!

(The people continue to stare, caught up by this revelation and wildly frightened.)

Woman: How come his car just up and started like that?

Sally: All by itself. He wasn't anywheres near it. It started all by itself.

(Don Martin approaches the group and stops a few feet away to look toward Les's car and then back toward the group.)

Don: And he never did come out to look at that thing that flew overhead. He wasn't even interested. *(He turns to the group, his face taut and serious.)* Why? Why didn't he come out with the rest of us to look?

Charlie: He always was an oddball. Him and his whole family. Real oddball.

Don: What do you say we ask him?

(The group suddenly starts toward the house. In this brief fraction of a moment, they take the first step toward changing from a group into a mob. They begin to head purposefully across the street toward the house at the end. Steve stands in front of them. For a moment their fear almost turns their walk into a wild stampede, but Steve's voice, loud, incisive, and commanding, makes them stop.)

Steve: Wait a minute . . . wait a minute! Let's not be a mob!

(The people stop, seem to pause for a moment, and then much more quietly and slowly start to walk across the street. Les stands alone facing the people.)

Les: I just don't understand it. I tried to start it, and it wouldn't start. You saw me. All of you saw me.

(And now, just as suddenly as the engine started, it stops, and there is a long silence that is gradually intruded upon by the frightened murmuring of the people.)

Les: I don't understand. I swear . . . I don't understand. What's happening?

Don: Maybe you better tell us.

Nothing's working on this street. Nothing. No lights, no power, no radio. *(then meaningfully)* Nothing except one car—yours!

(The people pick this up and now their murmuring becomes a loud chant filling the air with accusations and demands for action. Two of the men pass Don and head toward Les, who backs away, backing into his car and now at bay.)

Les: Wait a minute now. You keep your distance—all of you. So I've got a car that starts by itself—well, that's a freak thing, I admit it. But does that make me a criminal or something? I don't know why the car works—it just does!

(This stops the crowd momentarily, and now Les, still backing away, goes toward his front porch. He goes up the steps and then stops to stand facing the mob.)

Steve *(quietly):* We're all on a monster kick, Les. Seems that the general impression holds that maybe one family isn't what we think they are. Monsters from outer space or something. Different from us. Aliens from the vast beyond. *(He chuckles.)* You know anybody that might fit that description around here on Maple Street?

Les: What is this, a gag or something? *(He looks around the group again.)* This a practical joke or something?

(Suddenly the porch light goes on and then off. There's a murmur from the group.)

Les: Now, I suppose that's supposed to incriminate me! The light goes on and off. That really does it, doesn't it? *(He looks around at the faces of the people.)* I just don't understand this—*(He wets his lips, looking from face to face.)* Look, you all know me. We've lived here five years. Right in this

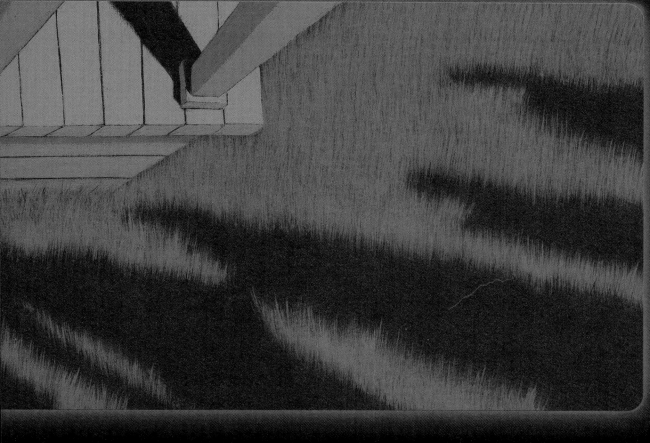

house. We're no different from any of the rest of you! We're no different at all. Really . . . this whole thing is just . . . just weird—

Woman: Well, if that's the case, Les Goodman, explain why—*(She stops suddenly, clamping her mouth shut.)*

Les *(softly):* Explain what?

Steve *(interjecting):* Look, let's forget this—

Charlie *(overlapping him):* Go ahead, let her talk. What about it? Explain what?

Woman *(a little reluctantly):* Well . . . sometimes I go to bed late at night. A couple of times . . . a couple of times I'd come out on the porch, and I'd see Mr. Goodman here in the wee hours of the morning standing out in front of his house . . . looking up at the sky. *(She looks around the circle of faces.)* That's right, looking up at the sky as if . . . as if he were waiting for something, *(pauses)* as if he were looking for something.

(There's a murmur of reaction from the crowd again. As Les starts toward them, they back away frightened.)

Les: You know really . . . this is for laughs. You know what I'm guilty of? (He laughs.) I'm guilty of insomnia. Now what's the penalty for insomnia?

(At this point the laugh, the humor, leaves his voice.)

Les: Did you hear what I said? I said it was insomnia. (a pause as he looks around, then shouts) I said it was insomnia! You fools. You scared, frightened rabbits, you. You're sick people, do you know that? You're sick people—all of you! And you don't even know what you're starting because let me tell you . . . let me tell you—this thing you're starting—that should frighten you. As God is my witness . . . you're letting something begin here that's a nightmare.

ACT TWO

SCENE 1.

(Fade in on Maple Street at night. On the sidewalk, little knots of people stand around talking in low voices. At the end of each conversation they look toward Les Goodman's house. From the various houses, we can see candlelight but no electricity. There is an all-pervading quiet that blankets the whole area, disturbed only by the almost whispered voices of the people standing around. In one group Charlie stands staring across at the Goodmans' house. Two men stand across the street from it in almost sentrylike poses.)

Sally (a little timorously): It just doesn't seem right, though, keeping watch on them. Why . . . he was right when he said he was one of our neighbors. Why, I've known Ethel Goodman ever since they moved in. We've been good friends—

Charlie: That don't prove a thing. Any guy who'd spend his time lookin' up at the sky early in the morning—well, there's something wrong with that kind of a person. There's something that ain't legitimate. Maybe under normal circumstances we could let it go by, but these aren't normal circumstances. Why, look at this street. Nothin' but candles. Why, it's like goin' back into the Dark Ages or somethin'!

(Steve walks down the steps of his porch, down the street over to Les's house, and then stops at the foot of the steps. Les stands there, his wife behind him, very frightened.)

Les: Just stay right where you are, Steve. We don't want any trouble, but this time if anybody sets foot on my porch, that's what they're going to get—trouble!

Steve: Look, Les—

Les: I've already explained to you people. I don't sleep very well at night sometimes. I get up and I take a walk and I look up at the sky. I look at the stars!

Ethel: That's exactly what he does. Why this whole thing, it's . . . it's some kind of madness or something.

Steve (nods grimly): That's exactly what it is—some kind of madness.

Charlie's Voice (shrill, from across the street): You best watch who you're seen with, Steve! Until we get this all straightened out, you ain't exactly above suspicion yourself.

Steve (whirling around toward him): Or you, Charlie. Or any of us, it seems. From age eight on up!

Woman: What I'd like to know is, what are we gonna do? Just stand around here all night?

Charlie: There's nothin' else we can do! (He turns back, looking toward Steve and Les again.) One of 'em'll tip their hand. They got to.

Steve (raising his voice): There's something you can do, Charlie. You could go home and keep your mouth shut. You could quit strutting around like a self-appointed hanging judge and just climb into bed and forget it.

Charlie: You sound real anxious to have that happen, Steve. I think we better keep our eye on you too!

Don (as if he were taking the bit in his teeth, takes a hesitant step to the front): I think everything might as well come out now. (He turns toward Steve.) Your wife's done plenty of talking, Steve, about how odd you are!

Charlie (picking this up, his eyes widening): Go ahead, tell us what she's said.

(Steve walks toward them from across the street.)

Steve: Go ahead, what's my wife said? Let's get it all out. Let's pick out every idiosyncrasy of every single man woman, and child on the street. And then we might as well set up some kind of a kangaroo court. How about a firing squad at dawn, Charlie, so we can get rid of all the suspects? Narrow them down. Make it easier for you.

Don: There's no need gettin' so upset, Steve. It's just that . . . well . . . Myra's talked about how there's been plenty of nights you spent hours down in your basement workin' on some kind of radio or something. Well, none of us have ever seen that radio—

(By this time Steve *has reached the group. He stands there defiantly close to them.)*

Charlie: Go ahead, Steve. What kind of "radio set" you workin' on? I never seen it. Neither has anyone else. Who do you talk to on that radio set? And who talks to you?

Steve: I'm surprised at you, Charlie. How come you're so dense all of a sudden? *(He pauses.)* Who do I talk to? I talk to monsters from outer space. I talk to three-headed green men who fly over here in what look like meteors.

*Myra Brand *steps down from the*

Myra: Steve! Steve, please. *(Then looking around, frightened, she walks toward the group.)* It's just a ham radio set, that's all. I bought him a book on it myself. It's just a ham radio set. A lot of people have them. I can show it to you. It's right down in the basement.

Steve *(whirls around toward her)* Show them nothing! If they want to look inside our house—let them get a search warrant.

Charlie: Look, buddy, you can't afford to—

Steve *(interrupting him):* Charlie, don't tell me what I can afford. And stop telling me who's dangerous and who isn't and who's safe and who's a menace. *(He turns to the group and shouts.)* And you're with him, too—all of you! You're standing here all set to crucify—all set to find a scapegoat— all desperate to point some kind of a finger at a neighbor! Well now, look, friends, the only thing that's gonna happen is that we'll eat each other up alive—

*(He stops abruptly as *Charlie *suddenly*

Charlie *(in a hushed voice):* That's not the only thing that can happen to us.

(Down the street, a figure has suddenly materialized in the gloom. In the silence we can hear the clickety-clack of slow, measured footsteps on concrete as the figure walks slowly toward them. One of the women lets out a stifled cry. The young mother grabs her boy, as do a couple of others.)

Tommy *(shouting, frightened):* It's the monster! It's the monster!

(Another woman lets out a wail, and the people fall back in a group, staring toward the darkness and the approaching figure. The people stand in the shadows watching. Don Martin joins them, carrying a shotgun. He holds it up.)

Don: We may need this.

Steve: A shotgun? *(He pulls it out of Don's hand.)* Good Lord—will anybody think a thought around here! Will you people wise up. What good would a shotgun do against—

(Charlie pulls the gun from Steve's hand.)

Charlie: No more talk, Steve. You're going to talk us into a grave! You'd let whatever's out there walk right over us, wouldn't yuh? Well, some of us won't!

(Charlie swings the gun around to point it toward the sidewalk. The dark figure continues to walk toward them. Charlie slowly raises the gun. As the figure gets closer and closer, he suddenly pulls the trigger. The sound of the shot explodes in the stillness.

The figure suddenly lets out a small cry, stumbles forward onto his knees, and then falls forward on his face. Don, Charlie, and Steve race forward to him. Steve is there first and turns the man over. The crowd gathers around them.)

Steve *(slowly looks up)*: It's Pete Van Horn.

Don *(in a hushed voice)*: Pete Van Horn! He was just gonna go over to the next block to see if the power was on—

Woman: You killed him, Charlie. You shot him dead!

Charlie *(looks around at the circle of faces, his eyes frightened, his face contorted)*: But . . . but I didn't know who he was. I certainly didn't know who he was. He comes walkin' out of the darkness—how am I supposed to know who he was? *(He grabs Steve.)* Steve—you know why I shot! How was I supposed to know he wasn't a monster or something? *(He grabs Don now.)* We're all scared of the same thing. I was just tryin' to . . . tryin' to protect my home, that's all! Look, all of you, that's all I was tryin' to do. *(He looks down wildly at the body.)* I didn't know it was somebody we knew! I didn't know—

(There's a sudden hush and then an intake of breath. Across the street all the lights go on in one of the houses.)

Woman *(in a very hushed voice)*: Charlie . . . Charlie . . . the lights just went on in your house. Why did the lights just go on?

Don: What about it, Charlie? How come you're the only one with lights now?

Les: That's what I'd like to know. *(A pause as they all stare toward Charlie.)*

Les: You were so quick to kill, Charlie, and you were so quick to tell us who we had to be careful of. Well, maybe you had to kill. Maybe Peter there was trying to tell us something. Maybe he'd found out something and came back to tell us who there was amongst us we should watch out for—

(Charlie backs away from the group, his eyes wide with fright.)

Charlie. No . . . no . . . it's nothing of the sort! I don't know why the lights are on. I swear I don't. Somebody's pulling a gag or something.

(He bumps against Steve, who grabs him and whirls him around.)

Steve: A gag? A gag? Charlie, there's a dead man on the sidewalk, and you killed him! Does this thing look like a gag to you?

(Charlie *breaks away and screams as he runs toward his house.*)

Charlie: No! No! Please!

(A *man breaks away from the crowd to chase* Charlie. *As the man tackles him and lands on top of him, the other people start to run toward them.* Charlie *gets up, breaks away from the other man's grasp, and lands a couple of desperate punches that push the man aside. Then he forces his way, fighting, through the crowd and jumps up on his front porch.*

Charlie *is on his porch as a rock thrown from the group smashes a window alongside of him, the broken glass flying past him. A couple of pieces cut him. He stands there perspiring, rumpled, blood running down from a cut on the cheek. His wife breaks away from the group to throw herself into his arms. He buries his face against her. We can see the crowd converging on the porch.*)

Voice One: It must have been him.

Voice Two: He's the one.

Voice Three: We got to get Charlie.

(*Another rock lands on the porch.* Charlie *pushes his wife behind him, facing the group.*)

Charlie: Look, look I swear to you . . . it isn't me . . . but I do know who it is . . . I swear to you, I do know who it is. I know who the monster is here. I know who it is that doesn't belong. I swear to you I know.

Les (*shouting*): What are you waiting for?

Woman (*shouting*): Come on, Charlie, come on!

Man One (*shouting*): Who is it, Charlie, tell us!

Don (*pushing his way to the front of the crowd*): All right, Charlie, let's hear it!

(Charlie*'s eyes dart around wildly.*)

Charlie: It's . . . it's . . .

Man Two (*screaming*): Go ahead, Charlie.

Charlie: It's . . . it's the kid. It's Tommy. He's the one!

(*There's a gasp from the crowd as we see* Sally *holding the boy.* Tommy *at first doesn't understand and then, realizing the eyes are all on him, buries his face against his mother.*)

Sally *(backs away)*: That's crazy. That's crazy. He's a little boy.

Woman: But he knew! He was the only one who knew! He told us all about it. Well, how did he know? How *could* he have known?

(Various people take this up and repeat the question.)

Voice One: How could he know?

Voice Two: Who told him?

Voice Three: Make the kid answer.

Man One: What about Les's car?

Don: It was Charlie who killed old man Van Horn.

Woman: But it was the kid here who knew what was going to happen all the time. He was the one who knew!

Steve *(shouts at his hysterical neighbors)*: Are you all gone crazy? *(pause as he looks about)* Stop!

(A fist smashes Steve's face, staggering him. The next few lines are spoken wildly, suggesting the coming of violence.)

Don: Charlie has to be the one—where's my rifle—

Woman: Les Goodman's the one. His car started! Let's wreck it—

Ethel: What about Steve's radio—he's the one that called them—

Les: Smash the radio. Get me a hammer. Get me something.

Steve: Stop—Stop—

Charlie: Where's that kid—let's get him.

Man One: Get Steve—get Charlie—they're working together.

(The crowd starts to converge around the mother, who grabs Tommy and starts to run with him. The crowd starts to follow, at first walking fast, and then running after him. Suddenly Charlie's lights go off and the lights in other houses go on, then off.)

Man One *(shouting)*: It isn't the kid . . . it's Bob Weaver's house.

Woman: It isn't Bob Weaver's house; it's Don Martin's place.

Charlie: I tell you it's the kid.

Don: It's Charlie. He's the one.

(People shout, accuse, and scream as the lights go on and off. Then, slowly, in the middle of this nightmarish morass of sight and sound, the camera starts to pull away until, once again, we have reached the opening shot looking at the Maple Street sign from high above.)

SCENE 2.

(The metal side of a spacecraft sits shrouded in darkness. An open door throws out a beam of light from the illuminated interior. Two figures appear, silhouetted against the bright lights. We get only a vague feeling of form.)

Figure One: Understand the procedure now? Just stop a few of their machines and radios and telephones and lawn mowers . . . throw them into darkness for a few hours, and then just sit back and watch the pattern.

Figure Two: And this pattern is always the same?

Figure One: With few variations. They pick the most dangerous enemy

they can find . . . and it's themselves. And all we need do is sit back . . . and watch.

Figure Two: Then I take it this place . . . this Maple Street . . . is not unique.

Figure One *(shaking his head):* By no means. Their world is full of Maple Streets. And we'll go from one to the other and let them destroy themselves. One to the other . . . one to the other . . . one to the other—

SCENE 3.

(The camera moves up for a shot of the starry sky, and over this we hear the Narrator's *voice.)*

Narrator: The tools of conquest do not necessarily come with bombs and explosions and fallout. There are weapons that are simply thoughts, attitudes, prejudices—to be found only in the minds of men. For the record, prejudices can kill and suspicion can destroy. A thoughtless, frightened search for a scapegoat has a fallout all its own for the children . . . and the children yet unborn. *(a pause)* And the pity of it is . . . that these things cannot be confined to . . . The Twilight Zone!

(Fade to black. The end.)

ROD SERLING

As a boy growing up in Binghamton, New York, Rod Serling enjoyed listening to stories on the radio. He could see the characters come alive in his imagination. It isn't surprising that he decided to make his career writing for radio and later for television and the movies. His first 43 freelance scripts were rejected. His breakthrough came in 1951 when he sold his first television drama. His critically acclaimed show *Patterns,* broadcast in 1955, was called a high point in television's evolution. In that era of live television, it was the first time a show was ever telecast more than once.

His best-known television series, *The Twilight Zone,* aired from 1959 to 1965 and can be seen now on reruns and videotape. Serling, who created, produced, and hosted the program, liked to deal with issues such as intolerance, fear, and prejudice on the show. "I think prejudice is a waste," he said, "and its normal end is violence." Serling received an Emmy Award in 1959 for his work on *The Twilight Zone.*

F E A R

Fear passes from man to man
Unknowing,
As one leaf passes its shudder
To another.

All at once the whole tree is trembling
And there is no sign of wind.

BY CHARLES SIMIC

METEORITE TIME LINE

Find some books about meteors and meteorites. What are the differences between them? Read about meteorites that have hit the earth. What was the result? Make a time line, showing prominent meteor showers and meteorite strikes within the last century.

RESPONSE

THE FEAR WITHIN

The play and the poem show how fear can cause us to become suspicious of one another. Do you believe fear can do this? With a small group, discuss how the play could have ended differently. Role-play a happy ending to the play.

THE RIGHT TO BEAR ARMS

There has been a lot of debate over the right to bear arms, or own guns. You and a partner should each find a different newspaper or magazine article about this issue. Write a brief summary of your article. Discuss with your partner what you read.

C O R N E R

WHAT DO YOU THINK?

- Who do you think are the monsters on Maple Street? Explain your answer.

- Why do people there begin accusing their neighbors of being monsters?

- What feelings other than fear do you think can spread from person to person in a group?

捕
星
鳥

The Star Fisher

BY LAURENCE YEP
ILLUSTRATED BY DEBORAH CHABRIAN

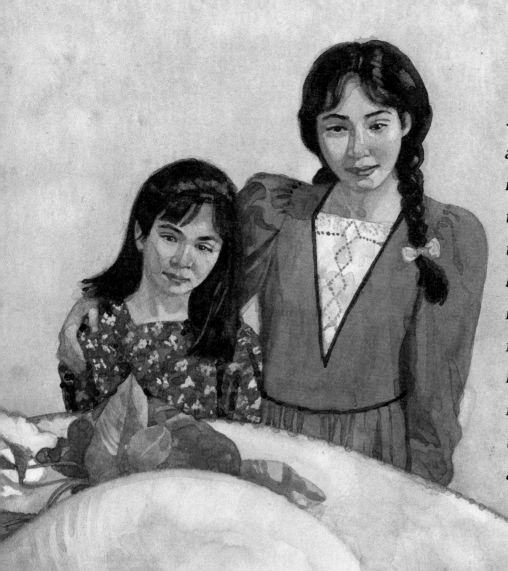

In 1927, Joan Lee and her family moved from Ohio to West Virginia to open a new business and start new lives. The family rented a house from a retired school-teacher who lived around the corner.

When I saw the woman, she reminded me of a bird. Though her hair was white with age, she walked with small, quick, lively steps. She was dressed in a long skirt that reached to the sidewalk almost, and she wore a little jacket with a kind of cape that was fastened in front with a large cameo brooch. There was a huge hat pinned to her head as well, and she carried a big basket over one arm.

When she saw us, she cocked her head to one side and leaned forward, the feather in her hat nodding. Her free hand tilted up the pair of wire glasses perched on her nose as she looked us up and down. *"Hello. Are you my new neighbors?"*

She sounded as if she were talking to someone her own age. Emily glanced around, but at the moment we were the only ones on the street.

The woman pursed her lips for a moment and then tried again. *"Do you speak English?"* Her eyes were bright with curiosity.

Putting away my novel, I got up. *"Yes, ma'am."*

She smiled at me and then put her hand under Emily's chin and studied her face. *"Goodness. What a cookie face."*

Emily stared up at her in fascination. *"Cookie face?"*

She studied Emily with the grave face of a doctor by a dying patient. *"What that face needs is a cookie. Then you'll start smiling."* Pinned by a chain to her jacket was a little watch with a gold knob at the top and a porcelain back with soft pink roses painted on it. When she straightened up, she glanced at the watch. *"It's almost four. Won't you come and have some tea?"*

I suddenly realized how thirsty I was; and from the way Emily was licking her lips, I knew she was, too. But before she could speak up, I did. *"Thank you, but I don't think we can."*

The woman's free hand darted to the handle of the basket so she could hold it in front of her. *"What intelligent children. Of course you shouldn't if you don't know me. I'm Miss Lucy Bradshaw, your landlady, and I live right next to you."*

Conversations in Chinese are in plain type. Conversations in English are in italics.

She nodded to a red brick building next to the school. *"And you're . . . ?"*

"Joan," I said with a self-conscious nod.

"And I'm Emily," she chimed in.

"Well, Emily, why don't you ask your parents if you can come to tea?" When Miss Lucy smiled, it made her long nose look even more like a beak. *"I'll wait here."*

Though we had been in the houses of our friends before, we had never sat down to tea. I knew enough from novels that tea was an important occasion for Americans. I had read descriptions of teas, of course, but I had never been at one; and that's a little like reading descriptions of an elephant and trying to match those with a real live one. Sheer curiosity made me want to go to her tea.

捕
星
鳥

I felt Emily tugging at my skirt, and when I leaned over, she warned in a whisper, *"Once we're inside the laundry, we probably won't ever get out again."*

"I'll talk to Papa," I answered back. Papa was always the one we went to when we needed something. I figured that it was all right to leave Emily alone with Miss Lucy for a few minutes. Opening the gate, I skipped up the steps and opened the door.

Mama was right there, industriously rubbing at some imaginary spot on the wainscoting. But I was sure she had been waiting by the door to make certain that we were all right.

"I'll help you in a little bit, Mama," I promised. "May we go to tea with the landlady?"

"Yes, you may," Mama grunted as she went on with her rubbing. But as I turned to the front door again, she added, "And don't go running to your papa every time you want something. I understand that much English."

Emily was leaning against the fence and chatting away with Miss Lucy when I came outside. *"Mama said it was all right,"* I announced as I closed the door.

Emily stared at me in amazement, but I ignored her as I opened the gate and stepped onto the street. *"This way,"* Miss Lucy said and led us along the sidewalk around the corner. The front door to her house faced Main, while the school faced Second.

Miss Lucy nodded down to Emily. *"After you, Emily."* Wiping her feet on the welcome mat, she opened the door. *"Come in,"* she said brightly.

Emily would have dashed in, but I caught her and made her drag her feet over the mat before I did.

There was a funny smell to the house—not unpleasant, but odd. And it took me a moment to realize it smelled like the museum we'd been to in Toledo. Miss Lucy had set her basket down and was unpinning her hat.

In the parlor, an upright piano squatted like a silent bull while thick, red velvet drapes fought back the sun. Overhead, a chandelier hung from the ceiling like a crystal spider. Beneath it, on a reading stand, sat an old Bible, its black leather cover much worn and the gold embossing almost rubbed away. Through the gold-edged sides of the paper stuck a little red ribbon like a snake's tongue.

"What's that?" Emily asked. She backed up so fast she bumped into me.

Miss Lucy set her hat down on a small table against the wall. "That's Rusty."

The dog sat on its haunches under a glass dome on the broad table. Its red hair and big floppy ears did not move as Emily and I peered so close that our breath began to frost the glass.

Coming over, Miss Lucy crooked an index finger and tapped the glass with it. Instantly Emily hopped back against me as if she expected the dog to bark. "Rusty's dead," Miss Lucy explained. "My grandfather's hobby was stuffing animals, and Rusty was my grandfather's favorite hunting dog." She waved her hand at the floor above us. "The rest of the animals are upstairs."

I couldn't help staring past the chandelier toward the white ceiling. Patterns of fruit and vegetables decorated it as well. I could almost imagine all the dark, furry shapes lurking up there. "What sort of animals?"

"Well, let's see. There's another dog and three cats." Miss Lucy looked up at the ceiling, too, as if she could see right through it. "A possum, an owl." She began to tick off the menagerie on her fingers. "A woodpecker, a raccoon that got in the way of Grandfather's buggy, and more birds than you could shake a stick at. In fact, there wasn't a dead pet that was safe from Grandfather."

"No lions or tigers?" Emily wondered, remembering the museum in Toledo.

Miss Lucy patted her hair, which had been done up in a bun. "There was a bear that Grandfather wanted to stuff. But Grandmother had enough of his dust catchers, so she put her foot down." She gave a little giggle that made her seem fifty years younger. "He got so mad that he threatened to stuff her if she died first."

I couldn't tell if she was joking or not, but Emily frowned up at Miss Lucy solemnly. "Did she?"

"No, he did." Miss Lucy took a handkerchief from her sleeve to wipe at the glass. "But his threat gave Grandmother quite a scare. I think they each stayed alive an extra ten years out of sheer stubbornness."

捕星鳥

Emily suddenly darted over toward a huge cabinet that rose almost to the ceiling. On shelf after shelf were rows of eggs of all sizes and colors. *"Did you dye these eggs?"*

Miss Lucy treated Emily as if they were the same age. *"No,"* she said as she came over, *"my great-aunt liked to collect them. She could shinny up a tree faster than a squirrel—and that was in full skirts."*

Emily pressed her nose so close to the glass that I pulled her back. Before every egg was a card with curly, delicate writing. *"Robin redbreast,"* she read slowly.

Miss Lucy clasped her hands in front of her. *"She said there was never a blue as nice as a robin's egg."*

I studied the egg with Emily. *"It's bluer than the sky."*

Miss Lucy looked at me thoughtfully. *"Why, I guess it is."*

I found myself liking Miss Lucy more and more. She wasn't stuck up like other grown-ups. Instead, she talked and acted toward us as if we were all equals.

Emily slipped away from my grasp and turned in a slow circle. Wherever she looked, there were cabinets full of odd objects. *"You certainly have a lot of things."*

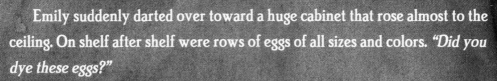

"*Every member of my family had a hobby.*" Miss Lucy spread out her arms grandly. "*This house is full of hobbies.*" She lowered her arms and added, "*And memories.*"

For a moment, surrounded by all of her family's memories in that great big house, Miss Lucy looked as small as Emily. As a giant grandfather clock loudly ticked off the seconds, Miss Lucy reminded me of a little girl lost in a museum.

Suddenly I felt sorry for her. I knew she must feel lonely—maybe as lonely as I had felt in the street. "*What's your hobby?*"

Miss Lucy unpinned her brooch and hung her cape over the back of a chair. "*People are my hobby. What's yours?*"

Emily piped up before I could. "*Food is my hobby.*"

"*Then*"—Miss Lucy winked mischievously— "*it's a good thing I invited you to tea.*"

捕
星
鳥

捕星鳥

RADISHES ONIONS BEETS LETTUCE CARROTS

I felt more and more as if we three were playing house, and Miss Lucy was only pretending to be our host and we were only pretending to be her guests. And suddenly I didn't feel strange or different. *"Yes, it's so very kind of you."* I dropped a curtsy as I had seen in a moving picture, and Emily did the same.

And to give Miss Lucy credit, she started to play the game as well. She might have had white hair, but she could be as lively as a little girl. *"This way."* Plucking up her dress between her fingers, she picked up her basket and led us grandly past more dim rooms full of furniture and brought us into the kitchen.

It was the sunniest room in her house and more typical of her than any other of those gloomy rooms. Thin lace curtains did not keep out the light but made shadowy patterns on the walls, and the back door was cut in half. That way the bottom half could be kept locked while

Miss Lucy kept the top half open for air and light. Unbolting the top half, she swung it back, revealing a small dirt courtyard between her house and our laundry. In one corner was a neat little garden of vegetables. Each row had a stake with a piece of paper that said what was in the row. I couldn't help thinking to myself that she had been a schoolteacher all right.

In the center of the kitchen was a big table with a worn top, and on pegs on its sides were rolling pins and other baking instruments hanging by leather thongs. Emily dragged out a chair and promptly sat down.

Unbuttoning her jacket, Miss Lucy hung that from a peg on the wall and took down an apron from another peg. *"But if people weren't my hobby, then food would be it."*

I helped her tie the apron behind her. *"Can I help?"*

There was a gas stove against one wall, looking as big and unmovable as a mountain. Next to the oven was a smaller door for the wood, and above the stove was a compartment for keeping things warm. Miss Lucy went over to it now and took a big teakettle from the top. *"Yes, you can get out plates, cups, and saucers."* And she nodded her head toward a cabinet against the far wall.

As I passed by the table, I poked Emily. "Ask her if she needs any help," I said, ignoring the glare she shot at me.

"I want to help, too," Emily announced.

"You can set the places," Miss Lucy said.

Emily scratched her head doubtfully, but she was afraid to ask what Miss Lucy meant. When she looked at me, I could only shake my head that I didn't know either. But I was just as reluctant to request an explanation as Emily. Even though we had been born here and could name all the presidents and the capitals of the states, there were so many little things that we didn't know—like place settings. In some ways, we were often like actors who were thrust onstage without a script, so that we had to improvise. And too often, up in Ohio, our ignorance had gotten us laughed at; and no one likes to feel like a fool.

But Miss Lucy must have been the kind of schoolteacher who had enormous reservoirs of patience. *"A place setting,"* she said. *"You know, knives and forks and napkins."*

"Oh, yes, of course," Emily nodded her head wisely like a little owl. *"That kind of place setting."*

With a sigh of relief that that crisis had passed, I went to the cabinet; but all I could find were cups and plates of thin, delicate china on which birds were painted. They were too fine for everyday use, so I turned to Miss Lucy. *"Am I by the right cabinet?"*

Going over to the sink, Miss Lucy turned the tap and water splashed into the metal kettle with a hollow drumming sound. *"Yes, that's it."*

With Miss Lucy to direct her, Emily had found the napkins and put them out. Since she was not sure how many utensils to use, she was setting out three spoons, two knives, and four forks at each place. Taking one of the plates, I held it up uncertainly. *"One of these?"*

Miss Lucy had set the kettle on the stove. *"You're company, aren't you?"* Miss Lucy looked at us over her shoulder. *"I need a plate, Emily."*

Emily came running over and took the plate when I handed it to her. When she brought it back, Miss Lucy had opened up a cookie tin and began to heap the plate with all sorts of different cookies, which she set on the table. *"Have some?"*

I was hungry enough to eat the whole plate, but I was also determined that Emily and I were going to behave like grown-up guests. "Don't be a pig," I said to Emily.

Glumly, Emily took the plate to the table and set it down in the center. *"I'll wait, ma'am."*

I set out cups of paper-thin china on saucers and put plates down by each setting. When the water had boiled, Miss Lucy poured it into a pot and added some tea leaves. When she had brought the teapot to the table and sat down, Emily, who had not taken her eyes from the plate, asked in Chinese, "Now can I eat?"

However, I knew Emily's habits all too well. "Just one," I instructed her in Chinese.

Emily looked at me in outrage. "One?"

"One," I said with a firm nod.

Emily leaned this way and that while she examined the contents of the plate for the largest cookie. Then, with all the delicacy of a surgeon, she slipped her choice out from the bottom and placed it in triumph upon her plate.

Miss Lucy must have guessed some of what we had said in Chinese. *"Well, I have an appetite, so excuse me."* She put a half-dozen cookies on top of her own plate. Then she tilted up the teapot so that a little bit of red-brown liquid poured from the pot into her cup. Deciding that it was all right, she finished filling the cup, the tea tinkling musically on the thin sides. *"Tea?"* she asked Emily.

Emily looked dubiously at the cup because the tea looked much darker and stronger than the tea we usually drank. *"I guess so."*

Picking up the saucer with the cup, Miss Lucy placed it in front of Emily and took Emily's in turn. *"Tea?"* she asked me.

"Please." I spread my napkin across my lap.

When she had poured my cup and handed it to me, she took mine and poured one for herself. In the meantime, Emily had been sniffing her tea suspiciously.

"Don't do that," I warned. "It's not polite."

"It smells funny," Emily protested.

Miss Lucy had been waiting politely for us to finish. Now she held up a small silver bowl shaped like a pumpkin. *"Sugar?"*

I had never before heard of having sugar in tea. In fact, we always drank ours plain; but neither Emily nor I wanted to behave like children.

"Please," Emily said politely.

Miss Lucy picked up a small spoon. *"One spoonful or two?"*

It was another anxious moment. *"Unh..."* Emily guessed wildly, *"six."*

"My, you have quite a sweet tooth." Miss Lucy did not even blink an eye as she spooned the sugar into Emily's cup. And then she turned to me. *"And you, Joan?"*

Six sounded like a nice, round, grown-up number to me, too. *"I'll have six."*

"I can see that sweet tooth runs in the family." But she added the sugar to the little cup as well until the cup was more sugar than tea.

I thought I should make polite conversation. *"My father says that when you do something, do it well."*

"He's a wise man." She held up a small silvery pitcher. *"Milk?"*

We'd never had milk in our tea either, but Emily gamely said, *"Please."*

"Say when," Miss Lucy instructed her and began pouring.

She might still be pouring if she had waited for Emily to tell her to stop. As it was, she stopped when she filled the cup to the brim. Taking my lesson from Emily, I told her to stop when my cup was almost full.

Emily and I were old hands at watching a host. When Miss Lucy put only one spoonful of sugar and a dash of milk into her tea, we both realized our mistakes. And when she stirred her cup, we tried to imitate her; but stirring was a bit harder for us at first with all the sugar inside the cup. Nonetheless, the spoon rang against the sides like the clapper in a delicate bell.

And when she raised the cup, she put out her little finger. With a glance at me, Emily stuck out her pinkie and raised her cup; and I did the same.

The tea was sweet enough to make my teeth shiver, so I put my cup down. Emily, however, had quite the sweet tooth and went on drinking.

Soon we were chatting like three old friends. Miss Lucy asked about our old town in Ohio, and we asked about our new home. (It had been the birthplace of the Confederate general Stonewall Jackson.) She asked about my family, and we asked about hers—she had a great-grandfather who'd fought in the Revolutionary War. Emily and I were both feeling very proud of ourselves when someone knocked on the door.

Immediately Miss Lucy became a grown-up again. *"Excuse me,"* she said. Dabbing her napkin at her lips, she put it on the table and went to the door.

"Yes?" Miss Lucy asked in her friendly way.

"Excuse me. I thought I heard my sisters." It was Bobby. *"My mother sent me here for them."*

"Of course, they're right here." Miss Lucy opened the bottom half of the door and stepped aside so Bobby could see us.

The game was over, but Emily wanted to finish it right. She held up her teacup. *"I'll be with you as soon as I finish my tea."*

"You're coming home now." An exasperated Bobby stormed into the kitchen and grabbed Emily's hand.

Embarrassed that her brother was treating her like a child, Emily got so angry that she forgot her manners and tried to kick him. "Let go."

But Bobby pulled stubbornly. "We can't start dinner until you're home."

"Watch out," I said, getting up from my chair. To my horror, I saw the fragile cup slip out of Emily's hand. It seemed to fall in slow motion: the tea flowing out of the cup, the cup itself tumbling through the air. Bobby tried to catch it, but his hands moved even slower.

It crashed with a tinkling sound. Dozens of pieces sprayed across the floor. "You broke it," Emily wailed.

Bobby had grown very pale, while I knelt down right in the tea and began picking up the pieces. *"We're sorry,"* I said to Miss Lucy. *"We'll do chores until we pay you back."* That would probably take us into next year from the look of that exquisite cup.

"Fiddlesticks." Miss Lucy had gotten a broom. *"I have tons of cups just like that."* She tapped me with the broom straws until I stood up. *"Collecting china was my mother's hobby."*

That only made me feel worse, though. *"Then it must have some sentimental value,"* I objected.

"New memories are just as good as old ones. I haven't had such a nice tea in ages." She winked at me as if our game were our special secret. And I knew the little girl was still there inside Miss Lucy. She was just hiding from Bobby and the rest of the world.

I tried to play the grown-up guest. *"Then,"* I said with a polite smile, *"we must have tea again."*

Laurence Yep

捕星鳥

Ilene Cooper, writer and children's books editor for *Booklist* magazine, spoke with Laurence Yep about *The Star Fisher*.

Much of *The Star Fisher* is based on your own family history, isn't it?

That's true. My grandfather originally came to San Francisco from China. We have a picture of him, a young man in his 20s wearing a Western suit, but his hair still in a braid wrapped around his head. Unfortunately, he arrived just a few days after the San Francisco earthquake in 1906, and so

there was no work for him. He moved to Pittsburgh where his brother lived and then moved on to West Virginia to open a laundry. Eventually, my grandparents took the family back to San Francisco because they wanted their girls to marry Chinese boys, and of course there were hardly any Chinese in West Virginia.

What else in *The Star Fisher* comes from real incidents?

There was a landlady who befriended the family. The girls in the story both contain bits of my mother, and my Auntie Mary did go off to the neighbor to have tea, but she was much younger than the girls in the story, about three or four. During her nap time she would sneak out of her crib to visit a neighbor, and her parents didn't know about it for months.

Did you live in a Chinese neighborhood when you were growing up?

No, I lived in an African American neighborhood. But I came to Chinatown after regular school to learn Chinese. I did that for four years, though I can't really speak the language. Today, I go into a Chinese store and point at an item and try to say the name—not very successfully usually.

So your family has always lived outside the mainstream culture.

That's true. But I think that's the way it is for any immigrant group. You go where the economic opportunities are, and that often takes you into another culture.

You have so many histories and stories from your family. How do you decide what you're going to write about?

I usually begin with one incident. For *The Star Fisher* it was remembering my grandmother learning to cook American style. She told me that whenever there was a church social, her apple pies always sold out first. That seemed so interesting to me, a Chinese woman perfecting American cooking. My grandmother really came to life when she came to America and West Virginia. She was from that tough survivor stock, cut off from family, from everything she had ever known really, and yet she thrived. She did learn to read and write English, but her one regret was that she never learned American math. She did all her business numbers in her head, using a Chinese-style of calculation.

Laurence Yep

PASSPORTS TO

Human beings are more alike than unalike, and what is true anywhere is true everywhere, yet I encourage travel to as many destinations as possible for the sake of education as well as pleasure.

It is necessary, especially for Americans, to see other lands and experience other cultures. The American, living in this vast country and able to traverse three thousand miles east to west using the same language, needs to hear languages as they collide in Europe, Africa, and Asia.

A tourist, browsing in a Paris shop, eating in an Italian *ristorante*, or idling along a Hong Kong street, will encounter three or

BY MAYA ANGELOU

UNDERSTANDING

four languages as she negotiates the buying of a blouse, the paying of a check, or the choosing of a trinket. I do not mean to suggest that simply overhearing a foreign tongue adds to one's understanding of that language. I do know, however, that being exposed to the existence of other languages increases the perception that the world is populated by people who not only speak differently from oneself but whose cultures and philosophies are other than one's own.

Perhaps travel cannot prevent bigotry, but by demonstrating that all peoples cry, laugh, eat, worry, and die, it can introduce the idea that if we try to understand each other, we may even become friends.

DISCUSS HOBBIES

HOBBY TRADING CARDS

Miss Lucy has a house full of hobbies. Along with classmates, make a trading card that tells about your special hobby or collection. On the front of the card, draw a picture of your hobby. On the back, write your name. Put everyone's card in a bag. Then take turns drawing cards. Find the person whose card you draw. Learn about his or her hobby.

ROLE-PLAY A PARTY

WELCOME, MISS LUCY!

Imagine that Miss Lucy is coming to your house for a visit. Plan a simple afternoon party. What will you serve? Plan a special surprise for Miss Lucy. With a partner, role-play Miss Lucy's visit to your house.

DO RESEARCH

ANOTHER COUNTRY

Emily and Joan's parents were born in China. Was anyone in your family—or among your ancestors—born in another country? Find information about that country. Imagine what it would be like to live there now. Write about the differences and similarities between living in the United States and living in that country.

WHAT DO YOU THINK?

- What do Miss Lucy, Emily, and Joan learn about each other?

- If you were Joan, would you have accepted Miss Lucy's invitation? Why or why not?

- Miss Lucy says, "New memories are just as good as old ones." What does she mean?

319

Theme Wrap-Up

The selections in this theme explore how people communicate with one another. In some cases, a misunderstanding based on prejudice can be overcome; in other cases, suspicion grows and the result can be fatal. From what you have learned in this theme, what could you teach others about how to celebrate differences?

What do you think Miss Lucy would have said to calm the residents of Maple Street?

ACTIVITY CORNER

Think about your family or a group of friends. How are you alike? How are you different? Create a poster with several Venn diagrams showing similarities and differences between you and your family members or friends. Talk about the ways you can learn from one another's differences.

TURNING

The following selections reveal something that is as true today as it was in ancient Greece and Rome: it may take many years to reach a goal, but a person's life or a community can be changed in an instant.

POINTS

TURNING

CONTENTS

POINTS

323

BOOKSHELF

Wilma Rudolph
by Wayne Coffey

This is the story of the young woman from Tennessee who overcame crippling illnesses and other problems to become the fastest female athlete in the world.
Signatures Library

Detectives in Togas
by Henry Winterfeld

In ancient Rome, six students band together to help a classmate by trying to solve the crime for which he has been blamed.
Signatures Library

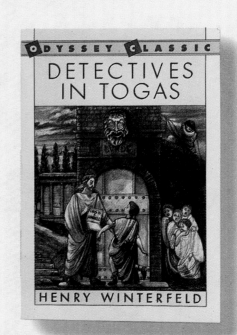

Cat Running
by Zilpha Keatley Snyder

Cat has always run to win, but one day her swiftness as a runner takes on life-and-death importance.
SLJ Best Books

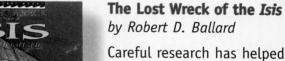

The Lost Wreck of the *Isis*
by Robert D. Ballard

Careful research has helped archaeologists re-create the final voyage of an ancient Roman tradeship.
Outstanding Science Trade Book

Volcano
by Patricia Lauber

The eruption of Mount St. Helens in 1980 gave scientists an exciting chance to see how nature rebuilds itself after great destruction.
Newbery Honor, ALA Notable, SLJ Best Books, Outstanding Science Trade Book

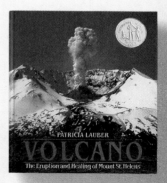

ATALANTA'S RACE

from *The Golden Fleece and the Heroes Who Lived Before Achilles*

by PADRAIC COLUM
illustrated by DAVID WILGUS

Newbery Honor

THE CLASSIC GREEK MYTHS ARE TALES OF HEROES AND ADVENTURERS. IN THE EVENING, PEOPLE WOULD GATHER IN THE KING'S PALACE TO LISTEN TO THESE STORIES. ONE NIGHT, ATALANTA, THE HUNTRESS, TOLD A STORY.

327

**T**here are two Atalantas, she said; she herself, the Huntress, and another who is noted for her speed of foot and her delight in the race—the daughter of Schœneus,[1] King of Bœotia,[2] Atalanta of the Swift Foot.

So proud was she of her swiftness that she made a vow to the gods that none would be her husband except the youth who won past her in the race. Youth after youth came and raced against her, but Atalanta, who grew fleeter and fleeter of foot, left each one of them far behind her. The youths who came to the race were so many and the clamor they made after defeat was so great, that her father made a law that, as he thought, would lessen their number. The law that he made was that the youth who came to race against Atalanta and who lost the race should lose his life into the bargain. After that the youths who had care for their lives stayed away from Bœotia.

Once there came a youth from a far part of Greece into the country that Atalanta's father ruled over. Hippomenes[3] was his name. He did not know of the race, but having come into the city and seeing the crowd of people, he went with them to the course. He looked upon the youths who were girded for the race, and he heard the folk say amongst themselves, "Poor youths, as mighty and as high-spirited as they look, by sunset the life will be out of each of them, for Atalanta will run past them as she ran past the others." Then Hippomenes spoke to the folk in wonder, and they told him of Atalanta's race and of what would befall the youths who were defeated in it. "Unlucky youths," cried Hippomenes, "how foolish they are to try to win a bride at the price of their lives."

Then, with pity in his heart, he watched the youths prepare for the race. Atalanta had not yet taken her place, and he was fearful of looking upon her. "She is a witch," he said to himself, "she must be a witch to draw so many youths to their deaths, and she, no doubt, will show in her face and figure the witch's spirit."

But even as he said this, Hippomenes saw Atalanta. She stood with the youths before they crouched for the first dart in the race. He saw that she was a girl of a light and a lovely form. Then they crouched for the race; then the trumpets rang out, and the youths and the maiden darted like swallows over the sand of the course.

---

[1] Schœneus (shō′nē·əs)
[2] Bœotia (bē·ō′shē·ə)
[3] Hippomenes (hip·om′ə·nēz)

On came Atalanta, far, far ahead of the youths who had started with her. Over her bare shoulders her hair streamed, blown backward by the wind that met her flight. Her fair neck shone, and her little feet were like flying doves. It seemed to Hippomenes as he watched her that there was fire in her lovely body. On and on she went as swift as the arrow that the Scythian shoots from his bow. And as he watched the race he was not sorry that the youths were being left behind. Rather would he have been enraged if one came near overtaking her, for now his heart was set upon winning her for his bride, and he cursed himself for not having entered the race.

She passed the last goal mark and she was given the victor's wreath of flowers. Hippomenes stood and watched her and he did not see the youths who had started with her—they had thrown themselves on the ground in their despair.

Then wild, as though he were one of the doomed youths, Hippomenes made his way through the throng and came before the black-bearded King of Bœotia. The king's brows were knit, for even then he was pronouncing doom upon the youths who had been left behind in the race. He looked upon Hippomenes, another youth who would make the trial, and the frown became heavier upon his face.

But Hippomenes saw only Atalanta. She came beside her father; the wreath was upon her head of gold, and her eyes were wide and tender. She turned her face to him, and then she knew by the wildness that was in his look that he had come to enter the race with her. Then the flush that was on her face died away, and she shook her head as if she were imploring him to go from that place.

The dark-bearded king bent his brows upon him and said, "Speak, O youth, speak and tell us what brings you here."

Then cried Hippomenes as if his whole life were bursting out with his words: "Why does this maiden, your daughter, seek an easy renown by conquering weakly youths in the race? She has not striven yet. Here stand I, one of the blood of Poseidon, the god of the sea. Should I be defeated by her in the race, then, indeed, might Atalanta have something to boast of."

Atalanta stepped forward and said: "Do not speak of it, youth. Indeed I think that it is some god, envious of your beauty and your strength, who sent you here to strive with me and to meet your doom. Ah, think of the youths who have striven with me even now! Think of the hard doom that is about to fall upon them! You venture your life in the race, but indeed I am not worthy of the price. Go hence, O stranger youth, go hence and live happily, for indeed I think that there is some maiden who loves you well."

"Nay, maiden," said Hippomenes, "I will enter the race and I will venture my life on the chance of winning you for my bride. What good will my life and my spirit be to me if they cannot win this race for me?"

She drew away from him then and looked upon him no more, but bent down to fasten the sandals upon her feet. And the black-bearded king looked upon Hippomenes and said, "Face, then, this race tomorrow. You will be the only one who will enter it. But bethink thee of the doom that awaits thee at the end of it." The king said no more, and Hippomenes went from him and from Atalanta, and he came again to the place where the race had been run.

He looked across the sandy course with its goal marks, and in his mind he saw again Atalanta's swift race. He would not meet doom at the hands of the king's soldiers, he knew, for his spirit would leave him with the greatness of the effort he would make to reach the goal before her. And he thought it would be well to die in that effort and on that sandy place that was so far from his own land.

Even as he looked across the sandy course now deserted by the throng, he saw one move across it, coming toward him with feet that did not seem to touch the ground. She was a woman of wonderful presence. As Hippomenes looked upon her he knew that she was Aphrodite, the goddess of beauty and of love.

"Hippomenes," said the immortal goddess, "the gods are mindful of you who are sprung from one of the gods, and I am mindful of you because of your own worth.

I have come to help you in your race with Atalanta, for I would not have you slain, nor would I have that maiden go unwed. Give your greatest strength and your greatest swiftness to the race, and behold! Here are wonders that will prevent the fleet-footed Atalanta from putting all her spirit into the race."

And then the immortal goddess held out to Hippomenes a branch that had upon it three apples of shining gold.

"In Cyprus," said the goddess, "where I have come from, there is a tree on which these golden apples grow. Only I may pluck them. I have brought them to you, Hippomenes. Keep them in your girdle, and in the race you will find out what to do with them, I think."

So Aphrodite said, and then she vanished, leaving a fragrance in the air and the three shining apples in the hands of Hippomenes. Long he looked upon their bright-ness. They were beside him that night, and when he arose in the dawn he put them in his girdle. Then, before the throng, he went to the place of the race.

When he showed himself beside Atalanta all around the course were silent, for they all admired Hippomenes for his beauty and for the spirit that was in his face; they were silent out of compassion, for they knew the doom that befell the youths who raced with Atalanta.

And now Schœneus, the black-bearded king, stood up, and he spoke to the throng, saying: "Hear me all, both young and old: this youth, Hippomenes, seeks to win the race from my daughter, winning her for his bride. Now, if he be victorious and escape death I will give him my dear child, Atalanta, and many fleet horses besides as gifts from me, and in honor he shall go back to his native land. But if he fail in the race, then he will have to share the doom that has been meted out to the other youths who raced with Atalanta hoping to win her for a bride."

Then Hippomenes and Atalanta crouched for the start. The trumpets were sounded and they darted off.

Side by side with Atalanta Hippomenes went. Her flying hair touched his breast, and it seemed to him that they were skimming the sandy course as if they were swallows. But then Atalanta began to draw away from him. He saw her ahead of him, and then he began to hear the words of cheer that came from the throng — "Bend to the race, Hippomenes! Go on, go on! Use your strength to the utmost." He bent himself to the race, but further and further from him Atalanta drew.

Then it seemed to him that she checked her swiftness a little to look back at him. He gained on her a little. And then his hand touched the apples that were in his girdle. As it touched them it came into his mind what to do with the apples.

He was not far from her now, but already her swiftness was drawing her further and further away. He took one of the apples into his hand and tossed it into the air so that it fell on the track before her.

Atalanta saw the shining apple. She checked her speed and stooped in the race to pick it up. And as she stooped Hippomenes darted past her, and went flying toward the goal that now was within his sight.

But soon she was beside him again. He looked, and he saw that the goal marks were far, far ahead of him. Atalanta with the flying hair passed him, and drew away and away from him. He had not speed to gain upon her now, he thought, so he put his strength into his hand and he flung the second of the shining apples. The apple rolled before her and rolled off the course. Atalanta turned off the course, stooped and picked up the apple.

Then did Hippomenes draw all his spirit into his breast as he raced on. He was now nearer to the goal than she was. But he knew that she was behind him, going lightly where he went heavily. And then she was beside him, and then she went past him. She paused in her speed for a moment and she looked back on him.

As he raced on, his chest seemed weighted down and his throat was crackling dry. The goal marks were far away still, but Atalanta was nearing them. He took the last of the golden apples into his hand. Perhaps she was now so far that the strength of his throw would not be great enough to bring the apple before her.

But with all the strength he could put into his hand he flung the apple. It struck the course before her feet and then went bounding wide. Atalanta swerved in her race and followed where the apple went. Hippomenes marveled that he had been able to fling it so far. He saw Atalanta stoop to pick up the apple, and he bounded on. And then, although his strength was failing, he saw the goal marks near him. He set his feet between them and then fell down on the ground.

The attendants raised him up and put the victor's wreath upon his head. The concourse of people shouted with joy to see him victor. But he looked around for Atalanta and he saw her standing there with the golden apples in her hands. "He has won," he heard her say, "and I have not to hate myself for bringing a doom upon him. Gladly, gladly do I give up the race, and glad am I that it is this youth who has won the victory from me."

She took his hand and brought him before the king. Then Schœneus, in the sight of all the rejoicing people, gave Atalanta to Hippomenes for his bride, and he bestowed upon him also a great gift of horses. With his dear and hard-won bride, Hippomenes went to his own country, and the apples that she brought with her, the golden apples of Aphrodite, were reverenced by the people.

Padraic Colum

Padraic Colum was born in Ireland in 1881. He didn't begin writing stories for children until he moved to the United States in 1914. But he said his childhood friendship with Charlie MacGauran, a neighborhood storyteller, was what inspired him to become a writer. MacGauran taught Colum that "the storyteller must have respect for the child's mind and the child's conception of the world. . . . Strange words do not bewilder children if there is order in the action and the sentences." Colum kept this in mind when he retold the classic Greek myths in *The Golden Fleece*, which was named a Newbery Honor Book in 1922.

David Wilgus

David Wilgus worked for many years as an advertising art director before becoming a full-time illustrator. His highly detailed pencil drawings graced a series of books written by Jane Yolen, including *Here There Be Dragons* and *Here There Be Unicorns*. Wilgus prefers drawing to painting because he loves the feeling of working in pencil. He used colored pencils to illustrate "Atalanta's Race."

RESPONSE CORNER

MYTH TELLING

Work with a small group to invent a myth. First, talk about the characteristics of myths. Then brainstorm the plot, characters, and setting for your myth. Be as creative as possible. Tell your myth to another group as though you were passing it down to another generation.

A HEALTHFUL PLAN

Healthy runners must follow a plan of exercise and nutrition. Look for information on rules for athletes in training. Write a one-week plan for meals and exercise that a runner could use.

LET THE GAMES BEGIN!

Work with one of four teams in your class to organize a sixth-grade Olympic Race. Team One directs the opening ceremony. Team Two makes the rules for running the races and then times the runners. Team Three maps out the race course on the school grounds. Team Four designs the prizes and directs the awards ceremony. Anyone who wants to run in the race can do so.

WHAT DO YOU THINK?

- Do you think that the race between Atalanta and Hippomenes is fair? Explain your answer.

- If you could be one of the characters in this story, whom would you choose to be? Why?

- How would the story ending be different if Atalanta had won the race?

GREAT SUMMER OLYMPIC MOMENTS

BY NATE AASENG

ILLUSTRATED BY DARRIN JOHNSTON

For more than a thousand years, the ancient town of Olympia in western Greece was the gathering place for the greatest athletes of the world. Every four years, nations stopped their wars while men boxed, ran, jumped, and threw objects in the first Olympic stadium. First prize was a wreath of olive—and fame throughout the land. After the ancient Olympic games were banned by the Roman emperor in the year 394, the Olympian ideal of peaceful athletic competition among the nations became a distant memory. The stadium and temples of Olympia fell into ruin.

About 1,500 years later, in the 19th century, a group of German archaeologists began to dig in the area of Olympia. Many people around the world read about the ancient buildings that were being dug up. Scholars and students studied historical writings and learned how the ancient games had been organized. They even discovered the names of some of the great athletes who had competed in the games. Finally, in 1896, a group of sports fans set out to bring the games back to life.

Most of the pieces for this noble experiment had already been assembled. The games had a tireless organizer (Baron Pierre de Coubertin), a host country (Greece), financing (courtesy of a wealthy Greek architect), and competitors (more than 300, from 13 different nations).

At first, the games failed to inspire. The athletic performances of the 1896 Athens Olympics seemed very ordinary compared to the stories of legendary heroes who had battled for Olympic honors in ancient Greece. As the games progressed, the failure of the host country to win any track and field events added to the disappointment of the fans. After lying dormant for 1,500 years, the Olympic games needed something extraordinary to bring them back to life.

Late in the competition, on April 10, 1896, a small group of men gathered at the Marathon Bridge. Marathon, a village north of Athens, was the site of an ancient Greek victory over Persian invaders in 490 B.C. According to a story passed down through the years, a Greek messenger had run all the way from the battlefield to Athens with news of the victory. After giving his report, the runner had collapsed and died from exhaustion. In honor of this legend, Baron de Coubertin had introduced a new event called the marathon. The runners would follow the road from Marathon to Athens, an incredible 40 kilometers (about 25 miles) away.

Nearly 100,000 spectators gathered at the stadium to witness the finish. All afternoon they anxiously awaited reports of the race's progress. Unfortunately, the early news was no more promising for Greece than the results of any of the other events had been. A French athlete named Lermusiaux had dominated the early portion of the race. Unable to maintain his own pace, Lermusiaux slowed, gave up the lead to Edwin Flack of Australia, and soon collapsed. A subdued Greek crowd passed along the latest information—Flack was just a few miles away and holding on to his lead.

Four kilometers from the finish line, Flack, a gold medalist in the 800 meters, faltered. Soon after, a Greek army major charged into the stadium on horseback to deliver the latest bulletin to the king and queen of Greece: A Greek was in the lead!

After running from Marathon, Greece, to Athens, the Greek runner Spiridon Loues closes in on the finish line amid the cheers of his homeland fans in the stadium.

The news spread rapidly throughout the stadium. Sports fans, who had been mildly curious onlookers, became excited and tried to will the Greek along to the finish. A long, resounding roar from outside the stadium signaled that the first runner was nearing the finish. When the small form of Spiridon Loues appeared on the stadium track, the spectators leapt to their feet, shouting their delight. Loues crossed the finish line nearly seven minutes ahead of the next finisher and was practically drowned in a sea of congratulations.

This unexpected triumph by a poor man, who had finished no better than fifth in the Greek pre-Olympic trials, provided the spark that was needed to bring the Olympic games to life.

Years later, in 1968, the Olympic games in Mexico City followed a similar pattern. For 10 days of competition, the Mexican hosts politely applauded the victories of visiting athletes. In all that time, the Mexican athletes had faltered.

The host country's best prospect for a gold medal appeared to be in a swimming event, the 200-meter breaststroke. A 17-year-old named Felipe "Pepe" Muñoz had not only qualified for the finals but had also recorded the fastest time of the trial heats. Muñoz was still a long-shot to defeat Vladimir Kosinsky of the Soviet Union, who held the world record. But 8,000 Mexicans crowded the poolside bleachers to cheer his effort.

Halfway through the race, the Mexicans' hopes were evaporating. Muñoz, swimming in fourth place, appeared out of contention. Suddenly, the young swimmer surged forward. As he moved into third place, the hometown fans began cheering loudly. The inspired Muñoz continued to catch up to Kosinsky.

All spectators were on their feet as Muñoz touched the wall for the final turn just inches behind Kosinsky. Amid indescribable bedlam, the teenager caught the Soviet halfway down the final length and touched home half a second ahead of him to claim the gold medal.

In the celebration that followed, Muñoz was pulled out of the water and carried around the pool area. Spectators hugged and kissed each other. Television announcers wept openly. The Olympics had again provided hometown sports fans with an unforgettable experience.

Every four years, thousands of the world's greatest athletes gather to compete in the Olympic games. The grandeur and the massive scale of the Summer Olympics have made it the world's greatest showcase for what the human body and willpower can accomplish.

JOAN BENOIT

BY BILL LITTLEFIELD

ALA Best
Books for
Young Adults

Teachers'
Choice

SAMUELSON

ILLUSTRATED BY BERNIE FUCHS

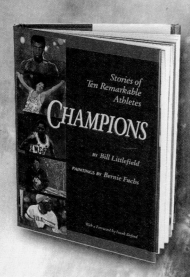

from *CHAMPIONS*

Stories of Ten Remarkable Athletes

IT IS TRUE THAT ALL RECORDS FALL, AND THE ONES JOAN BENOIT SAMUELSON SET IN THE BOSTON MARATHON IN 1983 AND THE 1984 OLYMPIC MARATHON WILL BE NO EXCEPTION. BUT LONG AFTER HER NUMBERS HAVE BEEN ECLIPSED, PEOPLE WHO SAW HER RUN WILL TALK ABOUT HER FIERCE AND STEADY DETERMINATION AND HER ASTONISHING RESILIENCE. AND THEN SOMEONE WILL REMEMBER THAT SHE WANTED TO CALL HER AUTOBIOGRAPHY *OUT ON A LIMP*, AND EVERYBODY WILL LAUGH. AND SOMEBODY ELSE WILL SAY, "YOU KNOW, THERE NEVER WAS A MORE DELIGHTFUL CHAMPION." AND EVERYONE WILL AGREE, BECAUSE THAT WILL BE TRUE, TOO.

March is not Maine's best season. Spring never comes early to northern New England, and the wind off the ocean in March stings a runner's cheek. But that discomfort was nothing compared to the pleasure of running near home, and so Joan Benoit was training in Cape Elizabeth, minutes from her family, in the middle of the March preceding the 1984 Summer Olympics.

There were other advantages to Cape Elizabeth. Though the roads and paths there are not free of traffic, there is still farmland to see. The view of the sea is fine, if you don't mind the solitude. And Joan Benoit knew all the routes up there so well that she was unlikely to be surprised or distracted from the business at hand. At one time she'd tried to keep to untraveled roads because running competitively had seemed so preposterous to her. As a schoolgirl she first discovered the joy running could bring her. It was all hers, and all she had to do to improve was run more. Her shyness was no handicap. Maybe it was even an advantage. She ran alone and loved it. But she was embarrassed about declaring herself a marathoner, saying it to the world by training seriously where anyone might notice. When cars would pass her in those days, she would sometimes stop running and pretend she was picking flowers. But now the solitude was simply one useful component to the concentration Joan Benoit had built to complement the joy. She'd acquired an iron sense of purpose that had been wearing down opponents for ten years, and that would drive Benoit through another decade of championship performances.

The run started off well. Why should it have been otherwise? Joan Benoit was the country's best female distance runner. She'd won the Boston Marathon twice, the second time the previous April (1983) in a world record time: 2 hours, 22 minutes, 43 seconds. She'd won major marathons in Eugene, Oregon, and in New Zealand as well, and too many shorter races to count. At least *she* hadn't counted them. And now, in the best shape of her career, she was pointing for the Olympic Trials, which were less than two months away. She'd picked the twenty-mile loop in Cape Elizabeth that day because it was a run that had always provided her with a sense of how well her training was going. She expected good news.

But with three miles to go, she felt an unfamiliar sensation in her knee. Later she would say it seemed as if "a spring were unraveling in the joint." She tried to run for another two miles, but the knee complained too loudly. When she could no longer stride, she hobbled. When she could no longer hobble, she walked.

"Injuries are part of the game." Maybe this is the most familiar cliché in all of sports. But each particular injury is new and ominous when it happens, and this one had picked a heck of a time to occur. Nearly every girl and boy who has ever run or jumped well enough to dream about excelling at it has entertained fantasies about the Olympics. Now here was Joan Benoit on the brink of the glorious realization of that fantasy. All she had to do was gradually bring her training to the peak she had learned to achieve for her biggest races and finish among the top three U.S. women in the marathon portion of the trials, which would be held in Washington State in May.

But you don't get to run in the Olympics if you don't qualify in the trials. And you don't run in the trials on a knee that feels like somebody's working on it with pliers.

"This was the most frightening moment of my life," Benoit said several years later in *Running Tide,* the autobiography she wrote with Sally Baker.

It was no exaggeration. Since childhood, Benoit had pushed herself to excel, first as a skier, then as a field hockey player, and finally as a runner. As a little girl, she had skied into the darkness of early evening rather than quit the slopes before she absolutely had to do it. A frostbitten fingertip was a small price to pay for the additional run or two that might make her more competitive. Once she'd begun running seriously, she'd always driven herself harder than any coach would. "I liked pushing myself to keep going after exhaustion set in," she has said. "It was a game I played."

Always the point of the game was to be as good as she could possibly be at what she was doing, and always that goal seemed to be just beyond the next marathon, the next ten-kilometer run, the next workout. Setting that sort of goal is a private way of motivating oneself, a way that lots of people might not understand. Winning races, especially races as famous as the Boston Marathon, might seem to be achievement enough to the people lining the course and clapping as the runners rush by, but winning has been almost incidental to Benoit. Even as a freshman at Bowdoin College she was uncomfortable with the praise she gained as an outstanding field hockey player. "I would squirm under the compliments," she remembers, "not in false modesty, but because I had a voice inside that said, 'Watch it.' I knew I was capable of more, and that kept me honest."

Even Joan Benoit's closest friends—the ones who best understood her determination and her enormous capacity to endure the rigors of long-distance running—were worried in the spring of 1984. The fluky injury was followed by weeks of indecision. Some days the knee felt fine. On other days it hurt just to walk upstairs, and that was when participation in the Olympic Trials couldn't have seemed more impossible. The most frustrating part of the ordeal was that the doctors Benoit consulted kept advising rest, the one suggestion she couldn't take seriously. Who could rest? When in the past had rest ever helped her prepare for a race? She'd always said, "Mileage is my safety blanket. I feel

I'm doing okay if I put in enough miles. And if I don't burn off my energy every day, I'm disoriented and grumpy." She was not likely to sit back and watch cartoons on T.V., even if that was what the doctor ordered. She was far more inclined to say, "When in doubt, run harder," and in her case "harder" meant more than the usual 100 to 120 miles each week.

March dragged into April, and the knee did not improve. In fact it seemed to be getting worse. Normally the doctors might have performed an arthroscopy, a procedure in which they insert a tiny scope into the knee and examine it to see if a ligament or cartilage has been torn. But with the Olympic Trials only weeks away, they were reluctant to do it. People recover from arthroscopy much more quickly than they do from more major knee surgery, but no surgery is truly minor. Even if they could diagnose and correct the problem with the arthroscope, the trauma of the surgery and the training time lost to it would certainly cost Benoit her shot at the Olympics.

To make matters even more improbably dramatic, the 1984 Olympics were particularly special for a number of reasons. The U.S. had boycotted the previous Games in 1980 to protest the presence of troops from the Soviet Union in Afghanistan. Hundreds of athletes, Joan Benoit included, had been denied the opportunity to participate in the spectacle by politics. Nobody, least of all Joan Benoit, wanted to be denied again. Beyond that, the 1984 Olympics were to be held in Los Angeles, so there would be an opportunity for U.S. athletes to perform before their countrymen and countrywomen. And finally the '84 Olympics would provide women with their first opportunity to run the marathon in the Games.

Under the curious assumption that females were somehow incapable of running twenty-six miles, the Olympic Committee had always limited them to shorter races. Even the growing popularity of marathoning among women and the triumphs of Benoit and other champions such as Ingrid Kristiansen, Rosa Mota, Grete Waitz, and Charlotte Teske hadn't earned female marathoners a chance to run in the Olympics until 1984. Now the opportunity was at hand, and there was serious doubt about whether the very best of all the American women runners would be able to compete.

Joan Benoit underwent arthroscopic surgery three weeks before the trials. Dr. Stan James found a fibrous mass called a plica that had become inflamed and was interfering with the normal movement of the knee joint. He removed it. Benoit awoke from the anesthetic and, still groggy, called a friend to ask if she could pick Joan up on her way home from work and take her running. It was a notion so goofy that even Benoit can't quite believe she ever had it.

Still, she was swimming and riding a stationary bicycle within days of her release from the hospital, and running again within a week. Drawing on her own determination and the support of her family and friends, she resumed her training, overcame a pulled hamstring muscle that resulted from favoring the knee, and appeared for the Olympic Trials as scheduled.

"Even as I was jogging to the starting line, I honestly didn't know if I could manage the race," she remembered afterward. She told her family not to come to the trials because she feared that she'd run badly if she ran at all. But when race day came, her brother and his wife were there. They claimed, transparently, that it was just one stop on a West Coast trip they'd been meaning to take anyway. Benoit admitted later that having them there had never been more important.

She ran conservatively that day and was surprised at the relative ease with which she covered the first twenty miles. The years of training and discipline seemed to carry her along automatically for a while. But with six miles to go, her legs suddenly remembered all the miles they'd missed over the past two months. The knee, only three weeks out from under the surgeon's scope, turned cranky. Benoit began concentrating on planting her feet with each stride to spare the joint unnecessary wobbling. She ran more and more slowly, more deliberately, less naturally, and although the commentators kept saying she was looking good, she knew otherwise. She kept sneaking peeks over her shoulder, wondering why some of the other runners were not moving up on her. That nobody did was a measure of her dominance of the U.S. marathoners.

Even as she crossed the finish line first, though, Joan Benoit was figuring that it would be different in the Olympics.

Perhaps it was partly doubt that drove her to train so effectively in the days between the trials and the Olympic Marathon itself. When that race finally came, it crushed other champions. The weather was so hot and miserably humid that Grete Waitz, one of the prerace favorites, later said, "I could have run faster, but I was afraid of dying." She was hardly overstating the case. Switzerland's Gabriela Anderson-Schiess was so dehydrated by the time she reached the finish line that she was disoriented and staggering.

Amid that drama, Joan Benoit was the picture of superb

Joan Benoit Samuelson runs past a mural of herself on the way to Olympic gold.

efficiency. This time she never looked back. A photograph taken during the race says it all. It shows Benoit running past a building upon which there is a huge mural that depicts her victory a year earlier in the 1983 Boston Marathon. Also in the photograph is Bill Rodgers, the great marathoner whom Benoit had idolized as a young woman. He is perched on the back of the pace truck, providing television commentary for the race. The photograph is splendidly full of meaning. Joan Benoit is running alone, of course, since she ran most of the race alone. (She led it wire to wire.) But it also seems to symbolize the way in which she consistently ran beyond her own previous triumphs. The win in Boston depicted in the mural established a world

record, but the central figure in this picture is not dreaming of a past victory; she is churning toward the next. And it is the man, Rodgers, who watches and talks about it, as the woman, Benoit, runs into history.

The Olympic course in Los Angeles ended in the Coliseum, an enormous stadium packed with fans from all over the world. In order to enter the stadium that day, Benoit ran through a tunnel. She was alone, and she knew she had won. She remembers thinking, "Once you leave this tunnel, your life will be changed forever," and she remembers that then she fastened her eyes on her shoes and turned her attention back to maintaining her pace. She concentrated on only that until she had crossed the finish line. Then she raised her arms over her head and ran a victory lap around the Coliseum, waving at the applauding crowd. Her smile was glorious, exulting, and grateful all at once.

Her life did change, as the lives of Olympic gold medal winners are likely to do. But it changed less than the lives of other winners who have not been so firmly grounded in values more substantial than winning. When she was asked where she could be found after the Games, Joan Benoit said, "Look for me in a berry patch in Maine." She was not entirely successful at keeping her distance from the clatter and clamor that inevitably follow a triumph as large and public as hers had been, but within a short while she had reestablished the calm that had always seemed to lie at the center of her running life and her life beyond running. Even under pressure from those who were competing for her attention, offering her endorsement opportunities, or merely calling to wish her well, she remained the quiet, somewhat shy young woman from Maine.

Julie Krone, jockey

BERNIE FUCHS

Bernie Fuchs is considered one of America's foremost illustrators. In 1962, at the age of thirty, he was the youngest illustrator to ever be inducted into the Society of Illustrators' Hall of Fame. That same year he was named "Artist of the Year" by the Artists' Guild of New York.

Fuchs was born in O'Fallon, Illinois, and attended the School of Art at Washington University. He began his career in St. Louis, where he illustrated automobile advertisements. Success at that job brought him recognition and assignments to produce illustrations for magazines such as *Redbook, McCall's,* and *Sports Illustrated.*

Fuchs's illustrations for *Sports Illustrated,* and books such as Bill Littlefield's *Champions: Stories of Ten Remarkable Athletes* (from which "Joan Benoit Samuelson" was taken), capture the grace and power of professional athletes at the top of their form.

Satchel Paige, baseball pitcher

Nate "Tiny" Archibald, basketball player

Susan Butcher, dogsled race

355

Response

MAKE A TIME LINE

And the Winner Is . . .

Work with a group to find out who holds the world and Olympic records set since 1984 for the men's and women's marathons. Then make a time line, listing each year and the two athletes. Share your work with other groups. Discuss the sources you used to find the information.

CALCULATE MILEAGE

Go Figure

Joan Benoit ran an average of 110 miles each week to prepare for running 26-mile marathons. If she ran five days a week, how many miles did she run, on average, per day? Per month? Per year?

Corner

WRITE A POEM

The Drive Inside

Reread the last two paragraphs of the selection. In the last paragraph, Joan Benoit says, "Look for me in a berry patch in Maine." What do you think she means by that? Write a short poem in which you explain what you think she means.

WHAT DO YOU THINK?

- What makes Joan Benoit different from other runners?

- What did you find out about athletes that you didn't know before?

- What are some things that people might learn about winning from Joan Benoit's story?

THE PARTHENON, a temple to the Greek goddess Athena, was built nearly 2,500 years ago.

ANCIENT GREECE

FROM *KIDS DISCOVER MAGAZINE*

Picture yourself in Athens in 500 B.C.—about 2,500 years ago. The days are hot and dry, so you wear a *chiton,* a loose-fitting tunic. If you are a girl, you stay at home and learn how to spin and weave from your mother. If you are a rich boy, you attend school from the age of seven, studying reading, writing, arithmetic, music, and debating. (Poor boys probably didn't go to school.) Instead of using pencils and paper, you use a stylus and a wax-covered wooden tablet. Pebbles or an abacus help you with your math. On lazy afternoons, you might enjoy knuckle-bones (a game similar to jacks). Perhaps you pick up a lyre and play your favorite tune. No doubt you participate in some sport, for sports honor the gods, and they help boys become excellent soldiers.

Most likely your house is made of sun-dried mud bricks and built around a central courtyard. Stairs lead to your upper-story bedroom. The servants' quarters are upstairs, too.

As you walk into the main entrance, a statue of the god Hermes greets you. It's there to prevent evil spirits from entering.

GREEK FOLK

FORGET ABOUT FAST FOOD!
Here's a typical Greek menu.

Breakfast: Bread and figs
Lunch: Bread with goat cheese or olives
         and figs
Dinner: Barley porridge or bread or fish, with
         some vegetable, such as carrots, peas,
         or cabbage
Snacks: Pomegranates, figs, apples, pears

BEES PROVIDED HONEY, the only sweetener available. Rich people ate more meat and fish than poor people, and they could afford bread made from wheat, not barley.

AS A CITIZEN, ONE of your duties was to defend the state as a hoplite (heavily equipped) warrior. Hoplites operated in a huge rectangular formation of many thousands of men. In this formation, all men were equal. No one was expected to be an individual hero. This is where the ancient Greeks' idea of fundamental political equality comes from.

WEALTHY PEOPLE wore jewelry of gold, silver, and ivory. Poorer people might wear jewelry of bronze, lead, iron, bone, and glass.

MUSICAL INSTRUMENTS, such as cymbals, lyres, and kitharas (harplike instruments), kept Greeks entertained and entertaining. Popular wind instruments were the syrinx, or panpipes, which were made of reeds, and the *auloi* (single pipes) or *diauloi* (double pipes).

EVERY CITY-STATE had one or more gymnasia, where Greeks fine-tuned their bodies so they could successfully defend their city-state. Gymnasia were also important meeting places for exchanging ideas.

DRESSED FOR COMFORT
Rich and poor Greeks wore the same type of clothing. Richer people, however, might wear dyed clothes.

WHEN A BABY was born, it was shown to its father, who had the right to accept or reject it. If it was rejected, it was abandoned. People who wanted a child could adopt it.

LASTING ACHIEVEMENTS

The influence of ancient Greeks can be found in almost every area of our lives, from medicine to philosophy, from astronomy to drama. Here are some of the lasting achievements of these ingenious people, and the great Greeks whose legacies live on.

PHILOSOPHY

Early Greeks looked to the gods for explanations of life and of how the world worked. But by the sixth century B.C., people desired more practical explanations. Some started asking questions and making precise observations and calculations about the world. The Greeks called these people *philosophers*, which means "lovers of knowledge."

MEDICINE

HIPPOCRATES (460–377 B.C.) is known as the father of medicine. The Hippocratic oath, taken today by all doctors, requires physicians to act ethically and morally.

SCIENCE

ANAXAGORAS (about 500–428 B.C.), an astronomer, explained that a solar eclipse is caused by the moon passing between the earth and the sun and blocking out the sun's light.

ARCHIMEDES (about 287–212 B.C.) is credited with having discovered a now widely accepted law of physics: a body displaces its own weight in water. Archimedes made his discovery in the bath. He also built a device that raised water from one level to another. Similar pumps are still used in parts of Africa today.

SOCRATES (469–399 B.C.) was one of the most famous philosophers of ancient Greece. His way of teaching, known as the Socratic method, incorporated questions and answers, not simply lecturing. When Socrates was old, the Athenians sentenced him to death by poison because he had criticized the government.

PLATO (427–347 B.C.), a student of Socrates, set down detailed rules in his *Republic* on the best way to govern a state. His ideas are highly regarded today. He wrote *The Apology* as a response to the enemies of Socrates.

ARISTOTLE (384–322 B.C.), a pupil of Plato, was a tutor to Alexander the Great, who ruled Greece in the fourth century B.C. Aristotle was probably the first person to promote the scientific method of observation, in which one first looks carefully and then comes up with a theory.

ZENO (around 460 B.C.), leader of the Stoic school of philosophy, believed that if people followed their inner reason and remained untouched by emotion and by the outside world, they would live a virtuous life.

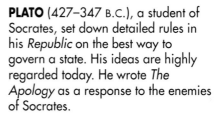

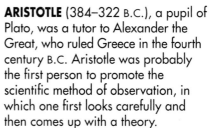

DEMOCRACY

Democracy in Ancient Greece was quite different from democracy as we know it. Today, we use the word *democracy* to describe a system of government in which everybody can vote. However, in the fifth century B.C. in Athens, many people—women, foreigners, and slaves—did not have the right to vote. Also, people in ancient Greece voted several times a year directly on the issues (direct democracy), whereas today, we vote once every several years to elect representatives who vote on issues (representational democracy).

There were no professional judges or lawyers, so citizens conducted their own cases in court. Over 200 men served on a jury to ensure that jurors were not bribed or intimidated. All citizens were expected to volunteer for jury duty.

JURORS' BALLOTS: The center token, above, with the hollow center, meant "guilty."

The Parthenon, built between 447 and 432 B.C., is considered by some to be the most beautiful building in the world. Parts of it still stand today, almost 2,500 years later. Inside the Parthenon stood a huge gold and ivory statue of the goddess Athena, patron of Athens, appearing as the goddess of warfare. On her right hand was a small winged figure of Nike, the goddess of victory.

THE GREEKS CREATED THREE IMPORTANT ARCHITECTURAL STYLES.

THE DORIC STYLE is simple, with thick, sturdy columns and plain capitals (tops).

THE IONIC STYLE has thinner columns than the Doric, and its capitals are decorated with two volutes (swirls).

THE CORINTHIAN STYLE has elaborate capitals decorated with acanthus leaves. Corinthian columns were not often used by the Greeks but became popular in Roman times.

HISTORY

Herodotus (about 480–425 B.C.) is known as the father of history because he was the first person to gather facts about events and write them down. His history of the Persian Wars was the beginning of Western history writing.

LITERATURE

Greek myths, stories about gods and heroes, are still popular today. In one, Daedalus makes wings for himself and his son, Icarus, so they can fly out of the maze in which they are imprisoned. The wings are attached with wax. Icarus flies too close to the sun and the wax melts, causing him to fall into the Aegean Sea and drown.

THE EARLIEST surviving examples of Greek literature are two epic poems, *The Iliad* and *The Odyssey,* credited to Homer, a blind poet who lived around the eighth century B.C. Little is known about him. His works give information about the Trojan War and about the hero Odysseus's return home from the war.

DRAMA

The origins of modern theater can be traced to ancient Greece. In its earliest form, Greek theater was songs and dances performed in the marketplace by a group of men called a chorus. Later, huge open-air theaters were built all over the Greek world.

SOPHOCLES

TRAGEDY

BY THE FIFTH century B.C., two types of plays emerged: tragedies and comedies. Tragedies were serious plays about past heroes who often came to tragic ends. Audiences today, as in ancient times, are spellbound by such tragedies as *Antigone* and *Oedipus Rex* (left), written by Sophocles (496–400 B.C.). Comedies were light-hearted plays that included a lot of clowning around, insults, rude jokes, and slapstick humor. Characters were everyday people who commented on politics and on famous people of the day.

COMEDY

THE 14,000-seat Epidaurus theater, cut into a hillside, was designed for excellent viewing and sound amplification.

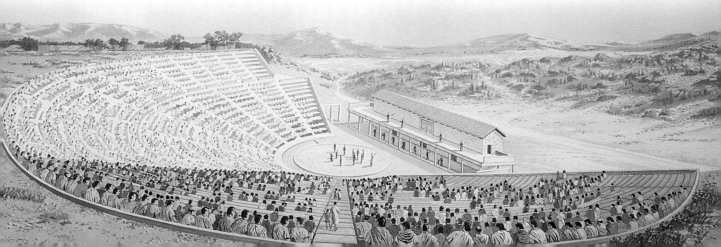

DIGGING UP THE PAST

Eventually, ancient Greek civilization was destroyed by war. For 27 years, Athens and Sparta, a city-state in the south of Greece known for its devotion to warfare, battled fiercely in the Peloponnesian War (431–404 B.C.). When it was finally over, Sparta was victorious, but not for long. Within about 50 years, the Macedonians from northeastern Greece had conquered both Athens and Sparta, along with many other Greek states.

Over time, other conquests took place. New rulers, customs, buildings, and ideas replaced old ones. How, then, do we know as much as we do about a way of life that thrived more than 20 centuries ago? Read on to find out.

A GREAT DEAL OF our knowledge of ancient Greece comes from the detailed painting on pottery, much of it black on an orange background (black-figure technique), or vice versa (red-figure technique).

A MINOAN colony on the island of Santorini was buried over 3,000 years ago by an enormous volcanic explosion—one that spewed ash so high that it reached Greenland, more than 3,500 miles away! Parts of Santorini sat under 900 feet of ash, preserving wall paintings that vividly detail the Minoan way of life.

ONE WAY TO FIND out about the past is to examine shipwrecks. The oldest known shipwreck in the world dates from about 1200 B.C., during what is known as the Bronze Age. The wreck, discovered off the coast of Turkey in 1959, contained agricultural implements, weapons, bronze tools, amphorae (vases), and about six tons of copper—enough, when mixed with tin, to equip an army of over 300 men! From this and other findings, we know that extensive trade routes existed in the Mediterranean more than 3,000 years ago!

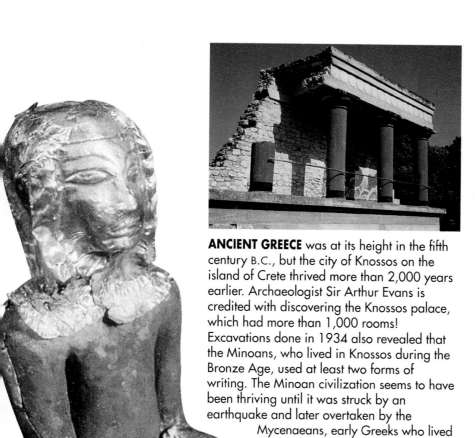

ANCIENT GREECE was at its height in the fifth century B.C., but the city of Knossos on the island of Crete thrived more than 2,000 years earlier. Archaeologist Sir Arthur Evans is credited with discovering the Knossos palace, which had more than 1,000 rooms! Excavations done in 1934 also revealed that the Minoans, who lived in Knossos during the Bronze Age, used at least two forms of writing. The Minoan civilization seems to have been thriving until it was struck by an earthquake and later overtaken by the Mycenaeans, early Greeks who lived on mainland Greece.

PEOPLE FIND OUT about the past by digging it up. In 1931, the enormous task of unearthing the ancient Athenian marketplace began. Houses that had been built over the agora were bought and torn down. Twenty-eight acres of soil were removed. Over 300,000 tons of earth were carted away before the ancient buildings were uncovered. Eventually, the stoa of Attalos was completely rebuilt and many other ancient monuments were brought to life.

HEINRICH SCHLIEMANN believed that the Trojan War was not simply a tale told by a blind bard named Homer but that it had actually taken place. Between 1870 and 1873, he began excavating where he felt Troy must have been. He unearthed many items (below), some going back 1,000 years earlier than Homer's poem: more than 8,000 gold rings, necklaces, bracelets, cups, and plates. Archaeologists today are fairly certain that Schliemann did, in fact, find the site of the Trojan War.

SOPHIA SCHLIEMANN wearing some of the jewelry discovered by her husband at Troy.

ART &

Autumn Leaves, Lake George, N.Y., by Georgia O'Keeffe, captures an image of nature's colorful change from one season to the next. In what ways is this painting similar to the selection you have read? In what ways is it different? If you could paint a picture of a turning point in your life, what would you show?

Autumn Leaves, Lake George, N.Y. (1924)
by Georgia O'Keeffe

Georgia O'Keeffe showed a talent for drawing when she was a child growing up in Wisconsin. She later studied art in Chicago and New York, and she taught school in Texas. Some of O'Keeffe's best-known works are of objects found in nature, such as flowers, rocks, and animal bones. When she then settled in New Mexico, she painted images of the canyons, mountains, bleached bones, and adobe buildings there.

LITERATURE

CITY

A Story of Roman Planning and Construction

by DAVID MACAULAY

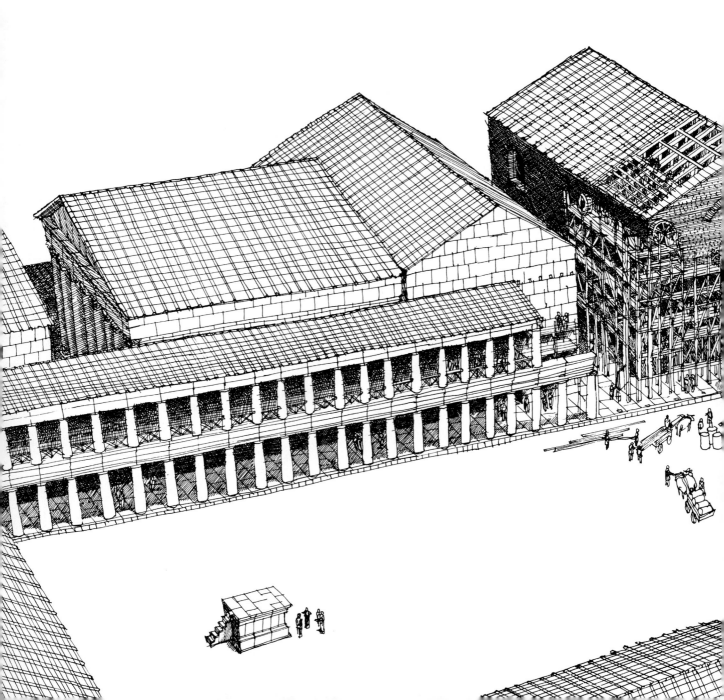

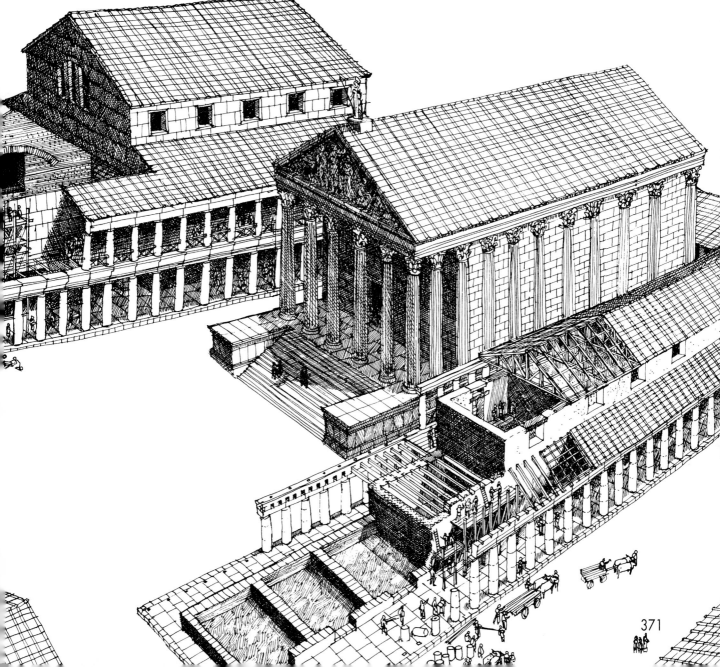

For almost two hundred years the wheat and grapes of northern Italy's fertile Po Valley had been collected in small trading villages and shipped to Rome. In 26 B.C. a disastrous spring flood destroyed the villages along the Po riverbanks as well as an important bridge. When news reached the Emperor Augustus he immediately dispatched to the stricken area forty-five military engineers, including planners, architects, surveyors, and construction specialists. They were to supervise the building of a new bridge and new roads and to lay plans for a new city. The city was named Verbonia, and—in honor of the Emperor—Augusta Verbonia.

Augustus hoped to combine all the remaining trading villages into one secure and efficient trading center and so increase the amount of produce coming into Rome. To speed up development of the new city, he retired to the area two thousand soldiers, who would not only help build Verbonia but also become its first citizens.

The new roads and bridge were completed before work began on the city itself. Once the surveyors had marked out a road with stakes, a ditch was dug on each side into which a row of curbstones was set. A deeper ditch was then dug between the two rows of curbstones which was filled with layers of stones of varying size. The top layer formed the pavement of the road and rose slightly in the center to force the rainwater into the side ditches. The pavement was constructed of flat stones that were carefully fitted together. Any spaces left between them were filled with smaller stones or pieces of scrap iron.

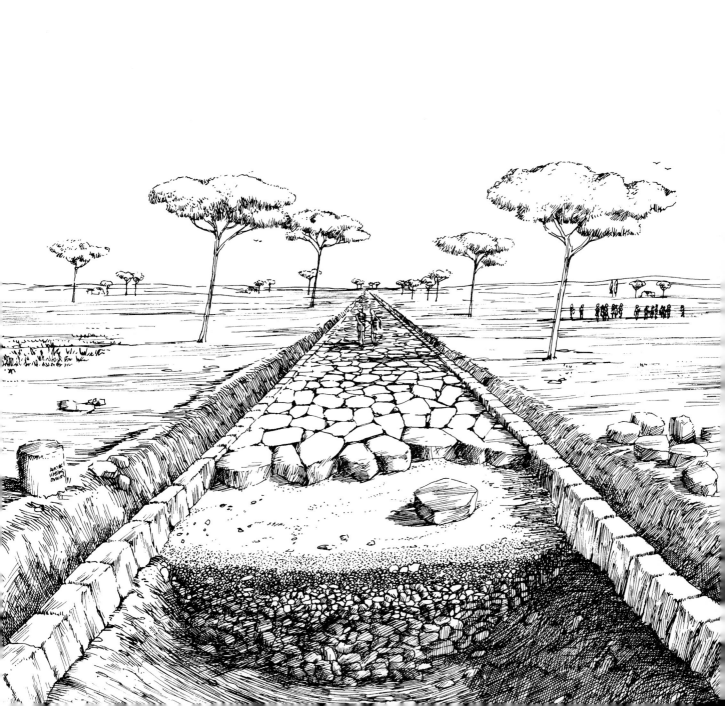

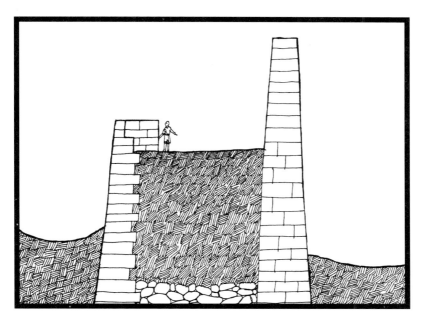

The city wall was built next. Two large ditches were dug along the furrow and the dirt was heaped into a high mound between them. A stone wall was built against each side for additional strength. The base of the outer wall went down thirty feet below ground level, making it almost impossible for anyone to tunnel under. On top of the outer wall alternating high and low sections called crenelations were built. The soldiers were protected behind the high sections while firing their weapons over the low sections. The inner wall was several feet higher than the outer wall to block the path of rocks and arrows that might be fired into the city.

Cranes on top of the mound lowered the stones into place. Four men standing inside a wooden wheel at the base of the crane provided the power. As they walked forward the wheel turned, rotating an axle which wound the rope. The engineers constantly checked to make sure each course of stones was level.

THE FORUM

By 19 B.C. the city walls were finished and work began on the first and most important public areas of the city—the forum and the market.

The forum was paved and covered two entire blocks. At one end the temple of Jupiter, Juno, and Minerva was built. Of all the temples to be built in the forum this was the most important. At the opposite end, facing the temple, was the rostrum. This was a raised platform from which speeches were made and decrees were read to the residents of the city. Along one side of the forum stood the Curia—the building in which the elected senators of the city met. Next to the Curia was the Basilica, the court of justice. The temple was constructed of polished limestone, while the other two buildings were brick-faced concrete covered with sheets of limestone. All the roofs were made of triangular wooden frames called trusses, covered by rows of clay tiles.

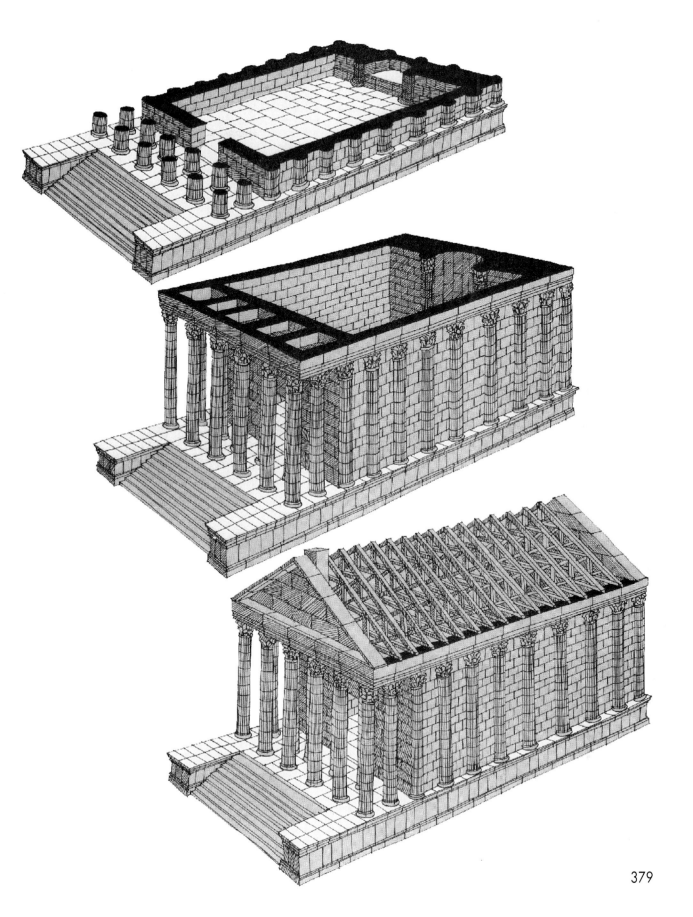

The buildings and the forum were surrounded by rows of columns called colonnades. The columns were either built of cylindrical stone blocks set on top of each other or they were constructed of brick and mortar covered by cement. A long two-story structure enclosed on both

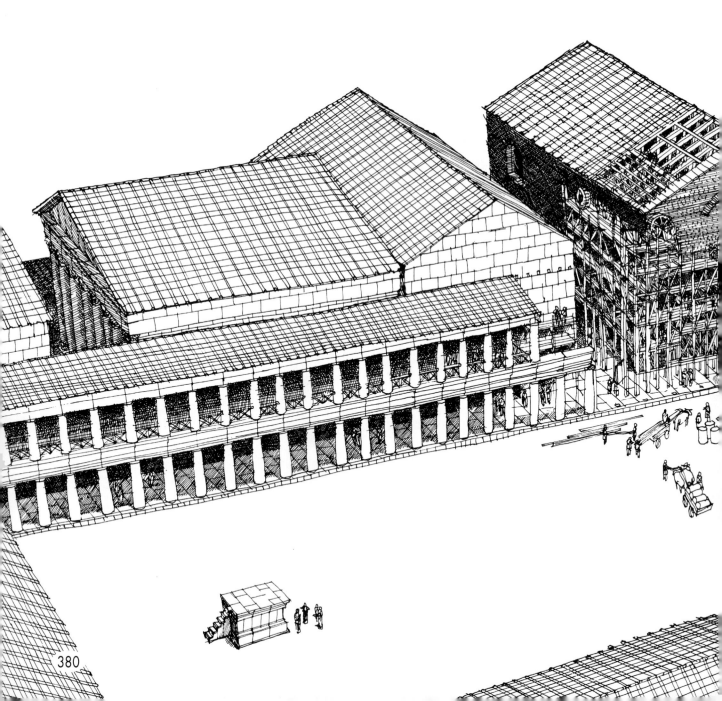

sides by colonnades was built to separate the forum from the busy streets. On the lower level were little shops which faced the street. On the second level were offices and schoolrooms which faced the forum.

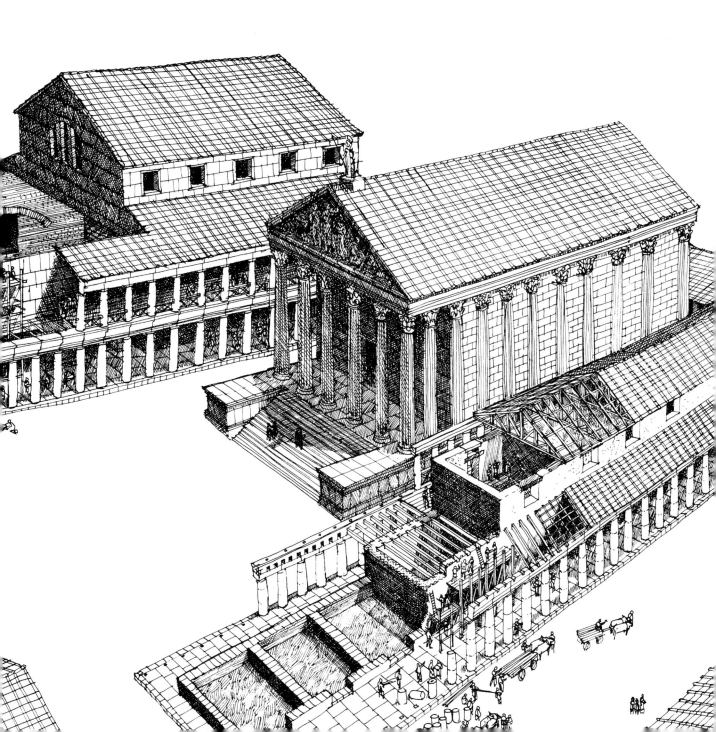

THE CENTRAL MARKET

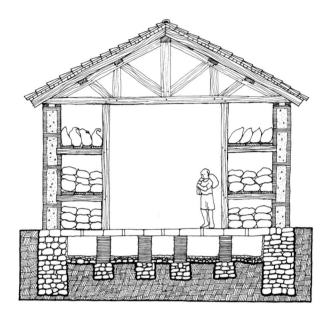

Because new temples were always being enlarged or replaced the forum really wasn't finished for two hundred years. But the central market across the street was finished in less than five. This was not surprising since Verbonia's main function was that of a trading center.

Along the streets that connected the markets, shops and workshops were built side by side. On one street Marcus Licinius, who came from Rome, built a bakery. Bread was one of the most important foods for the people of Verbonia and many bakeries were built throughout the city.

The main ingredient in the bread was flour, which was obtained by grinding grain in stone mills. Each mill consisted of two main pieces. The outer piece was rotated around the inner piece by pushing on the projecting arms. The grain was crushed or milled as it passed through the narrow space between the two. The flour that came out at the bottom of the mill was mixed with water and made into dough. Salt and leaven were then added. The dough was kneaded and formed into flat circular loaves and baked in a large brick oven.

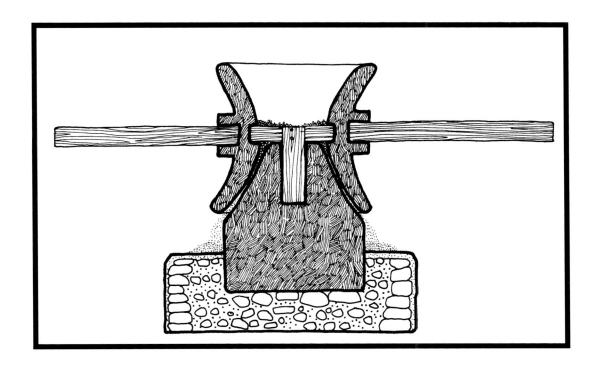

THE HOUSE OF MARCUS LICINIUS

The contractor who built Marcus' bakery also built his house. Like those of his neighbors, Marcus' house was quite large. The exterior walls were brick-faced concrete. Some of the interior walls were the same, while others were vertical wooden frames filled with small stones and mortar. All the walls were covered with a thick coat of plaster called stucco and painted.

There were many areas shown on the plan but two were much larger than the others. The first, at the front of the house, was called the atrium and was connected to the sidewalk by a narrow passage. The second, in the rear of the house, was a garden surrounded by a colonnade. This area was called the peristyle. The dining room, library, kitchen, and storerooms were located around the atrium, while the bedrooms and servants' quarters were on a second level.

Most of the activities took place in the atrium because of its size and the light that came through a square opening in the roof. Under the opening, called a compluvium, a shallow pool, called an impluvium, was sunk into the floor. Rain which fell into the impluvium ran through a small hole and into an underground tank. When water was needed the cover was taken off the tank and a clay jug lowered into it.

Marcus' favorite part of the house was the peristyle. It was quiet and private and very relaxing after a few hours in the bakery. It contained a fountain which could be turned off and on by a faucet. It also contained a shrine to the Lares—the gods who protected Marcus' house.

The floors of the atrium and peristyle were covered with mosaic—small black and white marble tiles that were pressed into wet cement in a variety of geometric patterns.

Because one house was built right up against another the only windows were located at the front facing the street. These were usually very small and covered with bars for security.

To brighten up the small dark rooms colorful pictures were painted on the walls. Many rooms contained jungle scenes full of wild animals and exotic plants. Imitation windows were painted in other rooms to make them seem less confining. In the winter the important rooms were heated by wood stoves.

On one side of the passage between the sidewalk and the atrium a toilet was connected to the sewer pipe and flushed by a continuous stream of water. On the other side a room that opened onto the sidewalk was rented out to a jeweler named Lucius Julius, who knew that a jewelry shop in Marcus' neighborhood would be very profitable.

Lucius was a former slave who had learned his craft in Egypt and had taken the name of the man who bought and eventually freed him. He and his family lived in an apartment in another section of the city.

All the buildings in Lucius' neighborhood contained two or more apartments. Many were owned by Marcus Licinius' neighbors and all contained shops opening onto the sidewalk. One of those shops was rented by a barber named Quintus Aurelius. The success of Quintus' business was mostly due to his willingness to gossip. For spreading news Quintus and Verbonia's other barbers were almost as important as the government decrees read in the forum, and they were definitely faster.

By the time of Augustus' death in A.D. 14, the streets of Verbonia were
lined with grocery shops, pastry shops, ceramic shops, furniture shops,
clothing shops, drugstores, wine shops, and snack bars.

Many of the craftsmen on a particular street often specialized in the same or related crafts. Most of the shops along a small quiet street near the forum were owned by highly skilled gold workers and the street eventually became known as "the street of gold." The craftsmen and their families lived in rooms behind or above their shops. As neighborhoods developed, families often got together to build shrines on their streets dedicated to the Lares.

Most of the snack bars were owned by Servius Vitellius, who also owned a chain of snack bars in Ariminum. The snack bars opened onto the sidewalk and each contained a concrete serving counter decorated with pieces of colored marble. Clay jugs embedded in the counter contained hot and cold drinks to be sold. A row of clay drinking cups marked with Servius' name stood on a marble shelf next to the counter.

At night and during the hot afternoons all the shops could be closed by fitting wooden panels into grooves on the tops and bottoms of the doorways. A lock was used to secure them in place. At night the city provided torch-carrying watchmen who patrolled the streets checking the locks and doors of all the buildings.

One hundred and twenty-five years after its founding, Verbonia had reached its limit. With the empire stronger than ever the walls once constructed to keep the enemy out were now serving a more important function—that of keeping the city in.

Although Verbonia is imaginary, its planning and construction are based on those of the hundreds of Roman cities founded between 300 B.C. and A.D. 150. No matter what brought about their creation, they were designed and built to serve the needs of all the people who lived within them. This kind of planning is the basis of any truly successful city. The need for it today is greater than ever.

DAVID MACAULAY

Making the complicated understandable is David Macaulay's great gift. He has done it in his many books that look at structures, from the pyramids to cathedrals. He has shown audiences how buildings are built and how they are unbuilt—in *Unbuilding,* he takes apart the Empire State Building. He has looked beneath the earth in *Underground.* He's been called "a born teacher with an interest in things nobody before had the skill or the courage to try to explain." Macaulay himself has said, "I consider myself first and foremost an illustrator, in the broadest sense, someone who makes things clear through pictures and teaches through pictures."

David Macaulay was born in England, and he remembers his early years there very happily. He liked to take his time getting to school and let his mind wander. "Whenever the opportunity to daydream presented itself, I did." At age 11, Macaulay moved to America with his family.

Although Macaulay had always enjoyed watching his mother draw scenes from family tales, it wasn't until he was a teenager that he discovered his own talent. He began drawing portraits of the Beatles, much to his classmates' delight. But when it was time to go to college, he thought it would be more practical to study architecture. That helped Macaulay learn a way of thinking that allowed him to understand how things worked.

After a year of teaching and working in an interior design studio, Macaulay became interested in book illustration. He also began writing stories. Although they weren't very good, as he admits, the illustrations that accompanied the stories were good enough to interest a publisher. There was a gargoyle in one of his stories, and it was that creature that made an editor suggest he write a book about cathedrals.

Since then, Macaulay has traveled to exotic places to research his books. He's been to France, visited Rome, climbed the Great Pyramid, all the while making sketches for his books. Macaulay is most interested in making his books realistic. He says, "One of the things I always try to do in a picture is to make the reader more of a participant than a spectator. I want him up on the roof of the building, and I want him to feel slightly sick because it's a long way up. If a reader can share that experience of being involved in a process, he will remember it. If I have any expertise at all, it is in that kind of communication."

CITY

BY LANGSTON HUGHES

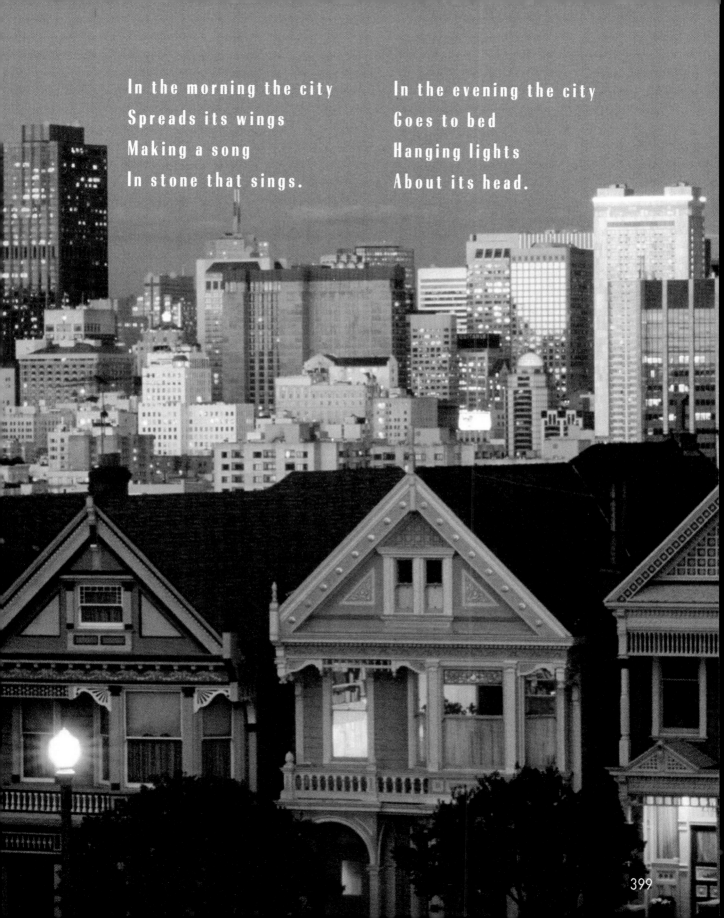

In the morning the city
Spreads its wings
Making a song
In stone that sings.

In the evening the city
Goes to bed
Hanging lights
About its head.

RESPONSE

COMPARE AND CONTRAST

SHOPPING SPREE

How is the city of Verbonia similar to a modern shopping mall? Write a paragraph comparing and contrasting the two. Use details from the selection.

DESIGN A MOSAIC

CARPET ART

The floors in Marcus Licinius' house were covered with mosaics. Work with a small group to design and make a mosaic using small pieces of colored paper. Display your mosaic in the classroom.

CORNER

CITY SIDEWALKS

Could the city in the poem be Verbonia? Write a paragraph stating your thoughts. Use details from both the story and the poem in your paragraph.

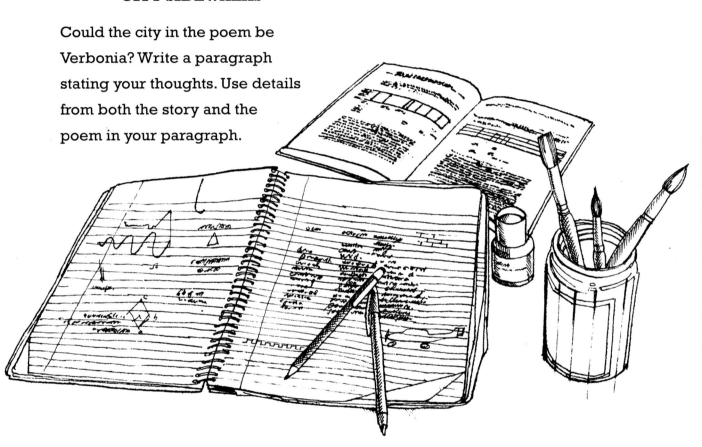

What Do You Think?

■ What are the most important ideas that you learned about the planning and construction of a Roman city?

■ What else would you like to learn about Roman cities?

■ How were Roman cities similar to modern cities? How were they different?

THE SECRETS OF
VESU

by Sara C. Bisel

with Jane Bisel and Shelley Tanaka

VESUVIUS

THE SECRETS OF
VESUVIUS
by Sara C. Bisel

Exploring the mysteries of an ancient buried city

IN THE SEASIDE TOWN OF HERCULANEUM (hər · kyoo · lāˊ nē · əm), THIS SUMMER MORNING SEEMED LIKE ANY OTHER. ON THE BEACHFRONT THE FISHERMEN PULLED UP THEIR BOATS IN FRONT OF THE SEAWALL. BREEZES FROM THE BAY COOLED THE WEALTHY ROMANS RELAXING IN THE GARDENS OF THEIR ELEGANT SUMMER VILLAS. NO ONE SUSPECTED THAT WITHIN HOURS THE TOP OF NEARBY MOUNT VESUVIUS WOULD BLOW OFF, BURYING THE TOWN AND MANY OF ITS PEOPLE UNDER AN ENORMOUS AVALANCHE OF SCORCHING MUD AND ASH.

Today the town of Herculaneum sits silently under the cone of the volcano that killed it. On the walls of its ruined villas, ghostly paintings and mosaics remind us of the thousands of people who once lived here. But what were these ancient Herculaneans really like and what happened to them on that fateful day in August, A.D. 79? Did most of them escape? One day an astonishing new discovery brought anthropologist Sara Bisel face to face with the actual victims of the fiery rage of Vesuvius.

A NEW ASSIGNMENT

Athens, Greece, June 1982

The telegram lying at my door was marked 'Urgent." As I bent down to pick it up, I hoped that it wasn't bad news. After spending a long hot day on my knees in the dusty ruins of an ancient Greek town, I was in no mood for surprises. When I ripped open the envelope I saw that it was from the National Geographic Society in Washington, D.C. They wanted me to telephone them immediately about a special project.

Why are they in such a hurry, I asked myself. As an archaeologist and anthropologist I have been involved in many expeditions. But my jobs are almost never emergencies. If something has been lying in the ground for a few thousand years, another week or two usually doesn't make much difference.

As I shut the door to my tiny apartment, I calculated the time difference between Athens, Greece, and Washington, D.C., and then dialed the long-distance number. My contact at the National Geographic Society wondered if I could spare a few days to examine some human skeletons that had just been found at the town of Herculaneum in Italy. Skeletons in Herculaneum, I thought to myself. Now *that* would be interesting!

Human bones are my specialty. In fact, I'm often called "the bone lady" because most of my work involves examining and reconstructing old skeletons. Believe it or not, bones are fascinating. They can tell you a great deal about someone, even if the person has been dead for thousands of years.

I can examine a skeleton and find out whether a person was male or female. If she was female, for example, I can tell you about how old she was when she died, whether she had children, what kind of work she might have done and what kind of food she ate. I can even glue dozens of small pieces of a skull back together like a jigsaw puzzle and show you what that person looked like.

The editor at *National Geographic* explained that workmen digging a drainage ditch near the ruins of Herculaneum had accidentally discovered some skeletons lying on what had once been the town's beachfront. Nearby, archaeologists had later uncovered some boat storage chambers in the ancient seawall. Much to their surprise, there were more skeletons inside these cave-like rooms. Here people had found shelter from the terrifying eruption of Mount Vesuvius in A.D. 79. As they lay huddled together in the dark, they were smothered by an enormous surge of scorching gas and ash from the volcano. Flowing hot ash, rock and pumice then buried them. Today, almost two thousand years later, the tangled remains of these ancient Romans lie as they fell, preserved in the wet volcanic earth.

This was an amazing discovery. Although archaeologists have been digging out Herculaneum for centuries, very few bodies had ever been found. As a result, experts had decided that almost all of the Herculaneans must have escaped before the disaster. We now knew that this was not true.

But even more exciting for me was the chance to study the actual skeletons of real ancient Romans. Because the Romans cremated their dead, they left behind plenty of urns full of human ashes but very few complete remains. So these Herculaneans represented the first large group of Roman skeletons ever found.

My job is to excavate and study the bones of people who lived and died many centuries ago.

When Vesuvius erupted, ash and gas came spewing out of the summit, forced straight up into the air by the pressure and heat of the blast. Eventually, this cloud cooled, and some of it collapsed, sending ash and hot gas racing down the slopes at speeds of up to seventy miles (110 kilometers) per hour, ripping the roofs off houses and overturning ships in the bay. These surges were followed by thick and glowing avalanches of fiery ash, rock and pumice—hot magma that has cooled so quickly that it is still full of volcanic gases, like a hard foamy sponge.

Vesuvius had not actually erupted for hundreds of years before A.D. 79, and the people of the area believed the volcano was extinct. But they could remember an earthquake seventeen years earlier that had caused much damage to the town. And in the days before the volcano erupted, occasional rumblings and ground tremors were felt, creating the odd crack in a wall, or causing a statue to tumble off its stand. And other strange things happened: wells and springs mysteriously dried up, flocks of birds flew away, and animals were exceptionally restless.

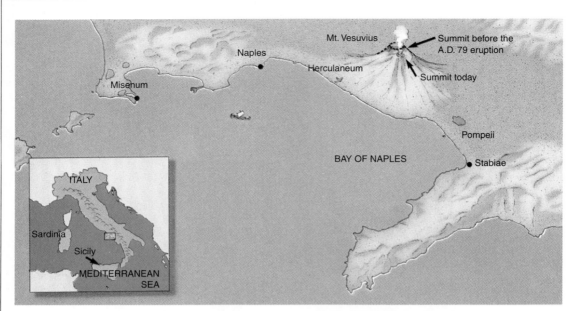

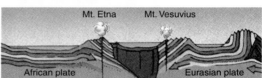

WHY DID VESUVIUS ERUPT?

Far below the earth's surface, gigantic plates of the earth's crust are constantly moving. Where these plates meet, one piece may rub against another, causing an earthquake. But if one plate pushes itself under another, it will melt and become liquid rock, or magma. The super-hot liquid rock creates gas and steam, building pressure until it blasts through weak places in the earth's surface. These weak spots are the world's volcanoes.

Above: Vesuvius is located in an area of the world where two plates of the earth's crust meet.

We know now that the dry wells were caused by the increasing heat and pressure that were building deep in the earth, and that animals are always more sensitive than humans to changes in the earth and the atmosphere. But, I wondered, were the people in Herculaneum aware that something was about to happen? Before the mountain actually erupted, did it occur to anyone that it might be a good idea to leave town? How many waited until the streets were so crowded that escape was almost impossible? Were they spooked by the tremors, their suddenly dry wells, or the nervous actions of their animals? Did they think the gods were showing their anger?

We will probably never know exactly what the volcano's victims were thinking in those days before the eruption. We do know that the glowing avalanches that buried Herculaneum and the nearby city of Pompeii created two time capsules of ancient Roman life that have not changed in almost two thousand years.

Sealed by volcanic ash and rock, the buried buildings have been protected from the wind and rain that would have worn down the columns and statues over the centuries. Wooden doors, shutters, stairs, cupboards and tables have not been exposed to the air to rot away, or been destroyed by fire. And unlike other ancient towns, the roads and buildings have not been repaired, or torn down and replaced by something more modern.

Instead, Herculaneum and Pompeii look the way they did so many years ago. The roofs of the houses may be gone, the mosaic floors cracked and the wall paintings faded. But we can still walk down the streets over the same stones that the ancient Romans walked on. We can see a 2,000-year-old loaf of bread, now turned to stone, or eggs still in their shells waiting to be served for lunch.

Herculaneum, which was less than three miles (five kilometers) from Vesuvius, was upwind of the volcano. Most of the falling ash blew in the opposite direction, leaving less than an inch lying over the town by the end of the day. Instead, at about 1:15 early the next morning, a violent surge of ash and hot gas poured over the town. By the time the waves of hot mud followed, everyone was dead. In a few hours, Herculaneum was completely buried under sixty-five feet (twenty meters) of hot volcanic matter, which, when it cooled, covered the town like a cement shield.

And so the town lay tightly sealed, for about 1,500 years.

HERCULANEUM

Herculaneum was covered by 65 feet (20 meters) of debris, while 12 feet (4 meters) of debris fell on Pompeii. Six different surges (the dark bands of ash on the diagram) poured down over Herculaneum, each followed by a scorching flow of debris. Only two of these surges reached Pompeii.

Flow (hot ash, pumice and rock)

Surge (hot gas and ash)

POMPEII

Then in 1709, a well-digger accidentally struck fine polished marble beneath the ground. An Austrian prince who was building a villa in the area realized that the marble was likely just the beginning of a major buried treasure, and he started to dig into the site.

Luckily for the prince, and unhappily for modern archaeologists and historians, the well-digger had found Herculaneum's ancient theater, one

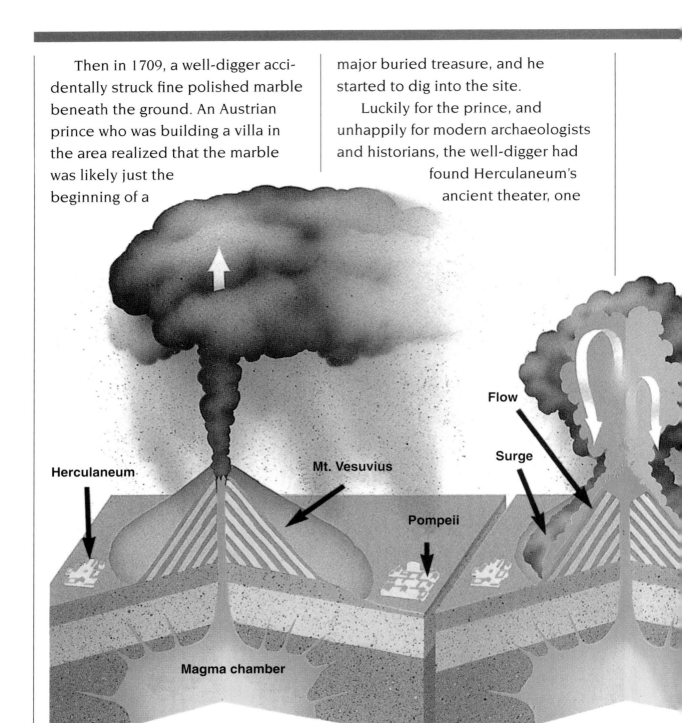

Flow

Surge

Herculaneum

Mt. Vesuvius

Pompeii

Magma chamber

1. *At midday on August 24, A.D. 79, Vesuvius erupts, sending a cloud of ash and pumice 12 miles (20 kilometers) into the air.*

2. *After midnight, the cloud collapses, sending a surge of ash and hot gas down the mountain, killing the Herculaneans. A flow of hot ash, rock and pumice eventually buries the town.*

of the most luxurious and treasure-filled buildings in the town. The prince wanted art and fine building materials for his villa, so he hired diggers who bored tunnels through the theater, not knowing what it was, and not caring in the least about the damage they were doing to the structure itself.

The prince plundered the building of its bronze and stone statues and vases. Marble was ripped off the walls and pillars, and the treasures were carted off to the prince's own house or those of his rich friends. Before long these valuable artifacts were scattered in museums and private collections all over Europe.

The prince's raiders, burrowing through the site like greedy moles sniffing out treasure, did more damage to Herculaneum than the volcano itself.

More raiding expeditions followed, and it was only in 1860 that serious archaeological work began.

But even with many of the most precious objects gone, the excavated town itself told historians a great

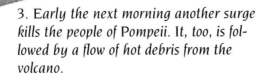

3. Early the next morning another surge kills the people of Pompeii. It, too, is followed by a flow of hot debris from the volcano.

413

deal about the ancient Romans and how they lived. Because the ruin had been snugly covered by a wet and heavy layer of earth, Herculaneum was even better preserved than Pompeii (which had suffered more damage under its airy blanket of ash and pumice).

Then just a few years ago came the most amazing discovery of all, when ditch-diggers accidentally found the group of skeletons on the ancient beachfront.

By the time these beach skeletons were found, scientists had discovered that we could learn a great deal about people by examining their bones. We could do much more than make plaster casts. Now we can analyze the bones themselves and reconstruct the skulls to see what the people looked like.

This is where I came in. In the morning, I would help to dig up these bones and begin to study them. For the first time, we would know more about the Romans than what books and paintings and sculptures had shown us. We would be able to see the people themselves.

I would be one of the first modern people to look an ancient Roman in the face.

When I got to the site, Dr. Maggi, the director of the excavation, was nowhere to be seen. Workmen sat around in small groups, drinking coffee out of thermoses. They eyed me curiously, then went back to their chat. I took a deep breath and decided to be patient. Later I would discover that waiting for Dr. Maggi's permission to begin work every morning was part of the routine. He made sure that excavation at the site was always closely supervised.

He arrived a few minutes later and introduced me to Ciro Formuola, the foreman of the work crew that was going to help me dig out the skeletons. These men were highly trained in doing delicate excavation work, and I knew I was lucky to have such experienced co-workers. In this business, a false move with a spade or trowel can do damage beyond repair.

A *wall painting showing a villa by the sea.*

414

When volcanic rock was chipped away from this room in the Suburban Baths, a beautiful statue of Apollo was discovered.

Volcanic flow burst through a window in the Suburban Baths throwing a heavy marble basin like this one *(above)* across the room. You can still see pieces of window glass in the bottom of the basin.

THE PEOPLE ON THE BEACH

Herculaneum, June 1982

t was quiet on Herculaneum's ancient beach. Above my head, drying sheets and underwear fluttered from the apartment balconies that now overlook the ruins.

Today this beach is just a narrow dirt corridor that lies several feet below sea level. But thousands of years ago, the waves of the Mediterranean would have lapped where I now stood, and my ears would have been filled with the gentle sound of the surf, rather than the dull roar of Ercolano's midday traffic.

To one side of me stood the arched entryways of the boat chambers, most of them still plugged by volcanic rock, their secrets locked inside. Only one chamber had been opened so far, and its contents were now hidden behind a padlocked plywood door.

I eyed the wooden door longingly, wishing for a sudden gift of X-ray vision. Dr. Maggi, the keeper of the key, had been called away

to a meeting with some government officials, and would not be back until sometime in the afternoon.

"*Dottoressa!*"[1]

Ciro was calling me from farther down the old beach. He was waving me toward a roped-off area

---

[1]Dottoressa (dō·tō·re´sä): Italian title for a woman who is a doctor or scholar

416

The beachfront, the ruins of Herculaneum and Vesuvius as they look today.

It didn't look like much at first—just a heap of dirt with bits of bone poking out. I knelt down and gently scraped earth off the skeleton, exposing it to the light for the first time in two thousand years. It almost looked as if the bones had been carelessly tossed there, they were so broken and tangled. I looked up.

surrounding three ordinary-looking piles of dirt.

I have examined thousands of skeletons in my life, but seeing each one for the first time still fills me with a kind of awe. As I walked over to the mound that Ciro was pointing at, I knew I was about to meet my first Herculanean.

Above me was the open terrace where Herculaneans had held sacred ceremonies. Above that was the wall of the town itself, most of the surrounding balustrade[2] now missing.

---

[2] balustrade (bal´ ə · strād): a handrail supported by posts

I closely examine each bone of a skeleton as I lift it from the wet volcanic earth.

Had this woman fallen from the wall above? Had some huge force propelled her from the town, perhaps a piece of flying debris, or the blast from the volcano itself, so that she smashed face down onto the ground? What had she been doing on the wall in the first place? Calling down to the people on the beach for help?

I picked up one of the bones and felt its cool smoothness in my hands. Because this was the first Herculanean I got to know, this skeleton was extra special to me. I named her Portia.

By measuring the bones, I could tell that Portia was about 5 feet 1 inch (155 centimeters) tall. She was about forty-eight when she died—an old woman by Roman standards—and had buck teeth.

Later, after a chemical analysis, we learned that Portia also had very high levels of lead in her bones. Lead is a poison, but in Roman times it was a common substance. It was used in makeup, medicines, paint pigment, pottery glazes, and to line drinking cups and plates.

On either side of Portia was a skeleton. One was another female. She lay on her side, almost looking as if she had died in her sleep. As I brushed dirt from her left hand, something shiny caught my eye as it glinted in the sunlight. It was a gold ring.

When we uncovered the rest of the hand, we found a second ring. And in a clump on her hip we found two intricate snakes' head bracelets made of pure gold, a pair of earrings that may have held pearls, and some coins (the cloth purse that had probably once held these valuables had long since rotted away).

We ended up calling her the Ring Lady. She was about forty-five when she died. She was not terribly good-looking; her jaw was large and pro-truding. There were no cavities in her teeth, but she did have gum disease, which left tiny pits in the bone along her gum line. If she had lived today, her dentist probably would have advised her to floss more often!

In fact, most of the Herculaneans I examined had very good teeth, with only about three cavities each. Today, many of us have about six-teen cavities each, in spite of all our fluoride treatments, regular dental checkups and constant nagging to floss and brush! But the Romans had no sugar in their diet. They used honey, but not much, because it was expensive. Instead, the Herculaneans ate a well-balanced diet, including much seafood, which is rich in fluoride. Not only that, but they had strong jaws from chewing and tearing food without using knives and forks. And they did clean their teeth, scrubbing them with the stringy end of a stick rather than using a brush and toothpaste.

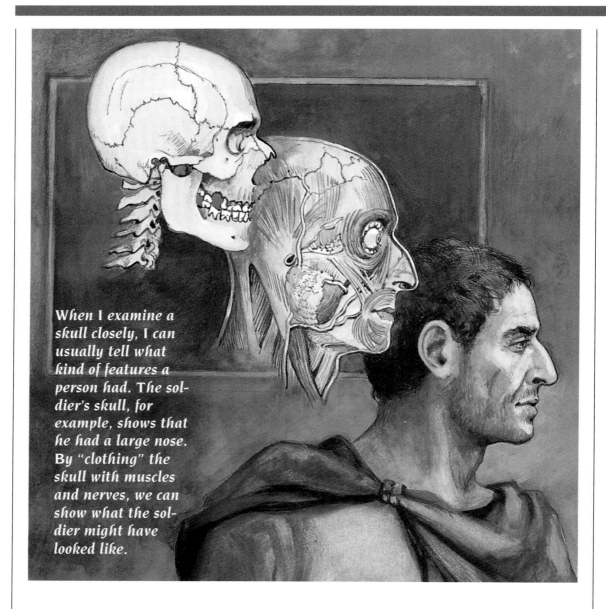

When I examine a skull closely, I can usually tell what kind of features a person had. The soldier's skull, for example, shows that he had a large nose. By "clothing" the skull with muscles and nerves, we can show what the soldier might have looked like.

On the other side of Portia we dug up the skeleton we called the Soldier. He was found lying face down, his hands outstretched, his sword still in his belt. We found carpenter's tools with him, which had perhaps been slung over his back. (Roman soldiers often worked on building projects when they were between wars.) He also had a money belt containing three gold coins. He was quite tall for a Roman, about 5 feet 8 inches (173 centimeters).

When I examined the man's skull, I could see that he was missing six teeth, including three at the front,

We found these coins in the soldier's money belt.

and that he'd had a huge nose. And when I examined the bone of his left thigh, I could see a lump where a wound had penetrated the bone and caused a blood clot that eventually had hardened. Near the knee, where the muscle would have been attached, the bone was enlarged slightly. This indicated that he would have had well-developed thighs, possibly due to gripping the sides of a horse with the knees while riding (Romans didn't use saddles).

Had the soldier lost those front teeth in a fight, I wondered. Had he been wounded in the leg during the same fight or another one? His life must have been fairly rough and tumble.

While members of the excavation team poured buckets of water on the three skeletons to loosen the debris, I continued to scrape off the dirt and volcanic matter with a trowel. Later,

in the laboratory, each bone and tooth would be washed with a soft brush. Then they would be left to dry before being dipped in an acrylic solution to preserve them. Finally, each bone would be measured, then measured again to prevent errors, and the figures would be carefully recorded.

By late afternoon my back and knees were stiff from crouching, and the back of my neck was tight with the beginning of a sunburn.

I stood up and stretched. There was still much to do before the three skeletons would be free of their volcanic straitjackets. I started to think about heading back to the hotel for a shower and bite to eat. But a flurry of activity down the beach caught my eye, and suddenly I no longer felt tired.

To my right, Dr. Maggi stood outside the locked wooden door I had seen earlier. He was unbolting the padlock. When he saw me, he waved. I put down my trowel, wiped my hands on my jeans and hurried over. Inside, I knew, was the only group of Roman skeletons that had ever been found—the twelve people who had huddled in the shelter and died together when the volcanic avalanches poured down the mountainside into the sea.

This surviving loaf of bread is now as hard as rock.

I could hear an odd echo from inside the chamber as Dr. Maggi clicked the padlock open. Behind me, a number of the crew members had gathered. We were all very quiet.

The plywood door seemed flimsy as Dr. Maggi pulled it open. From inside the chamber came the dank smell of damp earth.

A shiver crept up my neck. We were opening a 2,000-year-old grave. What would we find?

As I entered the cave-like boat chamber, I could barely see, even though the sun flooded through the door. Someone handed me a flashlight, but its light cast greenish shadows, making it feel even more spooky.

The light played over the back of the shelter, no bigger than a single garage and still crusted over with volcanic rock. I saw an oddly shaped,

Richard Steffy, a specialist in ancient boat construction, examines the fragile boat found on the beachfront.

lumpy mound halfway back. I took several steps into the chamber and pointed the light at the mound.

The narrow beam found a skull, the pale face a grimace of death. As my eyes grew accustomed to the dim light, I soon realized there were bones and skulls everywhere. They were all tangled together—clinging to each other for comfort in their final moments—and it was hard to distinguish one from another. But I knew that twelve skeletons had been found in all—three men, four women and five children. One child had an iron house key near him. Did he think he would be going back home?

I took another step into the cave. At my feet was a skeleton that was almost entirely uncovered. From the pelvis I could see it was a female, a girl, lying face down. Beneath her, we could just see the top of another small skull.

It was a baby.

I knelt down and gently touched the tiny skull. My throat felt tight as I thought about this girl, this baby, and what it must have been like for them in this dark cave in the moments before they died.

"*Allora, è la sorella?*"

I frowned, pulled my Italian-English dictionary out of the back

This wall painting from Pompeii shows what the boat from Herculaneum might have looked like under full sail.

pocket of my jeans and flipped through it. I realized Ciro thought these two skeletons belonged to a baby and its older sister.

"We'll see," I murmured. I knew it was important not to jump to conclusions. You have to question everything about bones, especially ones that have been lying around for two thousand years.

I struggled to free a bronze cupid pin and two little bells from the baby's bones. Whoever the child was, it had been rich enough to wear expensive ornaments. But I knew it would take many more hours of careful study before we knew the real story behind these two skeletons.

Later, in the laboratory, I gained enough information to put together a more likely background for the skeleton of the young girl.

Unlike the baby, she had not come from a wealthy family. She had been about fourteen, and from the shape of her skull I knew she had probably been pretty. When I examined her teeth I could tell that she had been starved or quite ill for a time when she was a baby. She had also had two teeth removed about one or two weeks before she died, probably giving her a fair bit of pain. And her life had been very hard. She had done a lot of running up and down stairs or hills, as well as having to lift objects too heavy for her delicate frame.

This girl could not have been the child of a wealthy family, like the baby. She had probably been a slave who died trying to protect the baby of the family she worked for.

And there were many others.

Excavators have nearly cleared one of these boat chambers, but the one next to it is still blocked by hard volcanic rock.

Near the slave girl lay the skeleton of a seven-year-old girl whose bones also showed that she had done work far too heavy for a child so young.

We found a sixteen-year-old fisherman, his upper body well developed from rowing boats, his teeth worn from holding cord while he repaired his fishing nets.

Though it is fascinating to reconstruct the life of a single person by examining his or her bones, for anthropologists and historians the most useful information comes from examining all of the skeletons of one population. This is one reason why Herculaneum is so important.

During the next few months we opened two more boat chambers. In one we discovered forty tangled human skeletons and one of a horse; in another we found twenty-six skeletons creepily lined up like a row of dominoes, as if heading in single file for the back of the chamber.

The skeletons represented a cross-section of the population of a whole town—old people, children and babies, slaves, rich and poor, men and women, the sick and the healthy. By examining all these skeletons, we can get some ideas about how the townspeople lived and what they were like physically.

We found out, for example, that the average Herculanean man was 5 feet 5 inches (165 centimeters) tall, the average woman about 5 feet 1 inch (155 centimeters). In general, they were well nourished. And we have examined enough people to know that although the rich people had easy lives, the slaves often worked so hard that they were in pain much of the time.

A coin box found on the beach.

Studying these skeletons closely can also help medical researchers and doctors. In ancient times, many diseases could not be cured by surgery or drugs. Instead, people kept getting sicker, until they eventually died. By examining the bones of these people, we can learn a great deal about how certain diseases progress.

By the end of my stay in Herculaneum, I had examined 139 skeletons. Their bones were sorted into yellow plastic vegetable crates that lined the shelves in my laboratory. And each box of bones has a different story to tell.

Even though I can't tell the good guys from the bad, and I can't tell you whether they were happy or not, I know a great deal about these people. I can see each person plainly. I even imagine them dressed as they might have been, lounging on their terraces or in the baths if they were wealthy, toiling in a mine or in a galley if they were the most unfortunate slaves.

Most of all, I feel that these people have become my friends, and that I have been very lucky to have had a part in bringing their stories to the rest of the world.

Among the ruins, archaeologists found these unusual glass beads with tiny faces on them.

Sara C. Bisel

Sara Bisel is one of the world's top experts when it comes to digging up facts about old bones. She is an archaeologist and physical anthropologist who graduated from the University of Minnesota in 1980. Bisel has studied ancient skeletons uncovered at archaeological sites in Greece, Turkey, and Israel. The National Geographic Society asked her to visit the ruins of the old Roman towns of Herculaneum and Pompeii and study the many well-preserved skeletons there. The results of her investigation of these buried cities were published in *Discover* magazine and *National Geographic*. The investigation was also recorded on film and shown on television by the National Geographic Society.

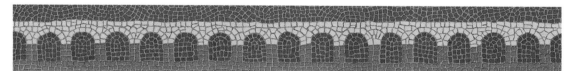

ANO

BY CONSTANCE LEVY

If you were a volcano,

asleep in the same spot

for a hundred years,

with old anger

rumbling and burning

your insides

wouldn't you awake

screaming with fire,

spitting rocks and ashes,

throwing a flaming fit

not caring who or what

you hit?

RESPONSE CORNER

RECORD YOUR DIET

SWEET TOOTH

The Herculaneans seem to have had healthy teeth because they ate no sugar. Record the number of grams of sugar you eat in one day. Compare your findings with those of your classmates. Discuss ways to modify your diet to make it more healthful.

DRAW A MAP

SAFETY FIRST

Draw a map of an escape route from your classroom in the event of a disaster. Mark a safe place for you, your classmates, and your teacher to go during such an emergency. Discuss your plan with the rest of your classmates.

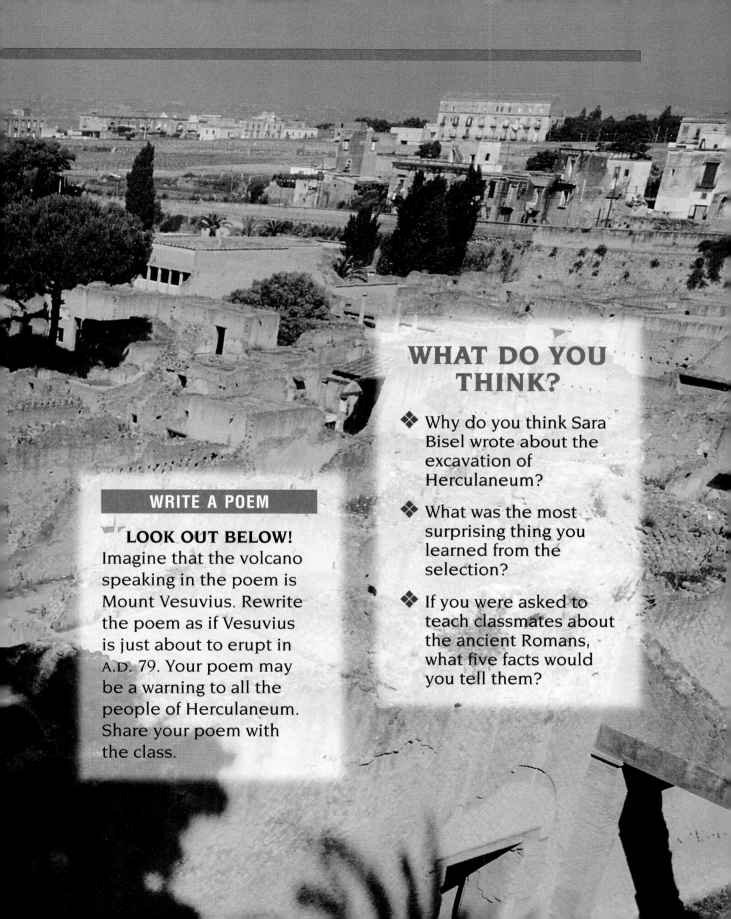

WRITE A POEM

LOOK OUT BELOW!
Imagine that the volcano speaking in the poem is Mount Vesuvius. Rewrite the poem as if Vesuvius is just about to erupt in A.D. 79. Your poem may be a warning to all the people of Herculaneum. Share your poem with the class.

WHAT DO YOU THINK?

❖ Why do you think Sara Bisel wrote about the excavation of Herculaneum?

❖ What was the most surprising thing you learned from the selection?

❖ If you were asked to teach classmates about the ancient Romans, what five facts would you tell them?

THEME

The people and communities in this theme are going through changes. Which of the people reach a turning point in their lives, and how does it come about? How do the communities change? What is the result of each change?

What kinds of things would Dr. Sara Bisel have uncovered if the site of her dig had been the city in "City: A Story of Roman Planning and Construction?"

ACTIVITY CORNER

Imagine that an archaeologist in the distant future is excavating a site that was once your neighborhood. What interesting objects will he or she find? Make a diorama showing a futuristic museum display of the archaeologist's most unusual finds.

WRAP-UP

THEME
MASTERPIECES

Artists who create masterpieces communicate powerful ideas through their creativity. The artists in the next selections provide stunning examples of creative expression through painting, photography, and architecture.

THEME

MASTERPIECES

CONTENTS

Journal of a Teenage Genius
by Helen V. Griffith

Zack, a teenage scientist, meets a girl whose family travels through time in this hilarious science fiction novel.
Award-Winning Author
Signatures Library

The Wright Brothers: How They Invented the Airplane
by Russell Freedman

Orville and Wilbur Wright began their careers as bicycle mechanics, but they ended up changing the course of history by inventing the airplane.
Newbery Honor
Outstanding Science Trade Book
Signatures Library

Round Buildings, Square Buildings, & Buildings That Wiggle Like a Fish
by Philip M. Isaacson

What makes architecture *art?* With stunning photographs and lively text, the author provides an entertaining discussion.
Notable Trade Book in Social Studies

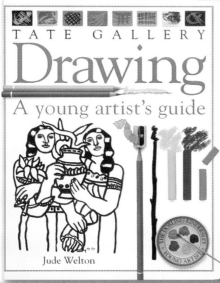

Drawing: A Young Artist's Guide
by Jude Welton

Works by some of the world's greatest artists help demonstrate the basics of drawing and composition.

Master of Mahogany: Tom Day, Free Black Cabinetmaker
by Mary E. Lyons

Tom Day's accomplishments as a cabinetmaker were all the more remarkable in an era when free African Americans had only limited opportunities.
Notable Trade Book in Social Studies

VELÁZQUEZ: SELF-PORTRAIT

Velázz

Diego Velázquez (dē·ā′gō bā·läs′kās) was born in Seville, Spain, on June 6, 1599, one hundred and seven years after Christopher Columbus left that city to sail to the Americas.

As a small child, Diego's drawings were so good that his parents sent him to study with Master Painter Francisco Herrera (frän·sēs′kō ā·rā′rä). But Diego soon wanted a greater freedom so he joined the studio of Francisco Pacheco (frän·sēs′kō pä·chā′kō), a teacher who allowed him creative artistic freedom. From this great teacher he learned the fine art of painting as well as literature and philosophy. Five years later, at the age of twenty, Diego married Juana, his teacher's daughter.

After rendering three portraits of King Philip IV, young Velázquez, at the age of twenty-five, was appointed the king's painter. With his wife and two daughters, he lived a happy life at court with plenty of time to fulfill his occupation as artist to the royal household.

Velázquez painted 121 outstanding canvases and became advisor and friend to his king. He died at the age of sixty-one, recognized as a great artist.

His paintings showed both the reality and the dreams of his times. This dedication to truth in art brought him fame in his lifetime.

From his devotion to art came the compassion and understanding that made him popular with both kings and commoners.

quez

BY ERNEST RABOFF

PHILIP IV ON HORSEBACK   PRADO, MADRID

"Philip IV on Horseback" shows us the vast knowledge Velázquez had of men and of horses. Both figures are powerful and alive with action yet are masterfully balanced by the artist so one does not overshadow the other.

Study the two heads. Study the posture of the rider and the position of the horse. Notice how Velázquez compares the sparkling armor of the king to the glistening brown coat of his mount.

This great portrait artist urges us to use our eyes to learn of men, horses, and all of life.

"Queen Isabella on Horseback" was painted to match the portraits of her husband, King Philip IV, and her son, Baltasar Carlos, both of whom were shown on horseback. By looking carefully at the horse's head and the raised hoof, you can see the artist's first painted outlines. He often repainted details in his constant striving for perfection.

Queen Isabella was the mother of Princess Maria Teresa, who became Queen of France.

In this graceful picture, the Queen's riding skirt, her arms, the horse's neck and prancing leg—even the clouds and the sloping hills—curve softly.

Velázquez was dedicated to reality and disciplined himself to painting precisely what he saw. He saw the world as it was and loved it. His joy in nature and human beings illuminates every painting and brightens those moments each of us spends in studying them.

QUEEN ISABELLA ON HORSEBACK   PRADO, MADRID

THREE MUSICIANS   STAATLICHE MUSEUM, BERLIN

"Three Musicians" is one of the paintings that Velázquez painted between the ages of eighteen and twenty-one. These youthful paintings tell a story. In this one we can learn about some of the instruments people played at the beginning of the seventeenth century. We can study the clothing, the hair styles, and the shapes of the drinking glasses of the time when the artist lived.

Velázquez warms the happy scene with glowing yellow colors. The boy, with his pet monkey looking over his shoulder, seems almost to invite us to join the fun and to share the food and drink.

JUAN DE PAREJA   PRIVATE COLLECTION

"Juan de Pareja" is a portrait of Velázquez's servant and pupil. He assisted the artist by grinding paints, cleaning brushes, and when necessary was a welcome traveling companion. At the age of forty-five, Pareja greatly surprised Velázquez by turning out his own fine paintings.

By carefully studying Pareja's shining eyes in this painting, we can get an idea of the bond of friendship and respect between these two men. This portrait inspires us with its quiet strength. The bronzed glow of Pareja's open, intelligent face is highlighted by the snow-white collar and the sensitively painted folds of the rich brown tunic and cape.

THE MAIDS OF HONOR   PRADO, MADRID

In "The Maids of Honor," called "Las Meninas" (läs mā·nē′näs) in Spanish, Velázquez has painted a tender story of the Spanish Court. The artist shows himself with his brush and palette at work on a life-size portrait of King Philip and Queen Mariana. You can see them reflected in the mirror hanging on the back wall of the studio.

The little Princess Margarita does not want to pose, even though her attendant is offering her a bribe. No one in the scene—her maids of honor, the two dwarfs, nor her teachers—can persuade her. Velázquez understood this moment, and by painting the scene just as it happened, he has recorded an intimate glimpse into family life at the royal court.

This is one of the most famous paintings in the world. Velázquez has vividly captured this moment of childhood and made it live eternally.

ERNEST RABOFF

Ernest Raboff was uniquely qualified to write about artists, since he himself studied art in two of the world's most influential art centers, Rome and Paris. Throughout his life, in fact, Raboff maintained his connection to the art world in a variety of ways, working not only as an artist, but as an art critic, collector, and gallery owner. By writing his "Art for Children" series, Raboff was able to share his lifelong passion for great art with younger readers. In each book of this series, Raboff provides a striking introduction to the work of a different artist, including full-color reproductions of some of the world's most famous masterpieces. His subjects range from Old Masters, such as Velázquez and Michelangelo, to revolutionary talents like Pablo Picasso and Paul Klee.

Response Corner

DRAW A PICTURE

MASTERFUL MOMENTS

The author states that in the painting "The Maids of Honor," Velázquez seemed to capture a moment of childhood and make it eternal. What is a memory that you wish to preserve forever? Draw a picture of this memory, and share it with a partner.

DIFFERENT STROKES

Which of the paintings featured in the selection do you like best? Write a brief description of the painting. Tell what you like most about this work and why.

BE ALL THAT YOU CAN BE

Velázquez had an ambition—to be a great painter. He was dedicated to his goal and disciplined in his work. What is one of your lifelong ambitions? Share with a small group your goal and how you plan to pursue it.

What Do You Think?

- What do you think the author wanted you to learn about Velázquez?

- Has this selection changed the way you feel about art? Explain your answer.

- How would you describe this selection to someone who has not read it?

449

I, JUAN DE PAREJA

Newbery Medal

Since his youth, Juan de Pareja (wän dā·pä·rä´hä) has been the personal slave of the great Spanish painter Diego Velázquez. Watching his master at work, Juan has developed a great love for the art of painting. Sadly, he has had to keep his own artistic talent a secret, for a law in seventeenth-century Spain forbids slaves from practicing the arts. The two men are now in the employ of King Philip IV, and Juan has chosen to entrust the king with his secret passion.

BY ELIZABETH BORTON DE TREVIÑO
ILLUSTRATED BY RICK FARRELL

he King was in the habit of coming often, at odd hours, to pass a short while in the studio. "You have only to see me as your sovereign when I speak," he told Master. "I wish to be able to slip in and out, quietly, without any formality, to sit and enjoy a painting of my choosing, and feel at peace." He had given me orders that I was not to "see" him either unless he spoke, whenever he came unaccompanied. "I wish to spend a little time in complete invisibility," he told us, smiling.

So cakes were always waiting for him in the studio, and one of his own easy chairs. His accustomed hour to drop in was late afternoon, before he had to dress for some court function.

Long ago I had heard some of the courtiers in Rubens' train say that the Spanish court was the stiffest and most boring in Europe. I am sure His Majesty found it so, but did not know what to do about it.

So he escaped, and sat gazing at some picture of Master's, which he had turned round from where they were stacked, and set up, at some distance from his chair.

I had secretly painted a large canvas, for Master was frequently in attendance on Mistress in her bedroom, where she rested many hours, and to which she called him to chat with her. She often felt lonely and needed him near.

My subject was the King's favorite hounds. All were dead, and they had not been contemporaries, but they had been favorites of his, and I knew that he would recognize them.

The three hounds (one of them was Corso) lay in a forest glade; a shaft of golden light came through the branches of the trees and lay warmly on them. One dog was turned toward me, tongue drooping from his mouth, the black doggy lips turned up in a smile; one looked away into the distance with pricked ears; and one dozed, nose on paws. I had taken their likenesses carefully from many paintings of Master, and I had worked out the setting with all the art of which I was capable.

Having received Communion and commended myself to Our Lady, I took that canvas and put it amongst those of Master turned against the wall, to await the King's pleasure. Then, trembling and already frightened, I awaited the hour when I would have to confess.

Several days went by. His Majesty was indisposed and remained in his apartments.

Master was painting another mirror arrangement, fussily moving his mirrors about, checking lights and reflections; he paid no attention to me and did not notice that I was nervous.

Then my hour struck.

It was late in the afternoon. Master was not painting, but sitting at his desk making out some accounts and writing to order special pigments from Flanders. The door of the studio opened quietly and His Majesty stepped in, looking around in his uncertain, apologetic way. He was dressed for some court ceremony: black velvet shoes and long black silk stockings, black velvet trousers, but instead of a doublet he wore

only a white shirt of thin cotton, and a dressing gown of dark silk brocade. I supposed that after contemplating a picture he meant to return to
his rooms, put on his doublet, call the barber to shave him and curl his
hair and mustache, and then attach his big white starched ruff at the last
moment.

He pulled out his chair, sat, and stretched his long legs with a deep
sigh. He smiled amiably at Master, who smiled back warmly, affectionately, and then went on with his accounts.

After a short time the King rose and went toward the wall. He stood
hesitating a moment, and then turned a canvas toward him. It was mine.

In the late light, the faithful hounds shone out
from the dark background, sunlight on their
glistening hides, light in their big, loving,
dark eyes. His Majesty stood transfixed;
he had never seen that canvas before.
I could watch his always-slow mind
adjusting to the fact that this was
a portrait of his own favorite
hounds.

I threw myself on my knees
before him.

"I beg mercy, Sire," I pleaded.
"The painting is mine. I have been
working secretly all these years,
with bits of canvas and color,
copying the works of Master, to

learn from them, and trying some original subjects by myself. I know very well that this is against the law. Master has never even suspected and has had nothing to do with my treachery. I am willing to endure whatever punishment you mete out to me."

I remained on my knees, begging the Virgin to remember my promise, praying and asking her forgiveness and her help. Opening my eyes, I saw the feet of His Majesty moving nervously about. Evidently he did not know what to reply. Then he cleared his throat and took a deep breath. The feet in the velvet shoes remained quiet.

"What . . . what shall we do . . . with this . . . this . . . disobedient slave?" I heard his voice lisping and stuttering, as he turned toward Master.

Still on my knees, I saw Master's neat small feet, in their shoes of Cordovan leather, approach and place themselves in front of my picture. He studied it some time in silence, and the King waited.

Then Master spoke. "Have I Your Majesty's leave to write an urgent letter before I answer?"

"You have it."

Master returned to his desk and I heard his quill scratching against the paper. His Majesty returned to his chair and threw himself into it. I remained where I was, praying with all my might.

Master rose, and his feet moved toward me.

"Get up, Juan," he said. He put a hand under my elbow and helped me to my feet. He was looking at me with the gentle affection he had always shown me.

He took my hand and put a letter into it. I have worn that letter sewed into a silk envelope and pinned inside my shirt ever since.

The letter said:

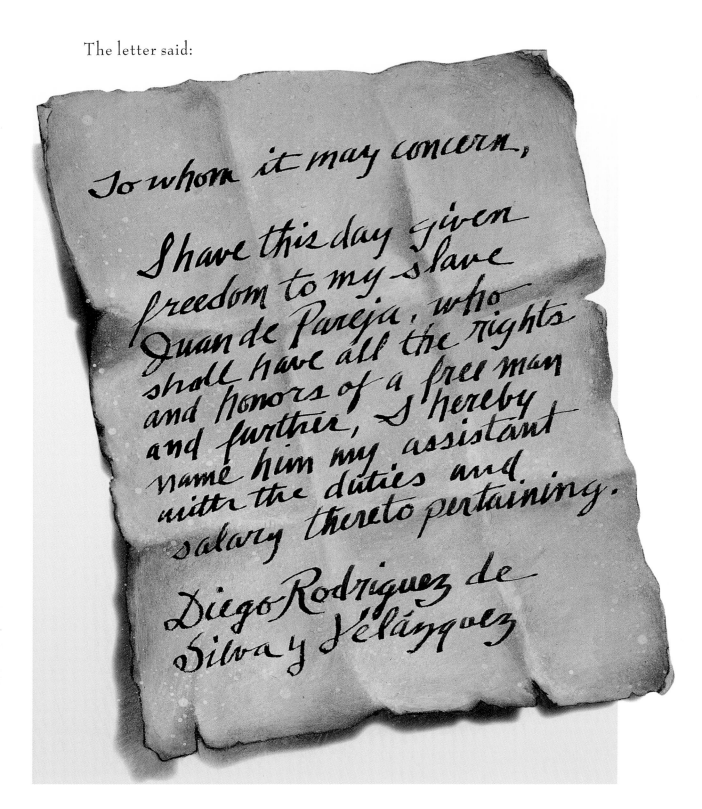

To whom it may concern,

I have this day given freedom to my slave Juan de Pareja, who shall have all the rights and honors of a free man and further, I hereby name him my assistant with the duties and salary thereto pertaining.

Diego Rodriguez de Silva y Velázquez

Master took the letter gently from my hand, after I had read it, and took it to the King who, reading, smiled radiantly. It was the first time in all those years that I had seen His Majesty smile. His teeth were small and uneven, but that smile seemed to me as beautiful as any I had ever seen.

The letter was given back to me, and I stood there, tears of joy streaming from my eyes.

"You were saying, Sire, something about a slave?" inquired Master softly. "I have no slave."

I seized his hand, to carry it to my lips.

"No, no," cried Master, snatching his hand back. "You owe me no gratitude, my good friend. The contrary. I am ashamed that in my selfish preoccupations I did not long ago give you what you have earned so well and what I know you will grace with your many virtues. You are to be my assistant if you wish, as you are my friend always."

"I am pleased," said His Majesty, and rose to his feet. At the door, before he left, he turned and said again, "I am pleased."

We waited, Master and I, side by side, bowing, as the King sailed down the corridor, his dressing gown billowing out behind him.

"Let us pack up our things, Juan," (he never again called me Juanico) "and go home. Mistress is fretful when I am not more often at her side. And I am tired."

"As your assistant, Master . . ."

"Now, do not call me Master anymore. Call me Diego."

"I cannot. You are still Master. My Master, as you were Master to the apprentices, and to other painters. Master means teacher, does it not?"

"Yes."

"I was never ashamed to call you my Master, and I am not ashamed now. I shall always give you the respect of that title."

"As you wish."

We were walking through the streets of Madrid toward our home. I took each step with a new spring in my knees, a new joy in my heart, for I walked as a free man, beside my Teacher.

"But, Master," I said, as we crossed the Plaza Mayor, "you were in error when you said that you had no slave. There is Lolis."

"Lolis belongs to my wife," he told me.

I determined to make this a day radiant in my memory in every way.

"Master, when we were in Italy, you told me that I could ask anything of this hand" (and I took his right hand lightly in my own) "and you would give it me. Now I know what to ask for."

He stopped in the square where the last rays of the sun struck level against us. "You want Lolis," he said, smiling.

"I wish to marry her. If she will have me."

"I will speak to my wife about it. I see no reason why you should not marry if you both wish it," he answered, and we continued to stroll in silence.

Inside our house—that house where I had lived so many years in peace of mind and spirit, even though I had not been free—everything now seemed new to me. The corridors, so much a part of my daily existence, the dark heavy carved furniture, the life-sized crucifix with its small glow and flicker of light always in a glass bowl at the feet of the Christ, the dark red velvet curtains now drawn against the declining day to keep out the humors[1] and evils of night—all were dear and known to me, but somehow fresh and new.

We had no sooner entered than Lolis came running toward us, finger to lip.

"The Mistress has been in much pain today," she whispered, "and I have just now been able to get her to sleep."

"I will not go up then," answered Master.

We went into the dining room. Very often Paquita[2] came, with her little daughter, but today the house was quiet and still. I could see that Master was worried, and I knew why. Mistress was more and more often ill and weak, and sometimes she lay and cried.

When I went into the kitchen later Lolis came and laid her head on my shoulder. She was not weeping—I have always been quick to tears, but I have never seen one glittering on her lashes—but she sighed deeply.

"My poor lady," she grieved. "I have come to be fond of her, Juan. And soon we will have to give her some opium to stop the awful paroxysms of coughing. The King could get it for Master. It will be a sad time now, Juan, until God calls her."

Actually, as sometimes happens, Mistress rallied and seemed much better a few days later. She got up and was dressed and began to eat some of the dainties Lolis had prepared for her. On the second evening she came to the supper table and smiled and seemed very happy, sitting at Master's side. She ate quite a bit of supper and did not cough once.

---

[1] humors: air currents that people once believed could affect the way a person feels
[2] Paquita (pä·kē´tä): the daughter of the Mistress and the Master

Master looked up at me suddenly and I could read his intention in his eyes. Turning to her, he said, *"Mi vida,*[3] I have given our good friend Juan his freedom and he is now my honored assistant. He will take many duties off my shoulders and I will rest more and be more often with you. I know you have been lonely with our daughter married and gone from the house."

"Ah yes!" cried Mistress, her thin face lighting up. "That is why I have been ailing. I have been lonely."

"And Juan wishes to marry. He has given his heart to you, Lolis. What do you say?"

Mistress clasped her hands. "Lolis!" she cried. "What is your answer?"

I remember that Lolis was wearing a dress of pale almond green, and she had bound back her hair with a rose-colored scarf.

"I can answer as I wish?" asked Lolis.

"Of course."

"My answer is No."

I felt as if my heart had been pierced with a dagger. Lolis saw the hurt in my face.

"It is not that I do not like him," she said, in her deep soft voice. "He is a good kind man, but I do not wish to bear any children into slavery."

Master's quiet voice was heard. "You are right, Lolis. Juan is now a free man. And I am sure my wife would like to give you your freedom, as a wedding gift. Isn't it so, my love?"

Mistress took her cue and answered at once, for she was always eager to please Master in every way she knew, and now that she was

---

[3] Mi vida (mē bē´ dä): love of my life

ill, more than ever, it seemed.

"It is so indeed. If you will hand me the paper and pen and inkpot, I will write the letter of manumission now."

Mistress wrote the letter and put it into Lolis' hand.

"My dear Lolis," she said, "you are as free now, as you have always been in your spirit, I think. But I would ask a favor of you. Please stay on as my nurse. Do not leave me . . . just yet."

Lolis put the letter in her bosom, and she looked with tenderness at Mistress.

"I am glad to be free," she said. "More than you can know. I never dreamed that it would come to pass so soon, though I had seen in the future that it would be so, one day. Just as I have seen that I would marry Juan. Yes, I shall stay with you, Mistress, as long as you want me. And I thank you."

Quietly she gathered up some dishes and left the room softly.

Master gave me permission with his eyes, and I followed Lolis out into the kitchen. She was in a corner, on her knees, praying.

"I was thanking God," she told me. "I have prayed for this every day of my life."

"And you will marry me, Lolis?"

"Yes. But you could have found a better woman, Juan. I am proud and haughty and sometimes I have a sharp tongue."

"It is you I want, just as you are."

She came into my arms then, and let me caress her hair, her cheek and her forehead.

"I have resented being a slave," she said. "I could not feel grateful in my heart, for deep inside me I resented being bound. I know that God made us all free and that no man should own another. I hated serving people because I was a slave and had to do their will. Only here in this house I had some peace because you are all kind and Mistress is sweet and affectionate. I will do my best to make her last days comfortable. But I am not like you, Juan, grateful and loving. I *hated* being owned! It was all I could do, some days, to keep the hot words inside my mouth and the resentment out of my voice."

"Never mind. Everything is different now. And if we have children, they will be born free."

"Yes. But many of our race are not, Juan. My heart aches for them."

"Some day," I assured her, "some day, I know that all men will be free."

ELIZABETH BORTON DE TREVIÑO

lizabeth Borton de Treviño was born on September 2, 1904, in Bakersfield, California. In 1934, while on a newspaper assignment in Mexico, she met Luis Treviño Gomez, whom she married a year later, and settled in Mexico, where she still lives.

I generally get story ideas from some true event or moment in history that fires my imagination. All of my books contain a little kernel of truth, something that really happened. Each of my stories tries to show some phase of love, that powerful emotion that makes the world go round.

It was my son, Luis, who, while studying painting, learned the true story of Juan de Pareja and told it to me. I loved the story, and when I saw a reproduction of the portrait Velázquez painted of Juan, I was determined to write about him, for his face seemed to be that of a dignified, noble, and proud person whose story should be told.

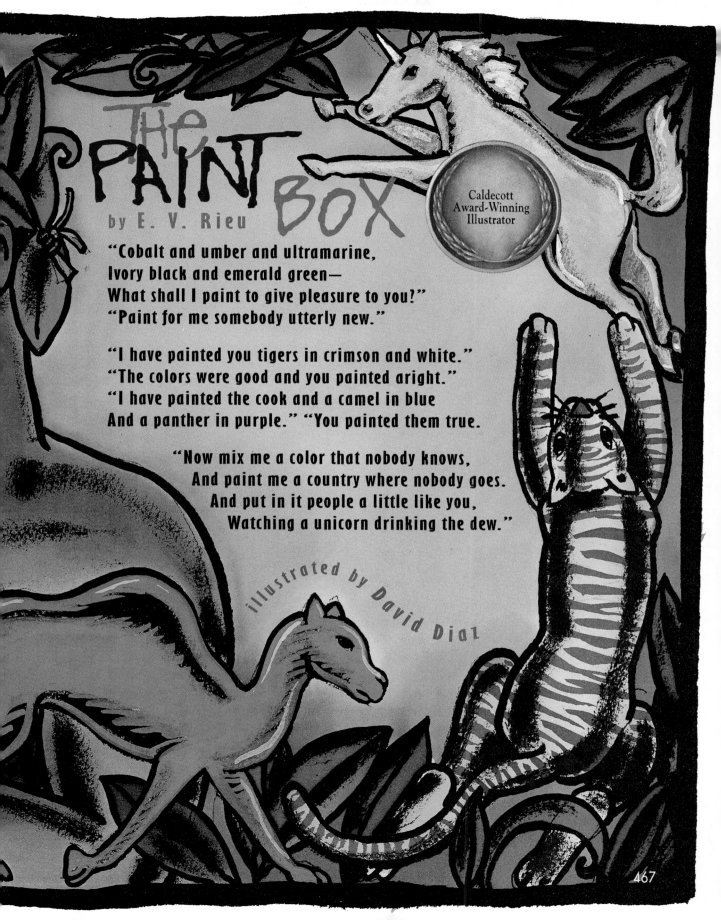

The PAINT BOX

by E. V. Rieu

Caldecott
Award-Winning
Illustrator

"Cobalt and umber and ultramarine,
Ivory black and emerald green—
What shall I paint to give pleasure to you?"
"Paint for me somebody utterly new."

"I have painted you tigers in crimson and white."
"The colors were good and you painted aright."
"I have painted the cook and a camel in blue
And a panther in purple." "You painted them true.

"Now mix me a color that nobody knows,
And paint me a country where nobody goes.
And put in it people a little like you,
Watching a unicorn drinking the dew."

illustrated by David Diaz

Response Corner

WRITE A PERSUASIVE PARAGRAPH

NO ART ALLOWED

Think about Juan de Pareja's talent as described in the story. Do you think the law barring slaves in seventeenth-century Spain from practicing the arts was fair? Write a persuasive paragraph stating your opinion.

WRITE A NOTE

¡MUCHAS GRACIAS!

Velázquez writes a letter declaring Juan's freedom. Imagine that you are Juan. Write a note of response to Master Velázquez. Use the appropriate format for a thank-you note.

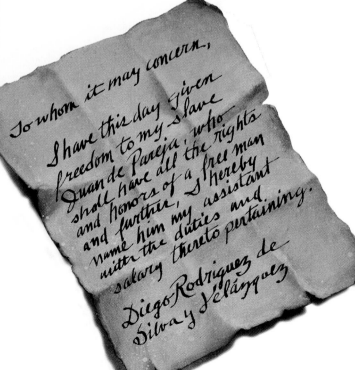

To whom it may concern,

I have this day given freedom to my slave Juan de Pareja, who shall have all the rights and honors of a free man and further, I hereby name him my assistant with the duties and salary thereto pertaining.

Diego Rodriguez de Silva y Velázquez

CREATE A CLASS BOOK

KEEPING THE DREAM ALIVE

The poem and the selection are about freedom of expression. Many African Americans expressed their longing for freedom and equality through the arts —painting, drama, music, and dance. Research an African American artist and write a report about that person's life. Bind your report together with those of your classmates in a book titled "Dream Keepers."

What do you think?

- What two problems does Juan de Pareja have to face in the story? How are these problems solved?

- How did you feel at the end of the story? Explain your answer.

- If the poet of "The Paint Box" were to describe Juan de Pareja's portrait of the hounds, what might he say?

ART & LITERATURE

Artists create masterpieces in a variety of ways. What are the artists in this painting creating? Can you think of ways in which making a painting and playing an instrument are similar? How is this painting like the paintings you have seen by Velázquez? How is it different?

Women Playing Koto, Samisen and Kokyu
by Katsushika Oi

Katsushika Oi, a 19th-century Japanese artist, was one of the few well-known female painters of her time. As a child, Oi showed a talent for painting. Later, she and her father—who was also a successful artist—shared a studio. They worked well together and enjoyed each other's company. *Women Playing Koto, Samisen and Kokyu* is one of Oi's best-known artworks. Like music, this painting includes rhythm and pattern. Can you find examples of these?

471

Margaret Bourke-White in High-Altitude Flying Suit, 1943

Flor Garduño in 1986

Two Women Photographers

from FOCUS: Five Women Photographers

FOCUS: *Five Women Photographers*

JULIA MARGARET CAMERON   MARGARET BOURKE-WHITE
FLOR GARDUÑO   SANDY SKOGLUND   LORNA SIMPSON

Sylvia Wolf

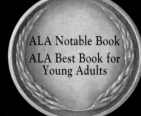

ALA Notable Book
ALA Best Book for
Young Adults

by Sylvia Wolf

When she was young, Margaret Bourke-White's best friends were the garter snakes she caught in the woods near her house. Margaret was a quiet girl—too serious to be popular with other children. But when she took her snakes to school, her classmates thought she was wonderfully strange. Margaret liked being different. She once wrote in her diary that she pictured herself "doing all the things that women never do."

Margaret Bourke-White was born to Minnie and Joseph White in the Bronx, New York, on June 14, 1904. (Margaret added Minnie's maiden name, Bourke, when she started her career in photography.) Margaret's mother was an avid reader with an adventurous spirit. She taught Margaret and her younger brother and sister to be curious, determined, and fearless. Her father was a mechanical engineer and inventor who worked for a printing company. He felt that hard work and striving for perfection were the highest human virtues. When Margaret was faced with a tough task, he would urge her to keep trying. "*You can,*" he would say.

When Margaret was eight years old, her father took her on a tour of a foundry, a place where iron and other materials are melted at very high temperatures to make steel. (The steel is then shaped into machine parts.) Margaret watched with fascination as flames jumped from the bubbling vats of molten steel. In the heat, noise, and fiery light of the foundry, she saw beauty and power. When Margaret became a photographer, her first and favorite subjects were factories and machines.

Margaret was introduced to photography by her father, an amateur photographer. As a young girl, she often helped him in his darkroom. When her father died during her first year in college, Margaret decided to pursue photography on her own. Apart from her science courses at

Columbia University in New York City, she took classes at the Clarence White School of Photography. Margaret attended five schools during her college years.

When she was twenty-three, Margaret moved to Cleveland, Ohio, in the hopes of getting a job as an architectural photographer. A booming industrial city, Cleveland was the perfect place for someone who loved buildings and factory machinery. Margaret made many photographs in the Otis Steel Company's foundries. In one, light shines behind cables, pipes, and a man bending over at work. The silhouettes in the hot, misty air give the scene a mysterious, exciting feeling. To make a picture like this, Margaret often stood so close to steam and molten steel that factory workers were afraid she might get burned. They tried to make her stay back, but Margaret would not listen. When it came to getting a picture she wanted, no one could stand in her way.

Henry Luce, publisher of *Time* magazine, saw Margaret's Otis Steel photographs and thought they were terrific. Luce was founding a new magazine, called *Fortune*. It would be the first to use photographs to bring industry and big business to life. Luce offered Margaret a job photographing for *Fortune* magazine, and she accepted.

Margaret quickly became known for taking pictures no woman—and few men—had taken before. During the winter months of 1929–30, she photographed construction work at the top of New York City's Chrysler Building as the skyscraper was being built. Eight hundred feet up, in cold wind, she teetered on a scaffold with her camera and tripod as the building swayed.

When the Chrysler Building was finished, Margaret rented a studio behind the stainless steel gargoyles that decorated the top of the building. She liked to climb out on the gargoyles and photograph the city below. Amazed by Margaret's fearlessness, newspaper and magazine reporters wrote about her daring. The stories were not just about her photographs—they were about *her*. Margaret Bourke-White was becoming a celebrity.

The photographs published in *Fortune* were so popular that its founders decided to start another magazine— one with even more photographs. The magazine, named *Life*, contained very little writing. Instead, in a new format called the "photographic essay," it let the pictures tell the story. Margaret joined *Life* when the magazine was formed in 1936 and was the only woman among the magazine's first four staff photographers. Except for a short time working for a daily newspaper in 1940, she stayed with *Life* until she retired twenty-one years later.

Early in 1945, Margaret photographed a famous American, Gen. George S. Patton, in Germany. Then she followed his troops as they pursued retreating German forces. On April 11 of that year, Patton's regiment arrived

*Buchenwald,
Germany,
the Day
after
Liberation,
April 1945*

at Buchenwald, one of many concentration camps built by the Nazis. In these camps alone, the Germans killed over four million Jews, along with gypsies and political prisoners.

At first, it was difficult for Margaret to take pictures of the dead and starving prisoners, but she knew that without photographs, people would not believe reports of the horror at Buchenwald. One image is of inmates lined up behind a barbed wire fence, staring blankly at the camera. These men have seen so much death and brutality that they have little spirit left. Although physically they are alive, they seem emotionally dead. Photographs like these shocked the American public. Few who saw them will ever forget them.

A year later, with the war ended, Margaret was sent to document India's struggle for independence from Great Britain. India's great peace leader, Mahatma Gandhi, agreed to pose for her. First, though, Gandhi's secretary insisted Margaret take a lesson in spinning cotton so that she could understand the Mahatma's philosophy. To Gandhi, the spinning wheel represented India's break from Britain. He believed that cotton grown in India should be spun there, not in British textile mills, as was done at the time. When Margaret photographed Gandhi, she positioned his spinning wheel in the foreground of the portrait. It fills almost half the frame. By giving it so much space and importance, she reminds us of Gandhi's desire for India to be free from British rule.

In late 1949, Margaret was sent to do a photographic essay on racial injustice in South Africa, where whites, who were in the minority, brutally mistreated native Africans. She traveled two miles underground into a gold mine to photograph men who did hard and dangerous work for little pay. These men were known not by their names, but by numbers tattooed on their arms. In Margaret's photograph, #1139 and #5122 stand facing the camera. Their sweat shimmers in the artificial light of Margaret's flash. She positioned the camera to fill the frame with their torsos. In spite of miserable conditions and racial oppression, the workers appear noble and monumental.

*Gold Miners,
Johannesburg,
South Africa,
1950*

479

This picture and ones Margaret made during the Korean War in the early fifties are among the last of her career. In 1954, when she was forty-nine, Margaret was diagnosed with Parkinson's disease, an illness that attacks the nervous system. She continued to work for *Life* until 1957. Then, for fourteen years, she fought Parkinson's disease with the same bravery and determination that had made her a great photographer. In 1971, at age sixty-six, Margaret died of her illness.

During her years with *Life*, Margaret Bourke-White's photographs were seen by over one hundred million viewers each year. Today, they are admired both as historical documents and as works of art; they can be found in history textbooks and in museum collections around the world. She became a legendary figure in photography and paved the way for future photojournalists, men and women alike. Margaret succeeded many times over in fulfilling her childhood dream of doing things women of her time did not do. She never forgot her mother's lessons in curiosity and fearlessness and her father's words "*You can.*"

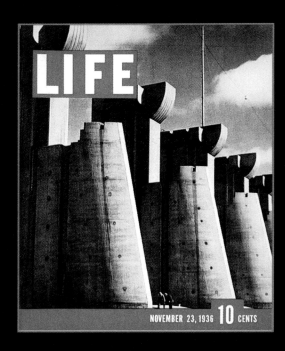

Dam at Fort Peck, Montana, 1936.
(First cover of *Life*.)

FLOR GARDUÑO (flôr gär • d͞o͞on' yō) was born the youngest of three children in Mexico City, Mexico, on March 21, 1957. Her mother, Estela, was a merchant, and her father, Gregorio, was a civil engineer. When Flor was five years old, her family moved to a farm outside of Mexico City. Flor's father had a strong love for animals and for life in the country. He often took the children on walks and pointed out animals, beautiful flowers, and fruit. It was from him that Flor developed her appreciation of nature.

From the time Flor was a girl, she knew she wanted to be an artist. At age eighteen, she left home to enter the San Carlos School of Fine Arts in Mexico City. For three years, she studied painting and drawing and read poetry, literature, and philosophy. She went to see films, sometimes two in one day. Then the teachers went on strike. Flor was anxious to keep learning, so she signed up to study with the only teacher who was not on strike, a photographer named Kati Horna.

Before then, Flor had not been interested in photography. She had watched photographers on the streets of Mexico City who took portraits of people for a few pesos. But their work looked boring to Flor. It was not until she studied with Kati Horna that Flor discovered how wonderful photography could be.

Horna was a Hungarian photographer who had moved to Mexico City during the Second World War. In Europe, she had been friends with many important artists who were pioneers of modern art. Horna considered photography to be a fine art equal to painting and sculpture.

When Flor was twenty-two, she left school to work as a photographer. Flor's first job was with the Mexican secretary of public education. Her assignment was to visit and photograph in remote villages throughout Mexico where native Indians lived. Before the sixteenth century, when Spanish conquerors arrived in Latin America (Mexico, Central America, and South America), this area was inhabited by native Indians. From region to region, they had different languages and cultures. Today, over forty million Indians occupy villages all over Latin America. They still speak native languages, and they maintain many of their old customs. Other customs are mixed with the Christian practices brought by the Spaniards.

In these Indian communities, Flor's task was to take pictures of everyday activities. Later, the photographs appeared in children's schoolbooks written in native languages as well as Mexico's national language, Spanish. The images were used to illustrate words and help children learn how to read and write.

One of these early pictures is of two brothers walking home from the fields in Tulancingo, Mexico. Each one carries a huge squash over his shoulder like a baseball bat.

Kings of Canes,
Tulancingo, Mexico,
1981

The squash has been dried and hollowed out to be used as a tool for getting sap out of the agave plant. The sap is then used to make *pulque* (pool´kā), once the sacred drink of the Aztec people, who ruled an empire in Mexico in the fifteenth and early sixteenth centuries. In the photograph, the boys look one way, and the squashes tilt the other. The bold but simple composition makes this a dynamic picture.

Flor worked for the secretary of education for two years. After that, she photographed sculptures and paintings for art books. Then an exciting thing happened. Francisco Toledo, one of Mexico's famous painters and a friend of Flor's, offered to publish a book of her photographs. He liked her pictures and thought other people would like them, too. This was a great honor.

Flor selected her favorite photographs for the book. One is of a dense cloud of hundreds of birds flying above a country farm. Flor had seen them from a distance as they landed in the trees. They were so beautiful that she drove closer and loaded her film as quickly as she could. She hoped to photograph the birds as they flew away. Just as she was ready, they took flight. Flor had barely enough time to take one quick picture before they were gone.

Cloud, Jocotitlán, Mexico, 1982

Flor's equipment made it possible for her to act spontaneously in taking this picture. Her cameras are small and light. Also, her film speed is fast. This allowed her to stop the birds' motion as they flew. Even so, she knew she was lucky. It is difficult to be in the right place at the right time. When that happens and Flor takes a picture she is happy with, she says it is one of the best feelings in the world.

When Flor's book, *Magic of the Eternal Game,* was published in 1985, she took it to the international book fair in Frankfurt, Germany. One company there liked her work so much that they asked her to publish a book with them. She proposed one on animals. (Flor has loved animals since her childhood days on the farm.) The company liked the idea and she got started.

While working on her book *Bestiarium* (the Latin word for collection of animals), Flor traveled with Adriano Heitmann, a Swiss journalist and photographer. Like Flor, he was interested in the Indian cultures of Latin America, and he had helped her plan the book. Over time, Flor and Adriano fell in love.

During the next few years, they visited Guatemala, Ecuador, Bolivia, Peru, and tiny villages throughout Mexico. One picture she took in Guatemala celebrates the beauty of nature and light. Flor was driving along a small country road when she saw a girl, about ten or twelve years old, walking with a basket of lilies balanced on her head. The girl wore the traditional dress of the area. Flor followed the girl to her house, then asked if she could take a picture. By positioning the girl half in shadow, half in light, she made a striking composition. The lilies shine in the sunlight like a floral crown.

*Basket
of Light,
Sumpango,
Guatemala,
1989*

In 1992, Flor published her third book, *Witnesses of Time*. The book became an instant hit. It won a Kodak award as one of the best photography books of 1992 and was translated from Spanish into five languages. That same year, an exhibition of photographs from the book began a tour of museums in Europe and the United States.

Flor's photographs are popular because they are stunning pictures as well as documents of timeless traditions. Though modern technology has come to many villages, native Indians have maintained their heritage. With the camera, Flor shows us the survival of Indian cultures in Latin America.

A year after *Witnesses of Time* was published, Flor gave birth to her first child, a baby girl named Azul. Today, Flor, her husband, Adriano, and Azul divide their time between two homes. For part of the year, they live in a small white house in the foothills of the Swiss Alps. For the rest, they live in the Mexican village of Tepoztlán. Flor will continue making pictures, and she may even return to painting someday. In the meantime, however, she is enjoying the success of her most recent book and her days and nights with Azul.

The Woman, Juchitán, Mexico, 1987

SYLVIA WOLF

Sylvia Wolf, a photographer and educator, works at the Art Institute of Chicago where she studies and lectures about the work of great photographers.

"All of us, at one time or another, have taken a photograph or had a photograph taken of us. Photography is something anyone can do with a little instruction. But to create art with a camera— to make images that capture beauty, that tell us about the world we live in, or that make us feel deep emotions—is a different thing entirely."

 Photograph

Award-Winning
Poet

He washed his feet for the picture,

even his knees,

and wondered about that man

who cared enough to want him to sit there

for a photograph

even though he didn't have

nothing good to hold in his hands,

nor even a dog to sit by his chair.

It gave him, briefly,

some sort of feeling

of just being

enough.

BY CYNTHIA RYLANT

PHOTOGRAPH BY WALKER EVANS

Response

Margaret Bourke-White

GENDER DEBATE

Margaret Bourke-White wished that she could do "all the things that women never do." Debate with a partner about something women normally don't do but could. Each of you should take one side of the issue. Allow equal time for each point of view to be expressed.

BEHIND THE LENS

Compare and contrast the life and work of Margaret Bourke-White and Flor Garduño. Using details from the selection, tell what is different about each woman's style of photography. Include a statement about which woman's photographs you prefer, and why.

Corner

Flor Garduño

DISCUSS IDEAS

SIMPLE SUBJECT

If you were a photographer, what subject would you shoot for a book or magazine? Why would you choose that subject? Discuss your ideas with a small group of your classmates.

What Do You Think?

- How did the early experiences of the two women prepare them for a career in photography?

- What did you learn from the selection that you thought was especially interesting or important?

- What do you think that poet Cynthia Rylant would say about Flor Garduño's photograph "Basket of Light"?

Notable Trade Book
in Social Studies

492

*Litton Industries, Beverly Hills,
California, 1968*

The Will and the Way

and the Way

PAUL R. WILLIAMS, ARCHITECT

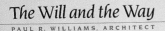

BY KAREN E. HUDSON

❖ *H*as anyone ever asked you what you want to be when you grow up? Maybe someone has suggested a road for you to follow. But what if you discovered that the road to your dreams hadn't been built yet?

This is the story of Paul Revere Williams, architect. Paul Williams didn't start out as an architect; he began as a kid, just like the rest of us. As a high school student, he made a commitment to himself to become an architect, and, in 1923, he became the first African-American member of the American Institute of Architects—later the AIA named him a Fellow, a prestigious honor. During a career that spanned nearly sixty years, he designed more than three thousand projects throughout the world—from Canada to Jamaica, Hawaii to Liberia, New York to Colombia, and, of course, in Los Angeles, his hometown. His vision and interests led him to build everything from houses to churches, schools, hospitals, office buildings, and public-housing projects.

Probably the only thing he loved more than architecture was his family. He was a loving husband, father, and—ultimately—a grandfather. That's where I come in. As his granddaughter I learned to wonder about the world around me. And when I grew up I became

Williams with grandchildren, Karen and Paul

curious about him, too. I knew Paul Williams—my grandfather—but I knew little about Paul R. Williams, architect. As I uncovered this side of him, I realized his life was a story that was meant to be shared.

First of all, no biography about Paul Williams would be complete without looking at his childhood, where the roots of the courage and fierce determination he exhibited throughout his life first took hold.

Paul was born on February 18, 1894, in downtown Los Angeles, at Eighth and Santee Streets. His father, Chester; mother, Lila; and brother, Chester, Jr.; had just moved there from Memphis, where his father had been a waiter at the Peabody Hotel. Los Angeles was full of opportunities. Chester, Sr., opened his own fruit stand at the Plaza, which is now known as Olvera Street. When Paul was a toddler, he and his mother would walk three blocks to the horsecar to take their daily ride to visit his father's stand. Sadly, Paul's mother and father both died by the time he was four. Orphaned, Paul was raised by loving foster parents, Mr. and Mrs.

Clarkson, while Chester, Jr., went to live with another foster family. Even though the brothers weren't able to see each other often, Chester was five years older and made an effort to keep in touch with his little brother.

The Clarksons lived in the neighborhood where Paul was born, so he continued to attend First African Methodist Episcopal Church (First A.M.E.), which is the oldest African-American church in Los Angeles. He was the only African-American in his class at Sentuous Avenue School on Pico Boulevard, where he was known as the class artist; otherwise his childhood experiences were like those of most people in early downtown Los Angeles. He lived in an integrated neighborhood. After school he and his playmates explored their surroundings. Sometimes they used wheat to catch the wild quail that roamed their street. At other times they visited their neighbors. The vegetable man taught them how to conserve natural resources, particularly water. They learned Chinese and German from the new kids who moved to the neighborhood.

His foster father worked as a janitor in a bank at First and Spring Streets. When he was still in elementary school, Paul began selling newspapers on the corner outside the bank to help support the family. Paul sold *The Record* and *The Express*, one for three cents or two for a nickel. U.S. Senator Frank Flint was a regular customer.

Although Paul traveled the world over, Los Angeles remained his home all of his life. Drawing was his lifelong love, too. By holding fast to his dreams and becoming an architect, Paul carved his own road and made it a little easier for more African-American architects to follow. (By 1993, there were 595 African-American members, including forty-two Fellows, in the AIA.)

In 1948, Paul became a grandfather for the first time. It was no small coincidence that his grandson, my brother, was named after him. Paul left us a legacy through his personal notes. Although the following notes are addressed to his grandson, we know he would be happy that we are sharing them with you. Maybe you'll want to take the road to an architectural career—or perhaps you'll decide that you, too, can blaze a new trail. Whatever you choose, remember to celebrate your creativity, learn from the accomplishments of others, and share your knowledge with those who follow.

Karen E. Hudson

Karen Elyse Hudson
Director
The Paul R. Williams Collection

Williams and his grandson, Paul Claude

> *"How can you, as an individual, fit into this pattern of tomorrow? First, we must be a part of the community in which we live and not apart from it."*

To my grandson:

I thought you'd never get here—but finally you've arrived! You should have seen the commotion at the hospital as Claude, your other grandfather, and I anxiously awaited your arrival. You're the first grandchild on both sides of the family. Your parents didn't get a chance to name you, because as soon as Claude and I found out you were a boy, we announced your name to be Paul Claude.

From the moment we heard you were due to join the family, I've kept a special notebook just for you. There's so much I want to tell you, so many experiences I want to share with you. I want you to know I love being an architect. . . . Perhaps you'll be an architect one day yourself. Don't let anyone keep you from achieving your dreams, Paul. You can be whatever you want to be—as long as you have the will and the way.

> *"To be sincere in my work, I must design homes, not houses.*
> *I must take into consideration each family's mode of living,*
> *its present economic problems, and its probable economic future."*

❖ When I was very young I drew pictures of animals. Soon I found myself drawing each building on my route to school. One day a family friend, who was a local builder, said I should become an architect. At the time I wasn't sure what it meant to be one, but I soon found out. I felt like a detective in a dime-store novel, questioning everyone I could about architecture. When I discovered that architects design homes, schools, churches, office buildings—and just about everything imaginable to live and work in—I decided this was the profession for me. Architects also draw the plans of how buildings should be built and supervise their construction. To think that something I drew on a piece of paper would become a building of bricks and boards was nothing less than magical!

When I entered high school the first question the counselor asked me was, "Why do you want to be an architect?" I told him I had heard of only one Negro architect in America, and I was sure this country could use at least one or two more. (The architect I knew of was Booker T. Washington's son-in-law, William S. Pittman. Of course, there were a few others, but they were back East and I wasn't aware of them.)

My career plans were not well accepted by everyone. Although my family encouraged me at every step, my guidance counselor continued to give me reasons why I would fail. I took architecture courses at Polytechnic High School, but when I told my adviser that I wanted to continue my studies at the university, he stared at me with as much astonishment as he would have had I proposed a rocket flight to Mars!

I suppose it was about 1912 when I made the commitment to become an architect. This was the turning point in my life because I realized I would forever question my right to be all that I could be if I allowed others to discourage me because of the color of my skin. I developed a fierce desire to prove to myself that I could become one of the best architects ever.

I knew I had the will. All I had to do was find the way.

Pool house and pool, Jay Paley residence, Bel Air, California, 1934

After graduating from high school I enrolled in the Los Angeles Art School and took a job as an architect's helper. The Beaux Arts Institute of Design of New York had a workshop in Los Angeles that accepted me as a student. After three years of study I won the coveted Beaux Arts Medal for excellence in design. Winning this competition reinforced my belief that I would succeed. I realized that the only chance I had of being accepted in the elite world of architecture was to compete on individual merit.

To find a job I went through the yellow pages and copied the addresses of all the architects listed. I arranged them in geographical order, put on my best suit of clothes, and called on each office. I asked if they were hiring or not. Next to each name I wrote down whether the answer was "no" or "maybe next week," and whether it was said with a smile or a frown. The following week I put my sketches in a smart portfolio and went back to each office where someone had smiled. Finally I was offered three positions. Three dollars per week was the highest salary, and one office paid nothing but gave me the chance to work in one of the most prestigious architectural firms in the city. I knew that this firm would give me invaluable experience, so I took the job. To my surprise they broke their contract and paid me three dollars beginning my very first week.

Shortly thereafter I began working for Wilbur D. Cook, a landscape architect and town planner. My first day in the office I informed the chief draftsman that I was a working-drawing man, meaning that I prepared drawings to be used on the job by construction workers. I bluffed my way through the day; then, at night, I took his drawings home and worked until daybreak. I went into the office early the next morning, laid out the drawings on my drafting table, and waited for the chief draftsman to drop by. He was astonished at how quickly I had completed the assignment. Thereafter, he considered me the fastest working-drawing man in the office. That's when I decided that I would do things faster, more efficiently, and better than others in order to be judged for my abilities rather than simply dismissed because of the color of my face.

In 1914, when I was twenty, my design for a neighborhood civic center in Pasadena, California, won the first prize of two hundred dollars,

Ambassador Hotel coffee shop, California, 1949

beating older and more experienced contestants. I won first honorable mention in architecture at the Chicago Emancipation Celebration in 1915 and the following year placed third for the Sperling Prize, an All-American competition held in New York. It was especially exciting to compete with other architects from across the country, because it's easy to be the best in your town and forget that there's a whole world of competition out there.

I thought drawing ability was all I needed to become an architect, but my boss told me how wrong I was. Even though I had some promising ideas, he explained that I'd never succeed if I only cared about the artistic part. That accounted for only about one quarter of an architect's job. I had not considered how architects obtain commissions to design buildings, only about how thrilling it was to work on them at my drafting board. Once again, my will wasn't enough. I had to find the way.

At the University of Southern California, I enrolled in an engineering program that included business classes. The degree required many math courses, and I was certainly glad I took them. The math helped me make the correct measurements on floor plans and gave me a foundation for the business side of architecture.

Meanwhile, I worked my way through college by making brass U's, S's, and C's for men's watch fobs and women's handbags. At one point

County Courthouse, Los Angeles, California

"Building styles change with time and fashion, but I measure my worth as an architect by my ability to please my client. Each home I design has something special and different from anyone else's home, but I've never made a house so trendy that, when the owners wanted to move, no one else would be interested in buying it."

The interior of the residence of E.L. Cord, an auto manufacturer. The drawing details how to build the staircase, which is shown in its final form.

five other students worked for me, and I made so much money that I considered changing my mind about school and architecture. Deep down inside, however, I knew the money was temporary and I'd grow bored. Becoming an architect would be a lot of work, but my future depended on staying in school. I took a hard look at my experience (or lack of it) and decided to attend three different art schools for intensive study in interior design, color harmony, and rendering.

With additional education and experience in landscaping under my belt, it was time to find a job that would give me experience in fine home design. I couldn't have asked for a better training ground than working in the offices of Reginald Johnson. Would you believe my first assignment was to design a $150,000 home? Up until then I'd never even been in a home that cost more than $10,000! I couldn't imagine how you could spend so much on a home, but then my employer sent me to look at homes in Santa Barbara, and I soon found out. That trip taught me more than where money was spent; it also taught me how it was spent. The most important lesson I learned was restraint. A room should have a single focal point, regardless of how much money goes into it. If not arranged well, a magnificent collection of furnishings can look like an expensive junk shop. Restraint, then, is a matter of choosing and carefully planning for the total effect.

Frederick Douglass, as shown in facade of the Twenty-eighth Street YMCA, Los Angeles

Paul Williams in front of the Los Angeles International Airport theme building

"Planning is thinking beforehand how something is to be made or done, and mixing imagination with the product—which in the broad sense makes all of us planners. The only difference is that some people get a license to get paid for thinking and the rest of us just contribute our good thoughts to our fellow man."

From that day on my motto became: "Good design is the pleasing assemblage of parts, not the assemblage of pleasing parts." I remember this whenever creative vision is involved. The same idea holds true whether you're getting dressed and putting an outfit together, redecorating your room, or setting the table. It even holds true when selecting people for a committee—it's important to choose people who work well together.

Satellite City, Paul Williams's vision of a city of the future

"Remember, imagination can be a tool in creative problem solving. Use your imagination, and you'll never give up on finding solutions to problems, whatever they are."

❖ *Karen Hudson* ❖

Karen Hudson says Paul Williams, her grandfather, could make a sketch come alive right before his clients' eyes. He would sit across the table from his clients and draw his sketches upside down. "A sparkle still comes to their eyes when they start talking about it," Ms. Hudson says.

Ms. Hudson talked to many of her grandfather's clients as part of her research for *The Will and the Way.* She realized that there were many remarkable things about her grandfather that few people knew. That's why she decided to write her book.

But putting the book together took a great deal of imagination and creativity. Ms. Hudson says one thing her grandfather always wanted her to do was use her imagination. She knew he would be proud if she tried to help others use imagination and creativity in their lives.

"It wasn't just important for him to inspire us to be architects," Ms. Hudson says. "It was important to him that we use imagination in our everyday lives, as a way to solve problems."

Ms. Hudson had problems finding information about her grandfather for the book. There weren't many public records about him, but Della Williams, her grandmother, had saved newspaper clippings about him since 1917.

As part of her research, Ms. Hudson also sent a questionnaire to the owners of the buildings her grandfather designed. The owners were eager to give her the information she needed. "I received most of the information through the generosity of others," Ms. Hudson says.

When her research was complete, Ms. Hudson realized that her grandfather's story could be inspirational to everyone, not only to kids who want to be architects.

"What you need to be is a person who contributes to your community," Ms. Hudson says. "That may or may not be as an architect. But if you listen, read, think, and use your imagination, you can apply that to anything," she says.

ON WATCHING THE CONSTRUCTION OF A SKYSCRAPER

BY BURTON RAFFEL

Nothing sings from these orange trees,

Rindless steel as smooth as sapling skin,

Except a crane's brief wheeze

And all the muffled, clanking din

Of rivets nosing in like bees.

❖ *Response*

A FINE EXAMPLE

Suppose you are Paul R. Williams's grandson. You have just read your grandfather's journal, which he wrote for you. Write a thank-you letter. Tell your grandfather how his journal has inspired you to reach your goals in life.

DESIGN A ROOM

ARCHITECTS IN TRAINING

Work with a partner to take measurements of your classroom. Draw a design of the room, indicating the measurements of each wall, window, doorway, and chalkboard. In your drawing, rearrange the items in the room in a way that is both functional and pleasing. With your classmates, vote on the design you like best.

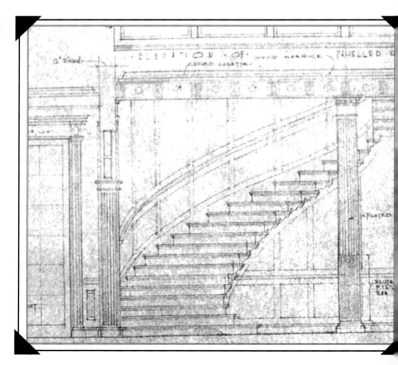

Corner

WRITE A POEM

WHERE THERE'S A WILL, THERE'S A WAY

Write the word *WILL* vertically on a sheet of paper. Using each letter as the first letter of a line, write a poem about the importance of having the will to accomplish a goal. Share your poem with your classmates.

WHAT DO YOU THINK?

- Do you think that the title of the selection appropriately describes the life of Paul R. Williams? Explain your answer.

- Which one of Paul R. Williams's designs was your favorite? Why?

- What do you think Paul R. Williams would say about the poem "On Watching the Construction of a Skyscraper"?

THEME
WRAP-UP

Would you consider the work of Margaret Bourke-White, Flor Garduño, and Paul Williams masterpieces? Explain your answer.

The artists in these selections show their creativity in different ways. What similarities do you see among them? How do they use their talents to help others?

ACTIVITY CORNER

What can you do to express your creativity? Think about different forms of creative expression that you enjoy, and create a masterpiece of your own. When you are finished, present it to the class.

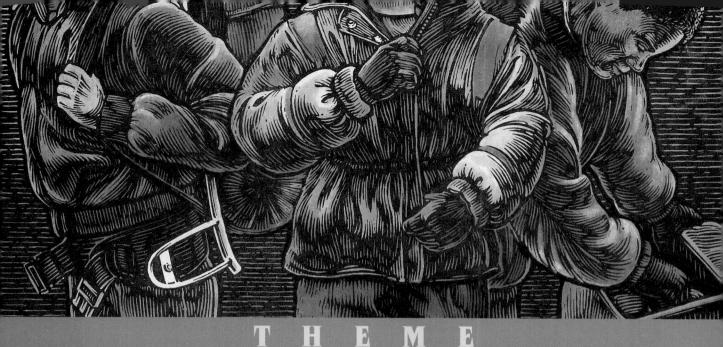

THEME

CONFRONTING NATURE

What would it take to overcome a disability and sail across the vast Atlantic Ocean? To battle a raging river? To survive in the frozen Arctic wilderness? The characters in the next selections rely on courage, strength, instinct, and common sense to survive.

CONFRONTING NATURE

CONTENTS

BOOKSHELF

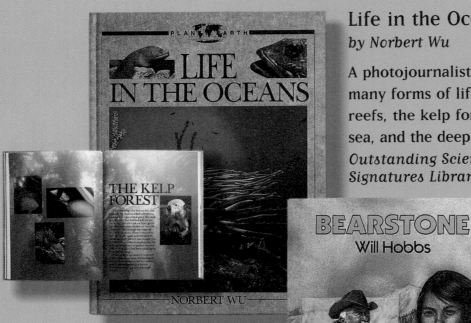

Life in the Oceans
by Norbert Wu

A photojournalist explores the many forms of life in the coral reefs, the kelp forest, the open sea, and the deep ocean.

Outstanding Science Trade Book
Signatures Library

Bearstone
by Will Hobbs

Cloyd finds strength in himself and in his Native American heritage when he must begin a new life in the mountains of Colorado.

ALA Notable Book, Children's Choice
Signatures Library

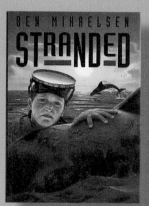

Stranded
by Ben Mikaelsen

Koby's physical disability has made her feel like an outsider. She finds a new sense of purpose, though, as she struggles to save two stranded whales.

Climb or Die
by Edward Myers

After a serious automobile accident, Jake and his sister must climb a mountain with improvised climbing gear to save their parents' lives.

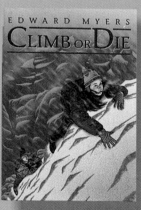

Making Sense: Animal Perception and Communication
by Bruce Brooks

Are five senses enough in the animal kingdom? Learn about the wonderful ways in which animals are able to make sense of their world.
Orbis Pictus Award

517

FREEDOM RI

When Liz and Pete Fordred decided to build a sailboat and cross the Atlantic, they knew nothing about boats or sailing. They had little money. And, in addition, they lived in Rhodesia (now Zimbabwe), a land locked country without many yachting experts to consult. Rhodesia was under worldwide sanctions at the time, so they couldn't import even a winch. But the greatest hurdle they faced was that they were both paraplegics, paralyzed from the chest down. Liz had been thrown from a horse in a riding competition and Pete had been in a car accident. What did they have going for them? Just grit, determination, and a complete misunderstanding of the word 'no.'

Liz and Pete Fordred

By Liz Fordred with Susie Blackmun

D E

I sometimes sit and ponder what we have done. Now that Pete and I own a house and a business in Fort Lauderdale and are busy being parents, our sailing trip seems like more than a mere decade ago. At times it doesn't even seem real. But if I close my eyes and allow myself to drift back in time, I can see Pete heading for the foredeck, clipped onto a lifeline as he scoots along on his bottom. . . .

Every time our boat climbs up a wave, he holds on with all the strength in his massive arms and waits for the plunge. When it comes, and the deck of Usikusiku (yoo·sē´koo·sē´koo) drops out from under him, he uses the momentary loss of gravity to slide farther down the deck.

After each plunge we hit bottom, and for a few seconds the sea spray blocks my view of him, but once I see the 18-foot running poles slowly rising into place I can relax.

I'm never comfortable when he's on the foredeck. What if he should go overboard? But that is a lapse into the negative, a state I refuse to enter. And, of course, we have planned and practiced a man-overboard procedure.

When Pete heaves himself back into the cockpit, he is exhausted by the enormous physical effort of moving around the boat and hoisting the poles. Without back or stomach muscles, he must do everything with his arms. At least our bodies are strong now, a far cry from their condition back in Rhodesia, in hospital beds. Wheelchairs might be permanent fixtures in our lives, but our quality of life is good.

Let's Build a Boat

During the first two years of our marriage, Pete and I were busy. He was in charge of an instrument workshop and I worked full time at the rehab center, where I'd been promoted to administrative assistant. Three times we represented Rhodesia in the South African Championships for the Disabled, which meant a lot of training. We organized sports activities for young disabled kids, and I was secretary for the Paraplegic Club. We went on two hilarious camping expeditions.

Somehow, all of that wasn't enough. We'd accepted our disabilities, but we weren't going to accept their restrictions. We wanted a challenge.

Both Pete and I had always wanted to travel. Now that we were paraplegics, though, traveling was tough. Going on an aircraft was practically impossible. You had to be carried up the steps because in Rhodesia passengers still went out on the tarmac to board, and once on the plane you couldn't use the bathroom. You couldn't get onto a train or bus, nor could you rent a car with hand controls. We liked camping so we tried to get a VW van, but the government wouldn't let us purchase the foreign currency to buy it. And with much of Africa in turmoil, South Africa was practically the only place to go. It was pretty frustrating.

One Saturday we were driving along a country road when Pete said, absolutely out of the blue, "Why don't we build a boat?"

I suppose it's hard to believe that two paraplegics could even dream of physically building a boat, let alone sailing it across an ocean. Why would we want to create more obstacles than we already had? The only answer I can come up with is that we weren't conventional people, even before our accidents.

The restrictions of being a paraplegic had made me want to scream at times. When Pete suggested building a boat, I felt suddenly free. It was almost like being on a horse again, galloping toward a difficult jump that others might think twice about but that I knew I could manage. It was a challenge, and I had always responded well to a challenge.

The goal would be regaining our independence. It never occurred to us that being in wheelchairs and building a boat was an unheard-of combination.

The closest either of us had been to a sailboat was looking at pictures, but you can't go through life doing only the things you know how to do, can you? We talked

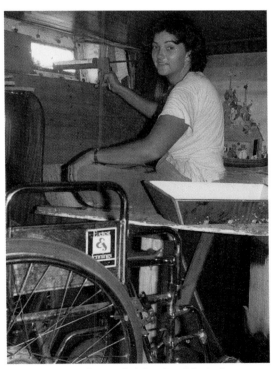

Liz works on the unfinished cabin in her mother's backyard in Salisbury, Rhodesia (now Harare, Zimbabwe).

521

about all the wonderful things future yachtsmen dream of. We envisioned sunny blue lagoons, palms and islands, white sand (sand and wheelchairs—we didn't think that one through very well).

In my normal fashion I went at the idea like a bull at a flag and found out as much as possible about buying or building a hull. Right in the middle of the countryside, hundreds of miles from the sea, I discovered a shipyard that fabricated hulls. A hull, though, represented only 10 percent to 15 percent of the work. The rest we would have to do ourselves.

During the four months it took for our hull to be built we saved like mad, read all we could lay our hands on and started planning the interior to suit our wheelchairs. We taped an outline of the cabin floor on Mom's veranda, so we could see where our chairs would fit and where everything would go. We knew there was nothing more frustrating than a wheelchair jamming and bashing into something at every turn.

When the 43-foot hull arrived, we put it into a huge hole we had had dug in Mom's backyard, so that the deck was brought down to ground level and we could just wheel right across in our chairs. Now our priority jobs were getting railings on the deck, so that we wouldn't roll off, and building a hydraulic lift to lower us inside.

As our commitment to building our boat grew, so did our realization that we could help other disabled people see that just because their bodies had been damaged didn't mean all their hopes and dreams were over. We also wanted to help able-bodied people understand that just because a person is physically disabled doesn't mean he or she is mentally incompetent as well.

Having a challenge and a goal were the most important steps we had taken since our accidents.

From Hull to Yacht

"I want to build something," I insisted after several evenings of passing tools to Pete while he had all the fun of doing the work. I wanted to do something constructive, even though I knew dangerously little about a T-square and tape measure.

Pete suggested that I start on the clothes cupboards on either side of the forward lift. He explained how

Liz and Pete with their boat in Durban, South Africa.

to go about it. I began with great enthusiasm, got absolutely tangled up with curves and angles, and let out what soon became a familiar cry for help. Pete would explain once again. Sometimes I would hurl the board as far away as possible and yell, "If you're so smart, *you* can do it!"

"Oh?" he'd say innocently. "I thought you wanted to learn."

Frustrations were plentiful. Things would continually fall off my lap. I'd pick them up and something else would fall. I'd back up and find I couldn't move because something was in the way of a wheel, or an electrical wire from the drilling machine or jigsaw had caught in the chair. It was worse when we first started to build, since the floor was the only place to put anything. Pete swore he would get a box and put everything that gave him trouble into it, and once we were sailing he would hurl it over the side. Humor was one way of coping with the frustration, so we often ended up laughing at each other.

I invented a way of getting up the sloping hull—up five feet and across two feet—by collecting bricks and stacking them against the side of the hull. Then I'd lay a plank from the bricks across to my armrest and drag my body across. We always found a way of doing a job. Sure, it might take an hour, whereas if we were able-bodied it would have taken five minutes, but it was best not to think of it like that; rather we should feel the satisfaction of trying and succeeding.

Slowly I learned new skills. I finally finished the first cupboard and got it all screwed into place. "Right," said Pete. "Now take it apart and glue it." I was rapidly losing patience with the cupboard and with Pete. I took it apart and glued it, although it did not fit as well the second time. Pete, who is a perfectionist, must have had to swallow hard to accept my cupboard.

In their spare time Pete and his dad were inventing a way for us to get down into the boat. This involved a lot of thinking, which taxed my patience. Whenever I saw Pete sitting there daydreaming, I would explode: "We have work to do!" He finally came up with an ingenious idea for a lift, all worked out to the last detail. I asked when he had done it. "While I was daydreaming," he said quietly.

We worked on the boat every second that we weren't occupied with our regular jobs; we could get in an average of six hours every night and 36 hours over a week-end. Making the wooden parts of the boat, such as the cabin and interior, are a normal part of boat building, but because we had little money for ready-made equipment—and because Rhodesia was under worldwide sanctions preventing us from importing much—we had to make nearly everything else as well. We made our own bolts out of brass rod. Pete and his dad fabricated the railings, wheelchair lift, steel rudder, self-tailing halyard winches and roller furling drums. Pete bought a reconditioned Mercedes engine and "marinized" it himself.

All of the physical activity made us more fit and agile and improved our balance, and the enormous feeling of satisfaction we got from even the smallest physical achievements made us soar. Life in wheelchairs had taken on some sort of meaning.

South Africa

We had been searching for a name for our boat. We finally settled on Usikusiku, an African word describing the hour between day and night, both dusk and dawn.

We hired a couple of workmen to trowel on epoxy to smooth out the hull. Then they rubbed it down and began to brush on paint. Suddenly it appeared we'd made major progress. Usikusiku looked like a yacht.

In order to properly finish the boat, and avoid making dangerous mistakes out of ignorance, we had to get her out of Rhodesia. We had to get to the sea so we could be around other yachtsmen and learn from them.

We hired a truck to make the 1,200-mile trip from Salisbury, Rhodesia (now Harare, Zimbabwe), to Durban, South Africa. After three months in dry dock, we were ready to launch. Usikusiku actually floated the first night in port. As we lay in our bunks, we were gently rocked to sleep by the lapping of water against the hull and the crackling of barnacles on the jetty walls. Already we were in a different world.

But during the time we were in Durban, nearly every member of every committee from the Durban Yacht Club came to inspect us. They told us we were attempting the impossible. The harbor authorities weren't impressed with us either. One continually came to visit us, telling us of all the horrors

525

we were going to face, then kicking our cabin and telling us it would come off with the first wave. We accepted these opinions as only to be expected. What really mattered was what we thought. We knew we were ignorant about sailing, but we weren't stupid and could learn.

Even nonsailors, more often than not, looked at us with disbelief. "You'll never make it," they told us bluntly.

Others wanted to know how we would sail the boat. "How will you go up the mast?" was a favorite question.

"We'll do it the same as everybody else does," I'd answer. "I'll winch Pete up in a bosun's chair."

"What happens if the engine stops?"

"Well, seeing as Pete is good with engines, that shouldn't be a problem. Besides, we're a sailboat."

"What will you do if the boat is sinking?"

"Having legs in a life raft is not absolutely necessary."

Sometimes I could have screamed.

Most of the world is unaware of the capabilities of wheelchair-bound paraplegics. I wanted my independence as much as anyone. I wanted to do as I liked, when I liked, but more often than not I had to fight to keep my independence. It was a constant battle when strangers made judgments without bothering to get to know us.

Fortunately, our supporters more than made up for the critics. A wealthy Greek businessman loaded us down with food, gear and advice. Several people we'd never even met sent us money. Many of the other yachtsmen pitched in by helping with the rigging, by teaching us to sail and navigate and by skippering the boat during our sea trials and the trip to Cape Town. In all we spent four years building our boat, and we couldn't have done it without the wonderful people who believed in us.

When the time came to sail, we were tense as we waved to the friends who'd followed us out of the bay. Once their shouts had faded, we were left with only the sounds of wind and water.

Bon Voyage

Looking back over the waves I could see Table Mountain looming over Cape Town in her grandeur. It was strange to be sailing alone with Pete for the first time, with

1,700 miles of the South Atlantic between us and St. Helena Island, our first stop.

As the wind increased, Usikusiku heeled toward the water, slowly picking up speed. The main sheet block should have zipped across the traveler, as it had on all our other sails, but it twisted and stuck.

"Let the sheet out a little," Pete said, but the traveler still didn't budge. What a good start!

On a regular sailboat the problem would have been simple because the traveler, which holds the end of the boom down, is usually at deck level. But we'd had to build ours so that it didn't block our wheelchairs when we were in port, and that meant putting it 4 1/2 feet above the deck. At sea, out of our chairs, the "roll bar," as we called it, loomed even higher over our heads. How could we get up there to untangle the snag?

While I pondered, Pete jumped (so to speak) into action. With his incredibly strong upper body, he grabbed hold of one of the traveler's vertical supports and pulled himself up, hand over hand, to the horizontal bar. Hanging from one arm, his body swinging with the motion of the boat, he stretched the other up and freed the block. The boom swung over with a crash.

Then Pete worked his way back across the bar and dropped safely onto his bottom into the cushioned cockpit.

We *could* do anything. Some things might require more thought and time, but we always got there in the end.

Around 5 p.m. the wind began to strengthen, so we furled the No. 1 jib and set the smaller No. 2. Pete connected the self-steering vane, though we ended up having to steer by hand since the seas were confused. I went below to fix our dinner, a stew I'd made the day before that I only had to heat up and ladle into deep dishes with lids that I could move in front of me without anything slopping over. We didn't eat much, out of excitement I suppose, with a bit of seasickness thrown in. My stomach was starting to churn—little did I know it wouldn't ever stop.

Because of my queasiness I suggested that Pete take the first watch while I tried to sleep. I tucked myself into the berth down below and set the leeboard to keep myself from rolling out.

Pete called me at midnight. When I finally got to the cockpit to relieve him, he announced that sleeping below was not going to work because it took too long to

Liz lowers Pete into the water in port so he can work on the propeller shaft.

get up on deck—in an emergency we could end up in a real pickle. He grabbed a blanket and stretched out in the cockpit.

That first night watch was tough as I struggled to stay awake. Once I fell asleep and the mainsail slammed from one side of the boat to the other. Pete didn't sleep well at all, and when he did get to sleep I had to wake him so I could visit the head. That made me feel sicker than ever and was exhausting because I had to hand crank the broken lift to get myself up on deck again. Halfway up I dropped the handle and had to go back down to fetch it. This happened twice!

Pete relieved me at 6 a.m. I slept until 9, then plotted our course, which made me feel awful. Pete was feeling sick too, so he went back to sleep. The porpoises, though, were enjoying it. Six of them showed off for us, moving incredibly fast and making fun of our five knots. They made us feel better and took the gloom out of our seasickness.

Later in the afternoon I made some soup and put it in a flask to keep our fluids up. Paraplegics are supposed to drink great quantities of fluids to flush the kidneys, so we kept pushing each other to drink. The pump flask I'd bought in Cape Town was a real life-saver. At night, when it was cold, we could have hot chocolate or soup. The only problem was getting it to the cockpit from below because, with the rolling of the boat, we could not keep it upright. It often fell, inevitably landing on its pump handle and spraying hot stuff everywhere, including on us. It became a matter of getting it to the cockpit as quickly as possible. It was not an ideal type of flask for the sailing environment, but it was best for us because we didn't have the abdominal and back muscles to hold a cup and pour from the usual kind, all the while balancing on a rocking boat.

We forced ourselves to wash and to change clothes daily, in order to keep sores away from our bottoms and legs, and we wore socks and high-top sneakers to protect our ankles and feet. One of the most important things we had to do if we were to succeed was avoid sickness and sores.

That second night the weather got worse, so we reduced sail again. The waves seemed to loom up all around us—better not to look at them or listen to the water washing through the cockpit and swishing through the spare gas bottles. I tried to sleep, telling myself it was no good being tired. It took me ages to get to sleep, unless I was on watch—then it was everything I could do to stay awake.

By the fifth day out we were getting used to the motion of the boat and didn't keep falling all over the place. Learning to live at sea was, in a way, like being a paraplegic for the first time because we had to relearn each task. Getting dressed was complicated for us at the best of times, but now we had to do it on a rolling boat while holding on. To put on my sneakers I had to lift my foot up with one hand and put the shoe on with the other. My foot would curl up with a spasm and refuse to go all the way in, then the boat would lurch and I'd end up lying on my back with my foot in the air, still trying to get the shoe on. Eventually we learned to use the motion of the boat to help us. It was hilarious watching each other slide about. When the cockpit cushions were wet we could move really quickly—we just had to make sure we ended up where we wanted to go.

Emotionally, sailing was the same for us as for other sailors. The first few days were more or less miserable. It was a chore to do everything. We felt sick, and sleep was hard to come by. Then we'd get a stretch of pleasant weather with reasonable winds and gentle seas—real picture-book sailing. We read, listened to BBC World Service and relaxed. We marveled at the flying fish and the porpoises and the miracle of this experience. We turned brown as nuts. One day Pete got into the wash basin on the aft deck, where he whistled and sang and sloshed about, while the basin, with him in it, slid around.

Then, just when we began enjoying the good, the unpleasant would rear its head. The wind and seas kicked up. The self-steering vane invariably quit, so we had to steer by hand, and the motion was so bad that we couldn't sleep. We were plagued by merciless seasickness and wondered what we were doing here. For four years we had worked for this? Feeling sick and having to hold on all the time?

"Sir Francis Drake must have been nuts to do this all his life," Pete would moan.

Then the weather would brighten again.

Sailing was a blend of extremes, and we reacted no differently than anyone else. Some practical matters required more ingenuity, but so had they when women began sailing, especially alone: They learned to use their intellect and the motion of the boat to compensate for their lack of brute strength.

We did the same to compensate for the parts of our bodies we couldn't use. We developed tricky ways of docking, of going for a swim, of getting in and out of the dinghy. For a long time we'd debated about sailing in our chairs (we could attach them to tracks) or out of them. Our sea trials had made it clear that *out* was the only way, so on deck we scooted about on our bottoms and down below we had false floors for use at sea. They raised us to a height where we could reach things in the saloon and galley and get in and out of our bunks, while Pete had access to his workbench.

Instead of letting our handicaps serve as obstacles, we simply found ways to work around them.

A porpoise entertains us.

Land Ho!

Being a new navigator, I grew increasingly apprehensive as we approached our first landfall. What if we were there and the island of St. Helena wasn't?

But one magical morning, 17 days after we'd left Cape Town, Pete woke me and told me to get the anchor ready. Was he being funny? No, there was St. Helena amongst the clouds, dead ahead. We hugged each other. My navigation worked! It really worked! Yahoo! Seventeen days at sea and out of the clouds loomed the blue outline of a mountain. Oh, how we wanted to dance for joy on the deck!

After another week at sea I found Ascension Island, too, which was memorable for the welcome we received. We'd been told that it would be difficult for us to get ashore on Ascension, but the islanders obviously had been warned by the St. Helenians that we were coming. As soon as we anchored, a boat came out to Usikusiku to fetch us. It motored straight to a crane, which lifted our boat and put it into a cradle on land.

"How are we going to get

down?" I whispered to Pete, but within minutes a forklift roared alongside and lowered us to our waiting chairs, while at least a hundred islanders looked on. I felt like a nit, but how wonderful it was that the islanders had thought of everything. Meeting people like these was another reward for all our hard work.

Our third and final leg across the Atlantic took two weeks and ended

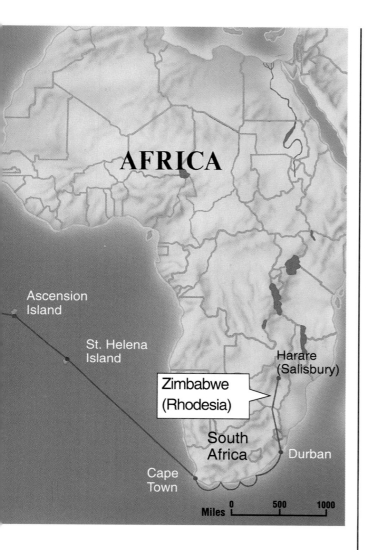

AFRICA

Ascension Island

St. Helena Island

Harare (Salisbury)

Zimbabwe (Rhodesia)

South Africa

Durban

Cape Town

Miles 0 500 1000

"Well, we made it," Pete said that night after we'd cleaned up and settled in.

"Of course, my love. There was never any doubt, was there?"

Pete got a job in Fortaleza, I began writing, and we settled in for the remainder of hurricane season. Then we made our way up the South American coast and entered the Northern Hemisphere for the first time in our lives. We cruised Caribbean islands in the manner we'd dreamed of, went aground in Puerto Rico and were rescued by the U.S. Coast Guard. We finally wound up in Fort Lauderdale, which we have made our home.

I can look back now and see how we have grown—mentally and physically. At the beginning of our rehabilitation, simple tasks like changing clothes were a real physical challenge that could bring tears of frustration. Pushing half a mile to the grocery store was unthinkable. Now all that seems like nothing, because we have overcome far bigger obstacles.

I might not be able to run wild with my dog through a field until I'm tired or jump on a horse and feel that exhilarating freedom under me, but there are plenty of other satisfying things to do in life. You just have to look for them.

with the most wonderful smell of wet earth and vegetation a full day before we saw land; I just couldn't stop breathing it in deeply. A few pretty butterflies flitted about Usikusiku, another indication that land must be close. With the following day's sunrise we could see Brazil ahead and the city of Fortaleza on our port bow. Yahoo! We were here! We had crossed the Atlantic!

Until I Saw the Sea

Until I saw the sea
I did not know
that wind
could wrinkle water so.

I never knew
that sun
could splinter a whole sea of blue.

Nor
did I know before,
a sea breathes in and out
upon a shore.

Lilian Moore

A Holiday, 1915
Edward Potthast

535

RESPONSE CORNER

SEAWORTHY SKETCH

Make a diagram of a sailboat. Label your diagram by adding the names of the boat parts mentioned in the selection. For more information, check an encyclopedia or books about sailing.

GOING FOR GLORY

Why do you think Pete and Liz were so determined to build the boat and sail it? Discuss your thoughts with a small group. Talk about a time when you showed determination in spite of obstacles.

TIME FLIES

For four years, Liz and Pete spent an average of six hours five nights a week and thirty-six hours every weekend working on their boat. Use a calculator to estimate the total number of hours it took Liz and Pete to build Usikusiku.

What Do You Think?

- How might reading this story change the way people feel about paraplegics and other people who are physically challenged?

- If you had met Liz and Pete before their trip, would you have encouraged them to go or not? Explain your answer.

- What images of the sea do you think the Fordreds might add to Lilian Moore's poem?

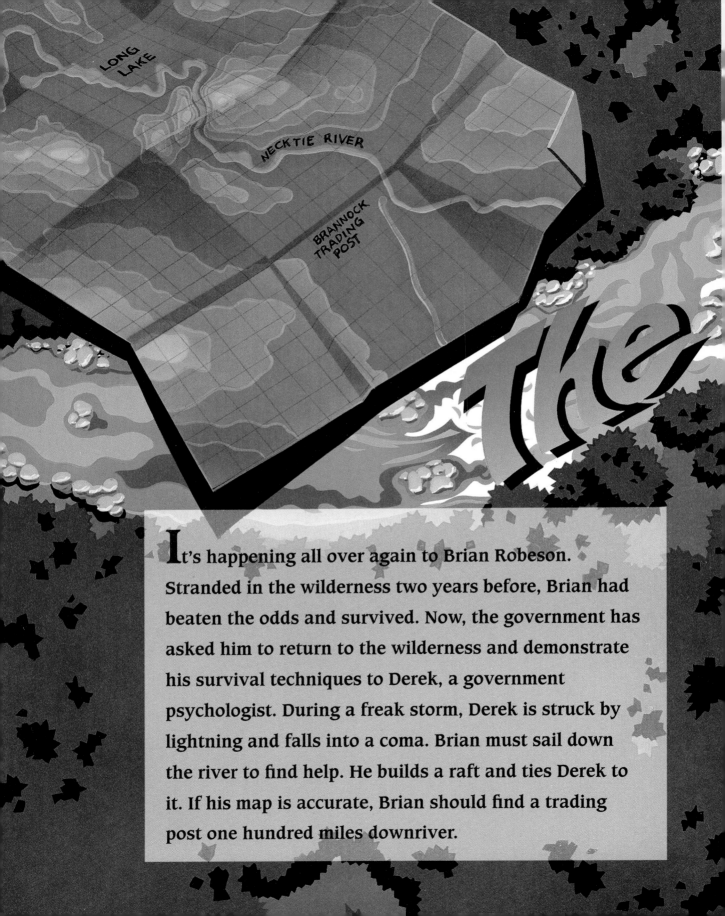

LONG LAKE

NECKTIE RIVER

BRANNOCK TRADING POST

The

It's happening all over again to Brian Robeson. Stranded in the wilderness two years before, Brian had beaten the odds and survived. Now, the government has asked him to return to the wilderness and demonstrate his survival techniques to Derek, a government psychologist. During a freak storm, Derek is struck by lightning and falls into a coma. Brian must sail down the river to find help. He builds a raft and ties Derek to it. If his map is accurate, Brian should find a trading post one hundred miles downriver.

River

Children's Choice
Young Adults'
Choice

BY GARY PAULSEN

ILLUSTRATED BY MARK REIDY

With the arrival of good light Brian took the map out and spread it on the briefcase.

The lake he had crossed did not show. He was positive. There were lakes, some large and small, but he was not moving fast enough to have reached any of them yet and that meant the map was not accurate.

It showed clean river with narrow banks where he guessed the lake to be and if it was inaccurate about this one thing then it might be wrong about all things.

Say the distance to the trading post. If the map had been made many years before and not updated, then the river might have changed direction, might not even go by the trading post any longer.

The trading post might not even be there.

The thought stunned him and he realized how foolish it had been to leave the lake and trust the map. There were so many variables, so many ways to go wrong.

He studied the map again and took some heart from it. It was so . . . so definite. It must be basically right. Close. Things could change, but not that much. The river was probably up a bit and the lake he had come through in the night was a low place that filled when the river ran high and not really a permanent lake that would be on the map.

Sure. There was logic there. All right. All he had to do was test the map, find some way to ensure that it was mostly right.

He put his finger on the river and followed it, tracing the path as the blue line cut through the green, followed it to where he thought he must be.

There.

If the map was right and he was guessing right, he should be about where his finger had stopped. It showed a long straight stretch and the contour lines were spread far apart, which would indicate a large low or flat area where there might be a lake.

Better yet, in a short distance—less than two miles—the contour lines came closer and closer together and showed two hills, one on either side of the river, just after a sharp *S* turn.

The raft was moving well now and the morning sun was cutting away some of the ache and tiredness of the night. He put the map back in the briefcase and checked on Derek. His face was swollen from the mosquitoes in the night, his eyes puffy and shut, and Brian used his T-shirt to wipe cool water on Derek's face. He rinsed it in the river and dampened Derek's mouth with fresh, clean water.

He wasn't sure if his eyes were being tricked or if it was real, but Derek looked thinner to him and he wondered if getting thinner was a sign of dehydration.

He dampened the T-shirt once more and put it over Derek's head. If he stays cool, Brian thought, cool and moist, it might help. If I can keep him out of the sun. . . .

If the raft had a canopy, a cover, it would help. He paddled to the shore and jammed the raft into some willows and grass. It took him a half hour to use some green willows and swatches of grass to arrange a crude awning over Derek. It did not cover the whole man, but kept most of him in shade, and when it was done Brian pushed the raft back out into the current and started moving again.

He watched for the hills. Hunger came with the morning and he started thinking about food. Cereal and milk, toast, bacon, fried eggs—the smells of breakfast seemed to hang over the raft.

It bothered him, but it was an old friend/enemy. He made himself quit thinking of food, thought instead of what to do, planning each move of the day.

Get a firm location, figure his speed, keep moving—a step at a time.

Time.

Time was so strange. It didn't mean anything, then it meant everything. It was like food. When he didn't have it he wanted it, when there was plenty of it he didn't care about it.

He stretched, sighed. "You know, if we were in a canoe and had a lunch and a cooler full of pop, we'd think this was the most beautiful place in the world."

And it was, he thought, truly beautiful. The trees, pines and spruce and cedars, towered so high they made the river seem to become narrow and in places where the bank was cut away by the moving water the trees had actually leaned out over the river until they were almost touching. They made the river seem like a soft, green tunnel.

The character of the river had changed. It happened almost suddenly, but with such a natural flow that Brian didn't notice it for a short time. The trees grew closer, the brush thicker and the banks higher.

Where they had been grassy and sloping away gradually, the banks were steeper and cut away, exposing the dirt and mud. The trees were so close and high that Brian would not be able to see the hills on the map when he came to them. He could see nothing but a wall of green.

He wiped Derek's face several times. All this time the raft had kept moving, and when his break was over he saw that they were coming into another bend.

He put the T-shirt back on, wet, and picked up the paddle and started to work, swinging the stern of the raft, keeping it in the middle of the current.

It would get hot soon and cook him, but he thought that it wouldn't matter. His hands were raw from the rough wood of the paddle and he thought that it wouldn't matter either.

All that mattered now was to keep moving.

He saw the hills from the map sooner than he thought he should see them.

But they were the right ones. He was sure of it. They rose steeply ahead and on either side, rounded but high, covered with trees.

It was just about noon and the sun was beating down on him. He reached under the shelter and used the damp T-shirt to cool Derek again.

"We're moving," he said, his voice thick with exhaustion, not believing it. "We're moving along now. . . ."

And when he said it he knew it was true. The raft was increasing in speed. Even as he watched, the speed seemed to pick up.

"We're hauling. . . ." He started, then trailed off as it dawned on him.

The contour lines being close together on the map meant that the banks steepened between the hills.

If there were hills and steep banks, the river might drop, fall a bit.

He reached for the briefcase to take another look at the map, but stopped with his hand halfway out.

A sound.

Some sound was there that at first he could not place. It was so soft, he could almost not hear it at all over the sounds of the birds.

But there it was again. A hissing? Was that it?

No.

It was lower than that. Not to be heard, but felt.

A *whooshing*—water.

A water sound.

A rumbling sound. The sound of water moving fast, dropping, falling.

Falling water.

A waterfall.

They were heading for a waterfall!

There was no time left. The river had narrowed slightly, but now there was more of a drop and the speed had increased dramatically.

They were dead in the middle of the river and Brian knew he had to get to shore, had to stop, but there was no time.

Twice as fast as he could walk, the raft was fairly careening now.

The sound was louder.

If he tried to paddle for shore, he would succeed only in turning the raft sideways. He was not sure how he could get over a waterfall—if indeed he could at all—but he was fairly certain he did not want to try it with the raft sideways. If it went the long way over the waterfall, it would be harder to roll over. Sideways and it would roll easily.

The sound was a definite rumble now, and in seconds they wheeled around a bend and Brian could see it.

"God . . ."

It was a whisper.

It was not a waterfall, but it might as well have been.

The river moved between two large stone bluffs that formed the sides of the two hills Brian had seen on the map.

The bluffs forced the river to a narrower width, deeper, and at the same time aimed it through some boulders that had split off either side and dropped in the middle.

All of this had the effect of making a monstrous chute where the water fought and roared to get through, smashing around the rocks in huge sprays of white water.

And the raft was aimed right down the middle of the chute.

Things happened so fast after that, there was not a way he could prepare for it.

The raft seemed to come alive, turn into a wild, crazy animal.

The front end took the river, swung down and into the current, grabbed the madness of the water and ran with it.

Brian had just time to look down at Derek, just time to see that he was still tied to the raft securely, and they were into it.

The raft bucked and tore at the water, slammed sideways. Brian tried to steer, using the paddle to swing the stern to the left and right, trying to avoid the boulders, but it was no use.

The water owned the raft, owned Derek, owned him. In the roaring, piling thunder of the river he had no control.

They were flying, the logs of the raft rearing out of the water on pressure ridges, slamming back down so hard it rattled his teeth.

In the middle of the chute was a boulder—huge, gray, wet with waves and spray—and the raft aimed directly at the center of it.

He had time to scream—sound lost in the roar of water—and throw himself on Derek. The raft wheeled slightly to the left and struck the boulder.

Brian thought for part of a second that they had made it.

Derek's body lurched beneath him and dropped back, the raft took the blow, flexed, gave, but held together; and Brian started one clear thought: we made it.

Then it hit. There was an underwater boulder next to the giant in the middle of the river. Hidden by a pressure wave, it lay sideways out and to the left, halfway to the left wall.

The nose of the raft made it, carried over by the pressure ridge, hung for a second, then dropped, plummeted down.

As it tipped forward the rear of the raft cut down into the water and came against the submerged ledge.

"Whunk!"

Brian heard it hit, felt the impact and the sound through his whole body. He grabbed, tried to hold on to the logs beneath Derek, but it was no use.

The stern kicked off the ledge, slapped him up and away, clear of the raft, completely in the air.

He hung for a split instant in midair, looking down on the raft, on Derek— then he plunged down, down into the boiling, ripping water.

Everything was madness—frothy green bubbles, hissing, roiling water.

He came up for a moment, saw the raft shooting away downstream carrying Derek, then he was down again, mashed down and tumbled by the pressure wave, smashed into the rocks on the bottom, and all he could think was that he had to stay alive, had to get up, get air, get back to the raft.

But the wave was a great weight on him, a house on him; the world was on him and he could not move up against it.

He fought and clawed against the rock, broke his face free, then was driven down again, hammered into the bottom.

Sideways.

He'd have to work sideways. Smashed, buffeted, he dragged himself to the side beneath the pressure wave.

It became stronger. He could not rise, could not get air, and his lungs seemed about to burst, demanded that he breathe, even if it was water. He willed the urge away, down, but it grew worse, and just when he knew it was over, when he would have to let the water in—when he would die—just then he made the edge of the pressure wave at the side of the boulder.

The current roared past the rock and took him like a chip, sucking him downstream.

He brought his head clear for one tearing breath, opened and shook water out of his eyes long enough to see that the raft was gone, out of sight—then he was driven back under, down to the bottom, smashing into boulders in a roaring green thunder, end over end until he knew nothing but the screaming need to breathe, to live, and then his head smashed into something explosively hard and he thought nothing at all.

Bright light flashed inside Brian's eyes—red and glaring—and he opened them to find that he was on his back, staring directly at the sun.

"Ecchh!" He rolled onto his stomach and spit and nearly choked on water.

He was in the shallows below the rapids, caught up in a small alcove in the shoreline.

The water was six or seven inches deep, with a gravel bottom. His senses returned and with them came the realization that he was all right. He was bruised, but nothing was broken; he had taken a little water, but apparently had coughed it out.

He was all right.

Derek.

The word slammed into him. Somehow, he had forgotten. . . .

He stood—his legs were a bit wobbly, but they held—and looked down the river.

It stretched away for half a mile, becoming more calm and peaceful as it dropped, nestled in trees and thick brush, a blue line in a green background. Birds flew across the water, ducks swam. . . .

There was no raft.

Brian turned, stood dripping, looking upriver into the rapids.

From below they did not look as bad. The pressure waves appeared smaller—even the boulder didn't seem as large. There was still the sound of the water—although that, too, was muted.

But there was no raft.

No Derek.

"Derek!"

He yelled, knowing it was futile.

He looked downriver again. There was no way the raft would have stopped in the rapids. It had to have come down, floated on downstream.

What had he seen? He frowned, trying to remember what had happened.

Oh, yes—the wave. The big submerged rock and the wave, the great wave had taken the raft and he had seen that—the raft moving off downriver. He did not think it had tipped; he seemed to remember that it was upright.

But Derek—was he still on the raft? He couldn't remember for certain, but it seemed that he was—everything was so confused. Tumbling in the rapids seemed to have shaken his brain loose.

He fought panic.

Things were—were what they were. If the raft rolled or if Derek fell off the raft, then . . . well then, that was it.

If not, Derek might still be all right.

"I have to figure he's still alive."

And if Derek was still on the raft, still alive, he was downriver.

Brian had to catch him, catch the raft.

He started to move along the bank, and did well for fifty or so yards. The bottom was gravel—spilled out by the rapids—but then it ended.

The river moved rapidly back into flatter country, swamps, lakes, and the first thing that happened was the bottom turned to mud.

Brian tried to move to the bank and run, but the brush was so thick and wild that it was like a jungle—grass, willows, and thick vines grabbed at him, holding him.

He moved back into the river—where the mud stopped him. If he tried to walk, when his weight came down, his feet sunk and just kept on going—two, three feet. The mud was so thick it pulled his right tennis shoe off, and when he groped to find it the mud held his arm, seemed to pull at him, tried to take him down.

He lost the shoe, clawed back to the bank and knew there was only one way to chase the raft.

"I'll have to swim."

But how far?

It didn't matter, he thought—Derek was down there somewhere. Brian had to catch him.

He shook his head, took off his remaining shoe, and left it on the bank.

He kept his pants on—they were not so heavy—and entered the river, pushed away from the bank until he was far enough out to start floating a bit.

He kicked off the mud and began to swim. Within three strokes he knew how tired he was—his whole body felt weak and sore from the beating he'd taken in the rapids.

But he could not stop. He worked along the edge, half swimming, half pushing along with his feet in the mud.

Downriver.

He had to catch the raft.

He became something other than himself that afternoon.

When he began to swim—after he'd overcome the agony of starting and his muscles had loosened somewhat—he tried to think.

The raft would move with the current, if it did not get hung up.

Brian would also move with the current, plus he had the added speed of swimming, and he should gain rapidly.

But when he rounded that first bend and did not see the raft, and cleared
the next bend two hundred yards further on and did not see the raft, worry
took him.

He stopped at the side and stood as much as he could in the mud.

It was nearly a quarter of a mile to the next bend and there was no raft.

Every muscle in his body was on fire. He slipped back into the water and
began swimming again, taking long, even strokes, kicking and pushing along
the mud; pulling himself forward.

Another bend, and another, always reaching, and always Brian's eyes
sought the still form, the thatched top of the raft.

Nothing.

The river seemed to have swallowed Derek. Altogether he rounded six
shallow bends and still there was no raft, the stupid raft that had hung up on
every bend when he was trying to steer it and now perversely held the center
of the river somehow. There was nothing but the green wall along either side,
the trees that grew higher and higher now that the rock hills were passed,
until they nearly closed over the top of the river; the green wall that closed in
and covered him as he slid along the water, wanting to scream, but pulling
instead, always pulling, a stroke, then another stroke, until there was not a
difference between him and the water, until his skin was the water and the
water was him, until he *was* the river and he came to the raft.

He nearly swam past it.

Brian moved near some willows, his face down in the water, reaching with his left arm and when he raised his head he was looking at the raft.

It had somehow come through all the bends and curves, and here must have caught a slight crosscurrent. The raft had moved to the outside of a shallow curve and had glided back beneath some overhanging willows and low trees.

All that showed was the rear end of the raft—and the bottom of Derek's shoes.

"Derek!"

Brian's hand had almost brushed the raft, but had he not looked up at the exact point that he had, he would have missed it.

He grabbed the raft, pulled himself up alongside.

Derek lay still, though his body had moved, twisted sideways on the raft.

"Derek," he said again, softer.

Derek's head was still to the side, the eyes half open, but if he had been pushed underwater in the rapids, even for a moment, it might be too late.

"Derek."

He looked done, gone, dead.

Brian tried his wrist, but could feel no pulse. He watched Derek's chest but it didn't seem to move. He leaned down, put his ear against Derek's mouth, held his breath.

There.

Softly on his ear, a touch of breath—once, then again, small puffs of air.

"Derek." He was alive, still alive.

It was as if everything came loose in Brian at the same time. His body, his mind, his soul were all exhausted and he fell across Derek, asleep or unconscious, fell with his legs still in the water.

"Derek."

Suddenly he was paddling.

His eyes were open and he was kneeling in back of Derek and he was leaning forward with the paddle and he did not have the slightest idea of how he'd come to be there.

He had a new paddle in his hands, carved roughly from a forked branch with a piece of Derek's pantleg pulled across the fork to form the face of the paddle. Brian was moving the raft and the sun was shining down on him and it was all, everything, completely new to him.

A different world.

"I must have slept, then moved in my sleep. . . ."

The briefcase was gone—torn off in the rapids—and with it the map. Not that it mattered.

The banks were just all green and the river went ahead to the next bend. The trees hung over the top and there was nothing to see but a slot of sky and the water ahead and the endless, endless green.

Nothing to match with a map.

He could no longer think anyway. He had no idea how far they had come, how many hours or days they had been traveling or how far it still was to the trading post. He could only pull now, only pull with the paddle.

He knew absolutely nothing, except the raft and the paddle and his hands, which had gone beyond bleeding now and were sores that stuck to the shaft of the crude paddle; knew nothing but the need, the numbing, crushing need to get Derek somewhere, somewhere, somewhere down the river. . . .

Food, hunger, home, distance, sleep, the agony of his body—none of it mattered anymore.

Only the reach.

The bend forward at the waist, the pull back with the arms, two on the left, two on the right.

Two left.

Two right.

Two.

Two.

Into that long day and that long night he moved the raft, so beyond thought now that even the hallucinations didn't come; nothing was there but the front of the raft, Derek, and the river.

The river.

Sometime in the morning of the next day, any day, a thousand days or eight days—he could not tell—somewhere in that morning the river widened and made a sweeping curve to the left, widened to half a mile or more, and he saw or thought he could see a building roof, a straight line in the trees that did not look natural and then he heard it, the sound of a dog barking—not a wolf or coyote, but a dog.

There was a small dock.

People had dogs that barked, and they had docks. He kept pulling, still not able to think or do anything but stroke, pulled to the edge of the river until the raft nudged against the dock, bounced, and then the paddle dropped.

He was done.

Above him on the bank he saw a small brown and white dog barking at him, its tail jerking with each bark, the hair of his back raised. As Brian watched, the round face of a young boy appeared next to the dog.

"Help. Help me," Brian thought he said, but heard no sound. The face of the boy disappeared and in moments two more people came, a man and woman, and they ran down to the dock and looked down at Brian and he was crying up at them, his torn hands hanging at his sides down in the water, down in the river.

The river.

"Derek. . . ."

Hands took him then, hands pulled him onto the dock; and the man jumped in the water and untied Derek and took him as well.

Hands.

Strong hands to help.

It was over.

Brian, Derek, and the raft traveled one hundred and nineteen miles down a river with an average current speed of two miles an hour, in just under sixty-three hours.

When Brian started, the raft weighed approximately two hundred pounds, but soaking up water all the way, it nearly doubled its weight by the time they reached the trading post—which was actually nothing more than a small cabin on the river where trappers could bring their furs. The post was owned and manned by a husband, wife, and one small boy, but they had a good radio and could call for help.

Derek's coma was low grade, and in truth he probably would have been all right even if Brian had not made the run—although he would have suffered significantly from dehydration. He began to come out of the coma in another week and had fully recovered within six months.

During the run Brian lost twelve pounds, mostly in fluids, though he drank river water constantly to make up for it, and his hands became infected from bacteria in the water. He healed rapidly—his hands became amazingly tough—and strangely suffered no real long-range difficulties from the run down the river, probably because his earlier time—the Time—had taught him so well.

His mother and father vowed never to let him go in the woods again, but relented after some little time when Brian pointed out that of all people who *were* qualified to be in the wilderness, he was certainly one of them.

About seven months after the incident, Brian was sitting alone at home wondering what to cook for dinner when the doorbell rang, and he opened the door to find a large truck parked in the street in front of the house.

"Brian Robeson?" the driver asked.

Brian nodded.

"Got some freight for you."

The driver went to the rear of the truck, opened it, and pulled out a sixteen-foot Kevlar canoe, with paddles taped to the thwarts. It was a beautiful canoe, light and graceful, with gently curving lines that made it look wonderfully easy to paddle.

Written in gold letters on each side of the bow were the words:
THE RAFT

"It's from a man named Derek Holtzer," the driver said, setting the canoe on the lawn. "There's a note taped inside."

He climbed back in the truck and drove away and Brian found the note.

"Next time," he read aloud, "it won't be so hard to paddle. Thanks."

GARY PAULSEN

Gary Paulsen was born in Minneapolis, Minnesota, in 1939. His father was in the army, so his family was always on the move. "The longest time I spent in one school was about five months," he remembers. "School was a nightmare and I was unbelievably shy, and terrible at sports."

One winter day he stepped into a library to get out of the cold. "The librarian walked up to me and asked me if I wanted a library card," he says. "When she handed me that card, she handed me the world. It was as though I had been dying of thirst and the librarian handed me a five-gallon bucket of water."

Paulsen has worked as a teacher, a farmer, a rancher, a truck driver, and a migrant farm worker. He was also an editor for a popular magazine. He says that working on the magazine was "the best of all possible ways to learn about writing."

Paulsen's stories are usually set in wild places and are about young people who learn more about themselves by facing the challenge of surviving in the wilderness. Besides writing, Paulsen loves dogsledding. He once entered the famous Iditarod dogsled race in Alaska. This experience was the inspiration for his book *Dogsong,* which was named a Newbery Honor Book.

Response Corner

MAKE A LIST

WATER TO THE RESCUE

Brian is worried that Derek may become dehydrated. Find out more about the causes and symptoms of dehydration. Make a list of tips to help prevent dehydration, and discuss your findings with your classmates.

WRITE A REPORT

ROW, ROW, ROW YOUR BOAT

Brian knows the technique of paddling the raft like a canoe. Work with a small group to write a report about the sport of canoeing. Include information about operating, maintaining, storing, and transporting a canoe. Share your report with the rest of the class.

TIME CAPSULE

Reread the section about *time* at the top of page 543. Do you agree with Gary Paulsen's thoughts about time? Write a poem that expresses your concept of time.

What Do You Think?

- Why are Brian and Derek on the river, and where do they end their trip?

- What would you have done about Derek if you had been in Brian's position?

- Do you think that Brian will go into the wilderness again? Explain your answer.

ART AND LITERATURE

What problem does the man in *The Gulf Stream*, by Winslow Homer, face as he confronts nature? How would you compare his problem with that faced by the Fordreds in "Freedom Ride" or by Brian in "The River"? Notice the many colors that Homer used in painting the water. How does this use of color help to create a mood of fear and suspense?

The Gulf Stream (1899)
by *Winslow Homer*

Winslow Homer, a self-taught artist, began his career making drawings for magazines at a time when photographs were not widely used. Homer gained fame for his realistic drawings of Civil War battles. Later, he painted scenes from country life as well as pictures that show the force and beauty of nature. His paintings provide a visual record of life in 19th-century America.

Julie of the Wolves

BY JEAN CRAIGHEAD GEORGE

ILLUSTRATED BY RICHARD COWDREY

JULIE
OF THE
WOLVES
by Jean Craighead George

Pictures by John Schoenherr

MIYAX, A THIRTEEN-YEAR-OLD ESKIMO GIRL, HAS LEFT HER HOME IN ALASKA AND IS HEADED FOR SAN FRANCISCO TOWARD AMY, HER PEN PAL, WHO CALLS HER JULIE. BUT SHE FINDS HERSELF LOST, WITHOUT FOOD OR A COMPASS, ON THE NORTH SLOPE OF ALASKA. SHE IS ALONE EXCEPT FOR A PACK OF ARCTIC WOLVES.

Upon discovering the wolves, she had settled down to live near them in the hope of sharing their food, until the sun set and the stars came out to guide her. She had built a house of sod, like the summer homes of the old Eskimos. Each brick had been cut with her *ulo*, the half-moon shaped woman's knife, so versatile it can trim a baby's hair, slice a tough bear, or chip an iceberg.

Her house was not well built for she had never made one before, but it was cozy inside. She had windproofed it by sealing the sod bricks with mud from the pond at her door, and she had made it beautiful by spreading her caribou ground cloth on the floor. On this she had placed her sleeping skin, a moosehide bag lined with soft white rabbit skins. Next to her bed she had built a low table of sod on which to put her clothes when she slept. To decorate the house she had made three flowers of bird feathers and stuck them in the top of the table. Then she had built a fireplace outdoors and placed her pot beside it. The pot was empty, for she had not found even a lemming to eat.

Last winter, when she had walked to school in Barrow, these mice-like rodents were so numerous they ran out from under her feet wherever she stepped. There were thousands and thousands of them until December, when they suddenly vanished. Her teacher

said that the lemmings had a chemical similar to antifreeze in their blood that kept them active all winter when other little mammals were hibernating. "They eat grass and multiply all winter," Mrs. Franklin had said in her singsong voice. "When there are too many, they grow nervous at the sight of each other. Somehow this shoots too much antifreeze into their bloodstreams and it begins to poison them. They become restless, then crazy. They run in a frenzy until they die."

Of this phenomenon Miyax's father had simply said, "The hour of the lemming is over for four years."

Unfortunately for Miyax, the hour of the animals that prey on the lemmings was also over. The white fox, the snowy owl, the weasel, the jaeger, and the siskin[1] had virtually disappeared. They had no food to eat and bore few or no young. Those that lived preyed on each other. With the passing of the lemmings, however, the grasses had grown high again and the hour of the caribou was upon the land. Healthy fat caribou cows gave birth to many calves. The caribou population increased, and this in turn increased the number of wolves who prey on the caribou. The abundance of the big deer of the north did Miyax no good, for she had not brought a gun on her trip. It had never occurred to her that she would not reach Point Hope before her food ran out.

A dull pain seized her stomach. She pulled blades of grass from their sheaths and ate the sweet ends. They were not very satisfying, so she picked a handful of caribou moss, a lichen. If the deer could survive in winter on this food, why not she? She munched, decided the plant might taste better if cooked, and went to the pond for water.

As she dipped her pot in, she thought about Amaroq. Why had he bared his teeth at her? Because she was young and he knew she couldn't hurt him? No, she said to herself, it was because he was speaking to her! He had told her to lie down. She had even understood and obeyed him. He had talked to her not with his voice, but with his ears, eyes, and lips; and he had even commended her with a wag of his tail.

[1] jaeger and siskin: types of birds

She dropped her pot, scrambled up the frost heave and stretched out on her stomach.

"Amaroq," she called softly, "I understand what you said. Can you understand me? I'm hungry—very, very hungry. Please bring me some meat."

The great wolf did not look her way and she began to doubt her reasoning. After all, flattened ears and a tail-wag were scarcely a conversation. She dropped her forehead against the lichens and rethought what had gone between them.

"Then why did I lie down?" she asked, lifting her head and looking at Amaroq. "Why did I?" she called to the yawning wolves. Not one turned her way.

Amaroq got to his feet, and as he slowly arose he seemed to fill the sky and blot out the sun. He was enormous. He could swallow her without even chewing.

"But he won't," she reminded herself. "Wolves do not eat people. That's gussak[2] talk. Kapugen said wolves are gentle brothers."

The black puppy was looking at her and wagging his tail. Hopefully, Miyax held out a pleading hand to him. His tail wagged harder. The mother rushed to him and stood above him sternly. When he licked her cheek apologetically, she pulled back her lips from her fine white teeth. They flashed as she smiled and forgave her cub.

"But don't let it happen again," said Miyax sarcastically, mimicking her own elders. The mother walked toward Amaroq.

"I should call you Martha after my stepmother," Miyax whispered. "But you're much too beautiful. I shall call you Silver instead."

Silver moved in a halo of light, for the sun sparkled on the guard hairs that grew out over the dense underfur and she seemed to glow.

The reprimanded pup snapped at a crane fly and shook himself. Bits of lichen and grass spun off his fur. He reeled unsteadily, took a wider stance, and looked down at his sleeping sister. With a yap he jumped on her and rolled her to her feet. She whined. He barked

---

[2] gussak: Eskimo term for white people

and picked up a bone. When he was sure she was watching, he ran down the slope with it. The sister tagged after him. He stopped and she grabbed the bone, too. She pulled; he pulled; then he pulled and she yanked.

Miyax could not help laughing. The puppies played with bones like Eskimo children played with leather ropes.

"I understand *that*," she said to the pups. "That's tug-o-war. Now how do you say, 'I'm hungry'?"

Amaroq was pacing restlessly along the crest of the frost heave as if something were about to happen. His eyes shot to Silver, then to the gray wolf Miyax had named Nails. These glances seemed to be a summons, for Silver and Nails glided to him, spanked the ground with their forepaws and bit him gently under the chin. He wagged his tail furiously and took Silver's slender nose in his mouth. She crouched before him, licked his cheek and lovingly bit his lower jaw. Amaroq's tail flashed high as her mouthing charged him with vitality. He nosed her affectionately. Unlike the fox who met his mate only in the breeding season, Amaroq lived with his mate all year.

Next, Nails took Amaroq's jaw in his mouth and the leader bit the top of his nose. A third adult, a small male, came slinking up. He got down on his belly before Amaroq, rolled trembling to his back, and wriggled.

"Hello, Jello," Miyax whispered, for he reminded her of the quivering gussak dessert her mother-in-law made.

She had seen the wolves mouth Amaroq's chin twice before and so she concluded that it was a ceremony, a sort of "Hail to the Chief." He must indeed be their leader for he was clearly the wealthy wolf; that is, wealthy as she had known the meaning of the word on Nunivak Island. There the old Eskimo hunters she had known in her childhood thought the riches of life were intelligence, fearlessness, and love. A man with these gifts was rich and was a great spirit who was admired in the same way that the gussaks admired a man with money and goods.

The three adults paid tribute to Amaroq until he was almost smothered with love; then he bayed a wild note that sounded like the wind on the frozen sea. With that the others sat around him, the puppies scattered between them. Jello hunched forward and Silver shot a fierce glance at him. Intimidated, Jello pulled his ears together and back. He drew himself down until he looked smaller than ever.

Amaroq wailed again, stretching his neck until his head was high above the others. They gazed at him affectionately and it was plain to see that he was their great spirit, a royal leader who held his group together with love and wisdom.

Any fear Miyax had of the wolves was dispelled by their affection for each other. They were friendly animals and so devoted to Amaroq that she needed only to be accepted by him to be accepted by all. She even knew how to achieve this—bite him under the chin. But how was she going to do that?

She studied the pups hoping they had a simpler way of expressing their love for him. The black puppy approached the leader, sat, then lay down and wagged his tail vigorously. He gazed up at Amaroq in pure adoration, and the royal eyes softened.

Well, that's what I'm doing! Miyax thought. She called to Amaroq. "I'm lying down gazing at you, too, but you don't look at *me* that way!"

When all the puppies were wagging his praises, Amaroq yipped, hit a high note, and crooned. As his voice rose and fell, the other adults sang out and the puppies yipped and bounced.

The song ended abruptly. Amaroq arose and trotted swiftly down the slope. Nails followed, and behind him ran Silver, then Jello. But Jello did not run far. Silver turned and looked him straight in the eye. She pressed her ears forward aggressively and lifted her tail. With that, Jello went back to the puppies and the three sped away like dark birds.

Miyax hunched forward on her elbows, the better to see and learn. She now knew how to be a good puppy, pay tribute to the leader, and even to be a leader by biting others on the top of the nose. She also knew how to tell Jello to baby-sit. If only she had big ears and a tail, she could lecture and talk to them all.

Flapping her hands on her head for ears, she flattened her fingers to make friends, pulled them together and back to express fear, and shot them forward to display her aggression and dominance. Then she folded her arms and studied the puppies again.

The black one greeted Jello by tackling his feet. Another jumped on his tail, and before he could discipline either, all five were upon him. He rolled and tumbled with them for almost an hour; then he ran down the slope, turned, and stopped. The pursuing pups plowed into him, tumbled, fell, and lay still. During a minute of surprised recovery there was no action. Then the black pup flashed his tail like a semaphore signal and they all jumped on Jello again.

Miyax rolled over and laughed aloud. "That's funny. They're really like kids."

When she looked back, Jello's tongue was hanging from his mouth and his sides were heaving. Four of the puppies had collapsed at his feet and were asleep. Jello flopped down, too, but the black pup still looked around. He was not the least bit tired. Miyax watched him, for there was something special about him.

He ran to the top of the den and barked. The smallest pup, whom Miyax called Sister, lifted her head, saw her favorite brother in action and, struggling to her feet, followed him devotedly. While they romped, Jello took the opportunity to rest behind a clump of sedge, a moisture-loving plant of the tundra. But hardly was he settled before a pup tracked him to his hideout and pounced on him. Jello narrowed his eyes, pressed his ears forward, and showed his teeth.

"I know what you're saying," she called to him. "You're saying, 'lie down.'" The puppy lay down, and Miyax got on all fours and looked for the nearest pup to speak to. It was Sister.

"Ummmm," she whined, and when Sister turned around she narrowed her eyes and showed her white teeth. Obediently, Sister lay down.

"I'm talking wolf! I'm talking wolf!" Miyax clapped, and tossing her head like a pup, crawled in a happy circle. As she was coming back she saw all five puppies sitting in a row watching her, their heads cocked in curiosity. Boldly the black pup came toward her, his fat backside swinging as he trotted to the bottom of her frost heave, and barked.

"You are *very* fearless and *very* smart," she said. "Now I know why you are special. You are wealthy and the leader of the puppies. There is no doubt what you'll grow up to be. So I shall name you after my father Kapugen, and I shall call you Kapu for short."

Kapu wrinkled his brow and turned an ear to tune in more acutely on her voice.

"You don't understand, do you?"

Hardly had she spoken than his tail went up, his mouth opened slightly, and he fairly grinned.

"Ee-lie!" she gasped. "You do understand. And that scares me." She perched on her heels. Jello whined an undulating note and Kapu turned back to the den.

Miyax imitated the call to come home. Kapu looked back over his shoulder in surprise. She giggled. He wagged his tail and jumped on Jello.

She clapped her hands and settled down to watch this language of jumps and tumbles, elated that she was at last breaking the wolf code. After a long time she decided they were not talking but rough-housing, and so she started home. Later she changed her mind. Roughhousing was very important to wolves. It occupied almost the entire night for the pups.

"Ee-lie, okay," she said. "I'll learn to roughhouse. Maybe then you'll accept me and feed me." She pranced, jumped, and whimpered; she growled, snarled, and rolled. But nobody came to roughhouse.

Sliding back to her camp, she heard the grass swish and looked up to see Amaroq and his hunters sweep around her frost heave and stop about five feet away. She could smell the sweet scent of their fur.

The hairs on her neck rose and her eyes widened. Amaroq's ears went forward aggressively and she remembered that wide eyes meant fear to him. It was not good to show him she was afraid. Animals attacked the fearful. She tried to narrow them, but remembered that was not right either. Narrowed eyes were mean. In desperation she recalled that Kapu had moved forward when challenged. She pranced right up to Amaroq. Her heart beat furiously as she grunt-whined the sound of the puppy begging adoringly for attention. Then she got down on her belly and gazed at him with fondness.

The great wolf backed up and avoided her eyes. She had said something wrong! Perhaps even offended him. Some slight gesture that meant nothing to her had apparently meant something to the wolf. His ears shot forward angrily and it seemed all was lost. She wanted to get up and run, but she gathered her courage and pranced closer to him. Swiftly she patted him under the chin.

The signal went off. It sped through his body and triggered emotions of love. Amaroq's ears flattened and his tail wagged in friendship. He could not react in any other way to the chin pat, for the roots of this signal lay deep in wolf history. It was inherited from generations and generations of leaders before him. As his eyes softened, the sweet odor of ambrosia arose from the gland on the top of his tail and she was drenched lightly in wolf scent. Miyax was one of the pack.

Jean Craighead George

Many of Jean Craighead George's books involve characters who must confront nature. Here writer Ilene Cooper talks with the author about how her interest in the natural world has shaped her writing and her life.

Cooper: You come from a family that's passionate about nature, don't you?

George: When my brothers and I were very young, my father took us into the woods along the Potomac River and taught us about plants and animals. He was so excited about natural history that it just followed that we would be, too.

Cooper: So when you were twelve years old, you were already a naturalist?

George: I was out in the meadow collecting wildflowers and insects, or raising polliwogs. I loved canoeing and camping. My brothers were expert falconers and they gave me a falcon of my own.

Cooper: What did you do when you couldn't be outside?

George: We had a whole attic full of the classics, and I read my way through them. In the summer, my mother always made us read for an hour after lunch. She was smart; she got some peace and quiet, and we got an education.

Cooper: Tell me a little bit about the trip to Alaska you took, where you did the research for Julie of the Wolves.

George: I was researching an article for the *Reader's Digest* magazine, and I went up there to do a piece on friendly wolves. The scientists at the Naval Arctic Research Lab were studying the plants and animals of the region, and their study of the wolves included communication. One of the scientists showed me how to approach them.

Cooper: Was it a little nerve-racking at first?

George: *(laughing)* No. The wolves are like dogs. In fact, all dogs are descended from wolves.

Cooper: At what point did you think there was a book in all this?

George: Not until I got home. The article fell through, and so there I was with all that research. Besides working with the wolves, I had been out in the tundra, looking at the plant life and the wildlife, like the lemmings. I also did some study of the Eskimos. My daughter suggested that I write a book, and that's how *Julie of the Wolves* came about. The book helped put the wolf on the endangered species list.

Cooper: Do you own any dogs?

George: Yes. I have an Alaskan malamute.

Cooper: Was there anything that you learned with the wolves that you were able to translate into useful approaches for training your dog?

George: Yes, you should put your hand over the dog's muzzle. That shows them you're the leader, and they adore their leader. And be sure to look them in the eye when you give them commands. If they are not looking right at you, giving commands does no good.

Cooper: You won the Newbery Award for Julie of the Wolves. *How did you react?*

George: I thought I had taken it quite calmly, but when the neighbors came to congratulate me, I brought out dog biscuits instead of cookies, and the next morning I found I had put the book in the refrigerator!

RESPONSE CORNER

CREATE A POSTER

SURVIVAL OF THE FITTEST

Several Arctic creatures are mentioned on pages 566 and 568. Research one of these birds or animals. Create a poster about the species. Tell how it survives in the Arctic environment. Display your poster in the classroom.

CALCULATE DISTANCE

MILE AFTER MILE

Look at a map of the United States. Choose a point on the northern slope of Alaska. Then find San Francisco, California. Calculate the number of miles Miyax has to travel to reach her destination.

DEMONSTRATE SIGNALS

A WAY WITH WORDS

The wolves in the story "communicate" with Miyax. Work with a group to find out more about wolf signals and what they mean. Demonstrate for your classmates what you learn.

WHAT DO YOU THINK?

- How do you know that Miyax is resourceful and sensitive to animals? Give examples from the story.

- Has this story changed your opinion of wolves? Explain why or why not.

- How do you think Miyax felt at the end of the story? Why?

TO THE TOP OF THE WORLD

ADVENTURES WITH ARCTIC WOLVES

Jim Brandenburg

JIM BRANDENBURG
To the Top of the World
ADVENTURES WITH ARCTIC WOLVES

ALA Best Book for Young Adults

SLJ Best Books Award

Jim Brandenburg spent one special spring and summer on Ellesmere Island near the Arctic Circle in Canada. This is the story of his adventures with a pack of wild wolves and how he observed them.

One of my first concerns was about how much I might interfere with the lives of these wolves. Would my presence cause them to abandon their den and disappear?

During most of the year, a wolf pack roams over its entire territory, making wolf study almost impossible. But each spring, the pack stays in or near one place. The mother must take to the den to have her pups, and the behavior of the whole pack revolves around feeding their young and ensuring their safety. This phenomenon makes study easier, but it also is a uniquely sensitive time.

How could I make it clear to the pack that I meant them no harm? That I would keep my distance and simply observe?

At first, I did not set up a permanent campsite in case the pack fled and moved to another den. I approached the den cautiously, alert to any signs that my presence might be causing stress in the pack. But the wolves never appeared overly nervous or bothered.

Meeting the Family

The den was set high on a hill. At its opening, rocks formed a kind of porch on which the pack members spent much of their time. The den opened into the earth from an entryway just large enough to fit snugly around the mother wolf. A hungry polar bear, in other words, could not squeeze in to make a snack out of the growing pups. Inside, a clean, bug-free layer of sand covered the ground leading into a cave twenty feet deep. The rock walls provided excellent protection from the bitter cold.

Pups spend their first weeks inside the den huddled around their mother, and each other, for warmth. I was eager and impatient for my first look at them. When they finally appeared outside the den, they proved well worth the wait.

There were six puppies, cute little gray bundles of fur waddling after the adults on short, fuzzy legs and oversized paws. I guessed that they were about five weeks old. It seemed impossible that by winter they'd be running alongside their parents.

Above left: The pups' narrow view of the world is seen from inside the den.

Above: The rocky outcropping at the den's entrance has been carved for eons by the winds of the High Arctic.

Several days later, I set up a camera about fifty yards from the den and was shooting photographs of the wriggling ball of pups. All seven adults looked in my direction, stretched, howled a few times at the sky, and took off on a hunt. I couldn't believe it! Not one adult stayed behind to bark at me and keep me away from the den. They trusted me with their precious pups. Finally, after all those frustrating years of wolf pursuit, I would be able to get close to an entire pack. And what a family it was!

The pups study the world outside their den.

The way adult wolves are constantly caring for the young in their pack is only one of many similarities with human families. Wolves mate for life, and the whole pack functions as an extended family of aunts and uncles, brothers and sisters. They take turns baby-sitting and teaching the pups what they need to know.

Wolves have very individual personalities. Bison and musk-oxen all behave much the same within their herds. Not wolves. It probably has to do with their intelligence and gifts of perception.

At first, however, *my* perceptions were not up to the task of telling the seven wolves in this pack apart. But over the weeks of watching and listening to the wolves, I found myself more and more aware of their differences, like body scars, facial expressions, and coloring.

I also noticed that some of them behaved in dominant ways, bristling and cocky. Others were more submissive, cringing when in the presence of a "superior" and always trying to keep the peace. In other words, a hierarchy became apparent, a ranking of the wolves according to their power in relation to the others.

At the top was the alpha male, Buster. He was usually first to attack on a hunt and the first to eat after a kill. Buster's eyes were extremely expressive. Sometimes they were piercing, threatening. Other times they were amused, haughty, or quizzical. Weighing less than 100 pounds, he was not the largest of the pack. But he stood proudly on thin, long legs, taller than even the largest German shepherd.

The adult wolves are excellent caretakers of their young charges.

Nearly his equal was the alpha female. I called her Midback because of a trail of dark fur running down her back. She was probably the most intelligent pack member. It was also clear that she was the *least* pleased to have me around. Midback's quickness and skill made her the best hunter among the pack.

Although scientists say that only the alpha pair has pups each spring, Midback was not the mother of the pups. There is no way to know why this alpha female did not give birth, but she was the most fiercely protective "parent" the pups had. She behaved like a dominant aunt who was often jealous of the pups' mother, whom I called, simply, Mom. Midback often rivaled Mom's authority over the pups.

Scruffy

Mom quickly became one of my favorites. She was a natural mother—gentle, tolerant, and devoted to the pups. Her facial expression can only be described as sweet and serene. And for some reason she seemed to have complete trust in humans. Maybe she simply got used to having me around because she was tied to the den.

The other wolf that could most often be found with the pups was my other favorite. He was an "adolescent" wolf, probably from the previous year's litter. His position in the pack was at the opposite end from the alpha pair—the bottom. I called him Scruffy because he was always a mess. His summer coat was scraggly, with huge balls of hair hanging from virtually every part of his hide.

Mom's serene disposition makes her the most tolerant member of the pack.

There was a kind of goofiness about Scruffy that endeared him to me, especially since he tended to follow me around a lot. He was usually left behind from a hunt, but baby-sitting was the perfect job for him because of his playfulness. It also gave him the chance to act dominantly over somebody, at least when Mom wasn't looking.

It was part of his job to play rough with the pups, knock them down hard enough to make them yelp. Though this kind of bullying may seem cruel, it is a necessary part of the pups' training. They have to learn the importance of knowing one's place in the hierarchy. This arrangement is crucial to the pack's unity and survival. Maintaining that ranking and its strict rules of behavior keeps the peace, avoids continual fights and injuries, maybe even death.

I knew less about the remaining three adults in the pack, mostly because they spent less time at the den site. Left Shoulder, a male named for a three-inch patch of missing fur on his left shoulder, was the largest, whitest wolf in the pack. Despite his size, he was submissive to the point of groveling in the presence of both Buster and Midback. The other two adults had even lower status in the pack, and I never got much of a sense of their personalities.

Many changes in the pack's membership would inevitably follow from one year to the next. But these seven adults and six pups made up the "family" as it existed one particular spring and summer on Ellesmere Island.

At times, the usually playful Scruffy must show his dominance over the pups by exposing his teeth and growling.

Left Shoulder shows no sign of favoring the wounded shoulder for which he was named; the wound was probably caused by the horn or hoof of a musk-ox.

While searching for an ideal campsite, I found a skull embedded in the powdery soil.

The story the skull told of the wolf's amazing survival skills intrigued me. Puncturing the lower jawbone was the tip of a musk-ox horn that had broken off, probably during combat. Bone tissue had grown thick across the point of injury, showing that he had lived for at least several months after the battle. The simple act of chewing must have been terribly painful, but his worn teeth indicated that he was very old when he died.

The discovery of this skull gave me an unusual glimpse into the harsh lives these wolves lead. It also provided a symbolic site on which to stake my own territorial claim for the spring and summer.

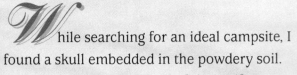

Living as Neighbors

This setting was a deep valley about a quarter-mile east of the den. A pair of binoculars allowed me to keep track of the pack's activities. My presence did not seem to affect the wolves in a negative way. They made regular trips to the camp, apparently to satisfy their curiosity. My goal was to blend in, to lie low without trying to hide or trick the wolves. There was, however, one unavoidable exception to this approach. It was my means of transportation, the Suzuki all-terrain vehicle (ATV).

I used this four-wheel buggy to carry my equipment and to keep up with the free-roaming pack. It's nothing for a wolf to travel forty miles at a steady pace of six miles per hour. It would have been impossible to keep up with them on foot.

Most of my time, of course, was spent not on the ATV but loitering within camera range of the den. Since the sun was up twenty-four hours a day at this point, I didn't think—or sleep—in night-and-day patterns. Besides, the wolves did not appear to have any regular sleep patterns either. As with their diet and hunting, wolves take opportunities when and where they can; they seem to know when it makes sense to be asleep and when it makes sense to be awake.

Often I found myself staying up twenty hours or more at a stretch, fearful that if I did fall asleep, the wolves would do something never before documented and I'd miss it. I would grab my sleeping bag and telephoto lens and curl up on the hillside overlooking the den, taking catnaps and every now and then cocking an ear or raising an eyelid toward the activity across the way.

More than once I fell asleep in spite of myself, only to wake to the curious sniffing of a wolf a few yards away. It was satisfying, at these times, to know that the creatures whom I was observing were keeping a similarly watchful eye on me.

A few words here about anthropomorphism, the common practice of giving human characteristics and feelings to non-humans. Throughout my career—even when I've felt closest to my wild subjects—I've always tried to preserve a boundary between us.

Yet, animals undoubtedly have more feelings than we give them credit for. To ignore this fact, or view their emotional range as smaller, *inferior* to ours, is just as wrong as thinking of them in strictly human terms.

I genuinely believe a magic exists in creatures as perceptive and intelligent as wolves, a magic that we may not be able to observe or measure in any scientific way.

Sometimes, during those days on Ellesmere, I would wonder how the wolves perceived me. Maybe they attributed wolflike feelings to my odd human behaviors. I wouldn't have been surprised.

The pack completely accepted my presence in their territory.

Exhausted from play sessions, Scruffy and the pups nap; a paw over the nose gives protection from the irritating mosquitoes.

During a high Arctic winter, the sun does not appear for four months and temperatures can drop to minus seventy degrees Fahrenheit. Add fierce winds, and you have a climate that seems unsuited to any living creature. But the  process of evolution produces characteristics in animals that allow them to adapt to the environment in which they live.

No matter how cold I felt it to be, I never observed a wolf who acted chilled. I suspect that even in the middle of the harshest winter Arctic wolves find a way to keep themselves comfortable. They probably spend much of their time in the position I saw them sleep in—curled up into tight balls with their bushy tails draped protectively over their noses. This position exposes the smallest possible amount of body surface to the cold.

Adaptation

Minus 60 degrees Fahrenheit; the orange glow is a product of the low-hanging March sun.

Since wolves appear to prefer sleeping outside, their winter coats and "leggings" must be superbly insulated. Their legs look twice as thick in winter as they do in summer. And they even grow long hair on the bottoms of their feet, which almost hides their footpads.

As warmer weather approaches, the wolves begin to shed. At one point or another, all the wolves had great gobs of shedding undercoat trailing up to two feet behind them. All summer, I waited for the moment when all the old excess hair would be gone and the wolves would be sleek and smooth. But such a day never came. The next winter's fur started growing in before the last one's could be entirely shaken or scraped free.

This messiness doesn't mean, however, that the wolves did not care about keeping themselves clean. Maintaining their white coats, of course, is necessary because it provides their camouflage during the winter. But they displayed individual differences, too, in how well-groomed they kept themselves. Left Shoulder and Scruffy represented the two extremes: The older wolf was always whiter, prettier than the rest, while Scruffy lived up to his nickname.

Buster, the alpha male, was another of the tidier individuals. This trait became evident in one of the most remarkable scenes I have ever witnessed in the animal world. Buster had turned almost black with mud in pursuit of an Arctic hare, but rather than lying down immediately to enjoy his meal, he took a long, careful swim, after which he shook himself dry—all with the dead hare clamped in his jaw. Only then did he sit down to his meal.

Another example of superb adaptation to environment is the wolf's legendary sense of smell. Some scientists have estimated that wolves can smell thousands of times better than humans can. Their snouts are always cocked in the direction of the prevailing breeze because it provides such important information about their world, especially the location of potential prey.

Buster, the alpha male, sniffs a bouquet of Arctic poppies.

Right: Puppies begin to practice howling very early in life; their amusing, high-pitched efforts add to the family songfest.

Below: Midback wakes up ready to hunt and howls to rouse her packmates.

Heavy winds, however, seem to annoy them with too much random information, and they avoid hunting altogether on such days.

On one occasion, I followed several of the wolves to a nearby beach where a dead fish had washed up on the shore. It had been dead for some time, and it smelled quite rank. The wolves took turns rolling around on the fish until they all shared in the stench. This behavior seemed odd to me, until they took off on their hunt. Evidently, they were masking their own scent so that a musk-ox or caribou could be reassured that it was only a dead fish stalking it, nothing dangerous.

The wolves' eyesight and hearing are in many ways as impressive as their sense of smell. Once it took me several minutes, *with* my binoculars, to detect an Arctic hare that Buster's eyes had been following for some time.

Their excellent senses allow these animals to do more than just locate prey efficiently. Wolves are probably one of the most social animals outside of the primates. The success of the pack depends strongly on a highly developed system of communication with neighboring packs as well as between individual pack members. Smell, vision, and hearing play crucial roles in such communication.

The most well-known form of communication wolves use is their howl. Howling begins at a very early age. Within weeks after emerging from the den, the pups cock their tiny snouts to the sky right alongside their parents.

I was often able to watch and listen to a songfest by the whole pack. Each had his or her distinctive voice and a preferred range of notes. Midback, for instance, had a high-pitched, almost whiny cry, whereas Left Shoulder would howl in the lower octaves.

A big hunt begins with a howling reveille.

Whatever their preferred notes, however, one thing was certain. Every wolf avoided hitting the same note as any of its packmates. When this happened by accident, one of the voices would frantically shuffle about until discord could be achieved once again. This phenomenon apparently has evolved to suit the scattered distribution of the Arctic wolves across an unfriendly environment, not always in safe numbers. With as many different tones as possible in its howling, a pack can give the impression of greater size and can intimidate possible intruders. I know I have been fooled by a distant pack's howls, estimating its size to be double what it turns out to be when I come across its members.

Wolves howl for many reasons beyond signaling their location to other packs. When part of the pack is off hunting, they howl to those left behind, perhaps letting them know their position. Wolves also will howl after a long sleep. Such howling seems to work up the group into enthusiasm for the next hunt, much as a team of athletes will shout in unison before a big game. But whatever practical purposes the wolves' howling might serve, it also seems to be for pleasure.

Wildlife photographer Jim Brandenburg spent twenty years looking for the perfect place to take pictures. He finally found it on Ellesmere Island, an isolated speck of land north of the Arctic Circle. What Brandenburg discovered on Ellesmere Island was so rare and unusual that no one had ever seen it before. He ended up staying on the island to take the photographs that would eventually go into his book *To the Top of the World.*

Brandenburg is considered one of the finest wildlife photographers. Because of his work on Ellesmere Island, he also became an expert on Arctic wolves.

But don't get the impression that Jim Brandenburg spent the twenty years before he found Ellesmere Island just hanging around. He stayed busy traveling to wild spots all over the world, bringing back pictures of places and animals that most people never see. More than a thousand of his photographs have been published in such magazines as *National Geographic, Life, Newsweek,* and *Smithsonian.*

BARKING UP A TREE

Jim Brandenburg noted a hierarchy among the pack of wolves he studied. Make a diagram of a "family tree" of the wolves mentioned in the selection. Compare your diagram with those of your classmates. Discuss any differences.

Response
Corner

PERSONALITY PLUS

Play a game with a partner. Describe the personality of one of the wolves from the selection. Have your partner guess which wolf you are describing. Keep score, awarding one point for each correct guess.

A NEW PERSPECTIVE

Suppose the selection were written from the perspective of a wolf. What might the wolf think of the presence and behavior of a human? Discuss your thoughts with a small group.

WHAT DO YOU THINK?

❖ What are the most important ideas you learned about wolves?

❖ Which wolf is your favorite? Why?

❖ Do you feel that the author gives the wolves human characteristics? Explain your answer.

THEME WRAP-UP

Some of the people in this theme choose to confront nature; others have no choice but to survive as best they can. Do you think that you would have taken the risks that the people in these selections did? Explain your answer.

If Miyax had the opportunity to share some of her knowledge about wolves with author Jim Brandenburg, what do you think she would tell him?

ACTIVITY CORNER

Picture yourself confronting nature either in one of the settings in this theme or in a setting of your own. Tape record a radio message you would send out to rescuers giving details of your situation and telling what you are doing to survive it.

Glossary

WHAT IS A GLOSSARY?

A glossary is like a small dictionary at the back of a book. It lists some of the words used in the book, along with their pronunciations, their meanings, and other useful information. If you come across a word you don't know as you are reading, you can look up the word in this glossary.

Using the

Like a dictionary, this glossary lists words in alphabetical order. To find a word, look it up by its first letter or letters.

To save time, use the **guide words** at the top of each page. These show you the first and last words on the page. Look at the guide words to see if your word falls between them alphabetically.

Here is an example of a glossary entry:

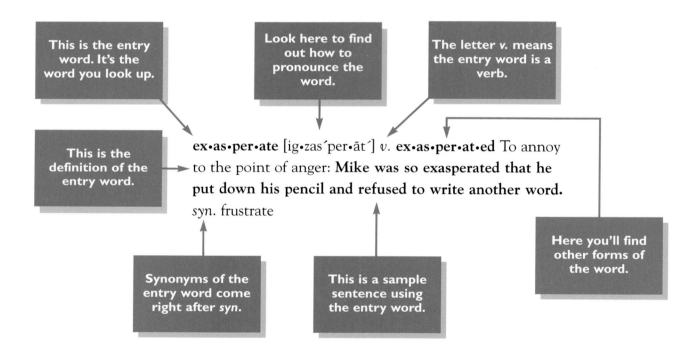

> This is the entry word. It's the word you look up.

> Look here to find out how to pronounce the word.

> The letter *v.* means the entry word is a verb.

> This is the definition of the entry word.

ex·as·per·ate [ig·zas´per·āt´] *v.* **ex·as·per·at·ed** To annoy to the point of anger: **Mike was so exasperated that he put down his pencil and refused to write another word.** *syn.* frustrate

> Synonyms of the entry word come right after *syn.*

> This is a sample sentence using the entry word.

> Here you'll find other forms of the word.

ETYMOLOGY

Etymology is the study or history of how words are developed. Words often have interesting backgrounds that can help you remember what they mean. Look in the margins of the glossary to find the etymologies of certain words.

Here is an example of an etymology:

archaeologist   This word is made up of two Greek words: *archaios*, which means "ancient or old" and *logia*, which means "knowledge." The *-ist* was added to show that it was talking about a person, giving the meaning "ancient-knowledge person."

Glossary

PRONUNCIATION

The pronunciation shows the important sounds of a word by giving a respelling within brackets; for example, [dis•pel´]. It will help you say the word correctly.

Below is the **pronunciation key.** It explains what the symbols in a respelling mean. A short **pronunciation key** appears on every other page of the glossary.

- • separates words into syllables
- ´ indicates heavier stress on a syllable
- ´ indicates light stress on a syllable

PRONUNCIATION KEY*

a	add, map	m	move, seem	u	up, done
ā	ace, rate	n	nice, tin	û(r)	burn, term
â(r)	care, air	ng	ring, song	yōo	fuse, few
ä	palm, father	o	odd, hot	v	vain, eve
b	bat, rub	ō	open, so	w	win, away
ch	check, catch	ô	order, jaw	y	yet, yearn
d	dog, rod	oi	oil, boy	z	zest, muse
e	end, pet	ou	pout, now	zh	vision, pleasure
ē	equal, tree	o͝o	took, full	ə	the schwa, an
f	fit, half	o͞o	pool, food		unstressed vowel
g	go, log	p	pit, stop		representing the
h	hope, hate	r	run, poor		sound spelled
i	it, give	s	see, pass		a in *above*
ī	ice, write	sh	sure, rush		e in *sicken*
j	joy, ledge	t	talk, sit		i in *possible*
k	cool, take	th	thin, both		o in *melon*
l	look, rule	t̶h̶	this, bathe		u in *circus*

Abbreviations: *adj.* adjective, *adv.* adverb, *conj.* conjunction, *interj.* interjection, *n.* noun, *prep.* preposition, *pron.* pronoun, *syn.* synonym, *v.* verb.

*The Pronunciation Key, adapted entries, and the Short Key that appear on the following pages are reprinted from *HBJ School Dictionary* Copyright © 1990 by Harcourt Brace & Company. Reprinted by permission of Harcourt Brace & Company.

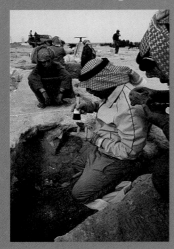

awe In Old Norse, *agi* simply meant "fear." Today the word *awe* expands on "fear" to include "respect" and "wonder."

brink This word is related to the word *break*. The Middle English word *brink* meant "the shore" or "the edge of the land." The shore is where the end of the land breaks off.

A

a·brupt [ə•brupt´] *adj.* Rude in speech and manner: **My aunt will not shop in that store because the clerks are *abrupt* and unfriendly.**

a·dorn [ə•dôrn´] *v.* **a·dorned, a·dorn·ing** To decorate: **The house was *adorned* with flowers and balloons for the party.**

ag·gres·sive·ly [ə•gres´iv•lē] *adv.* In a way that shows readiness to attack or fight: **The seagull *aggressively* chased the other birds away from the bread crumbs.**

an·tag·o·nism [an•tag´ə•niz´əm] *n.* Opposition to each other: ***Antagonism* had existed for years between the two countries.**

ap·point [ə•point´] *v.* **ap·point·ed, ap·point·ing** To select for a job: **Mrs. Ro was *appointed* spokesperson for the Parent-Teacher Association.**

ar·chae·ol·o·gist [är´kē•ol´ə•jist] *n.* A person who studies past times and cultures, usually by examining ancient artifacts: **The *archaeologists* were very excited when they discovered the lost city.**

av·id [av´id] *adj.* Enthusiastic: **My father is an *avid* golfer who plays every weekend, even when it rains.**

awe [ô] *n.* A feeling of wonder, fear, and respect: **Yoshihiro was in *awe* of his grandfather.**

B

bel·lig·er·ent·ly [bə•lij´ər•ənt•lē] *adv.* In an argumentative or challenging manner: **The wrestlers *belligerently* took their positions on the mat.**

be·stow [bi•stō´] *v.* **be·stowed, be·stow·ing** To give as a gift: **The king *bestowed* land and gold on his loyal soldiers.**

bi·zarre [bi•zär´] *adj.* Odd or unusual: **We were puzzled by the stranger's *bizarre* behavior.** *syns.* strange, weird

bond [bond] *n.* A force that holds things together: **The *bond* between true friends cannot be broken.**

brink [bringk] *n.* The point before something happens: **Scientists are on the *brink* of finding a cure for that disease.**

C

ca·pa·ble [kā´pə·bəl] *adj.*
Having the ability or skill for a task: **We were amazed that he was *capable* of doing so much work in so little time.**

car·cass [kär´kəs] *n.* The dead body of an animal: **The vultures picked at the rabbit *carcass* by the roadside.**

ca·ress [kə·res´] *v.* **ca·ressed, ca·ress·ing** To stroke lovingly and gently: **Dottie *caressed* the soft fur on the puppy's back.**

cas·u·al·ly [kazh´o͞o·əl·ē] *adv.* Done offhandedly or without thinking: **Their family dressed too *casually* for the wedding.** *syn.* informally

chant [chant] *n.* A simple, rhythmic melody sung or shouted: **The monks joined together to sing *chants* after their evening meal.**

cir·cum·stance [sûr´kəm·stans´] *n.* The condition surrounding an event or situation: **The *circumstances* of the accident still are not clear.**

clam·or [klam´ər] *n.* A loud and ongoing noise: **The *clamor* from the construction was so loud that Ellen had to cover her ears.** *syn.* racket

col·lapse [kə·laps´] *v.* **col·lapsed, col·laps·ing** To give way or fall in: **The floor *collapsed* under the weight of the machinery.**

co·ma [kō´mə] *n.* A lasting unconsciousness caused by injury or illness: **The family was overjoyed when little Eddie came out of his *coma*.**

con·sist [kən·sist´] *v.* **con·sist·ed, con·sist·ing** To be made up of: **The software package *consisted* of two disks, a manual, and a hint book.**

con·tem·po·rar·y [kən·tem´pə·rer´ē] *n.* A person who lives at the same time as another: **My *contemporaries* and I like the same kind of music.**

cor·dial·ly [kôr´·jəl·ē] *adv.* With friendliness and sincerity: **Smiling with delight, Mr. Cortez greeted his guests *cordially*.** *syns.* warmly, heartily

crev·ice [krev´is] *n.* A narrow opening or split in a rock or in the ground: **The *crevice* in the rock was caused by an earthquake.**

cru·cial [kro͞o´shəl] *adj.* Extremely important: **The energy supply was *crucial* to the space station.** *syn.* essential

caressed

crevice

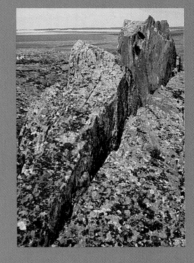

a	add	o͝o	took
ā	ace	o͞o	pool
â	care	u	up
ä	palm	û	burn
e	end	yo͞o	fuse
ē	equal	oi	oil
i	it	ou	pout
ī	ice	ng	ring
o	odd	th	thin
ō	open	t̶h̶	this
ô	order	zh	vision

ə = {
a in *above*
e in *sicken*
i in *possible*
o in *melon*
u in *circus*

curtsy

curtsy

debris

614

---

curt·sy [kûrt´sē] *n.* A bow made by women by bending the knees and lowering the head and shoulders as a sign of respect: **Dinah made a deep *curtsy* before the queen.**

D

de·bris [də•brē´ *or* dā•brē´] *n.* Scattered leftover pieces: **The workers cleaned up the *debris* left from the repairs to the wall.** *syn.* rubble

de·vo·tion [di•vō´shən] *n.* The act of giving oneself completely to: **No one questioned her complete *devotion* to environmental issues.** *syn.* dedication

di·ag·nos·tic [dī´əg•nos´tik] *adj.* Having to do with analyzing or evaluating a condition or situation: **The *diagnostic* exam helped the school determine which grade the new student belonged in.**

dis·card [dis•kärd] *v.* **dis·card·ed, dis·card·ing** To throw away or get rid of: **Sasha *discarded* the expired coupons.**

---

dis·dain·ful·ly [dis•dān´fəl•lē] *adv.* In a scornful or disgusted manner: **Claudia *disdainfully* looked at the old dress her sister had given her.**

dis·pel [dis•pel´] *v.* **dis·pelled, dis·pel·ling** To drive away: **Max's mother *dispelled* his worries about the trip by telling him about the wonderful things he would see.**

dis·tinc·tive [dis•tingk´tiv] *adj.* Easy to tell apart; standing out: **His *distinctive* laugh could be heard clear across the room.**

dis·tract [dis•trakt´] *v.* **dis·tract·ed, dis·tract·ing** To take one's attention away from something: **The music *distracted* Jason while he was doing his homework.**

dom·i·nance [dom´ə•nəns] *n.* Power, influence, or authority: **He defeated his enemies one by one until his *dominance* over the entire land was complete.**

du·bi·ous [d(y)oo´bē•əs] *adj.* Not sure or certain; having doubt: **Tai Wong was *dubious* about leaving without permission.**

E

ef·fi·cient [i·fish´ənt] *adj.* Working well with little waste: **The most** *efficient* **light bulb gives off the least heat.**

em·bark [im·bärk´] *v.* **em·barked, em·bark·ing** To start a project: **The city** *embarked* **on building a new bridge as soon as the floodwaters went down.**

ex·as·per·ate [ig·zas´pə·rāt´] *v.* **ex·as·per·at·ed, ex·as·per·at·ing** To annoy to the point of anger: **Mike was so** *exasperated* **that he put down his pencil and refused to write another word.** *syn.* frustrate

ex·ca·va·tion [eks´·kə·vā´shən] *n.* The digging up and uncovering of something: **Mila is working on an** *excavation* **of dinosaur bones in Montana this summer.**

ex·tinct [ik·stingkt´] *adj.* No longer living or active; often used to refer to a species: **The whooping crane is in danger of becoming** *extinct.*

F

fas·ci·na·tion [fas´ə·nā´shən] *n.* Great interest: **Li-Yuan's** *fascination* **with the building of models led to a career in architecture.**

for·bid·ding [fər·bid´ing] *adj.* Unfriendly and frightening: **The desert at noontime was** *forbidding* **and hot.**

frag·ile [fraj´əl] *adj.* Easily broken: **The sign next to the pottery display said, "Fragile—handle with care."** *syn.* delicate

fran·ti·cal·ly [fran´tik·lē] *adv.* In a wild and nervous way, full of fear or worry: **When the horses felt the earthquake, they** *frantically* **started running.**

func·tion [fungk´shən] *n.* The purpose something serves; use: **The** *function* **of this saw is to cut wood.**

fu·tile [fyo͞o´təl] *adj.* Useless; not effective: **It was** *futile* **to try to stop the floodwaters.**

excavation

frantically The Greek word *phren* referred to the mind, and *phrenitikos* was "a disease of the mind" in which someone was acting without thinking.

a	add	o͝o	took
ā	ace	o͞o	pool
â	care	u	up
ä	palm	û	burn
e	end	yo͞o	fuse
ē	equal	oi	oil
i	it	ou	pout
ī	ice	ng	ring
o	odd	th	thin
ō	open	t͟h	this
ô	order	zh	vision

ə = {
a in *above*
e in *sicken*
i in *possible*
o in *melon*
u in *circus*

H

hal·lu·ci·na·tion
[hə·lōō´sə·nā´shən] *n.*
Something one sees that is not
really there: **The intense heat
caused the hikers to
experience *hallucinations*.**

harsh [härsh] *adj.* Rough: **The
strong winds and rain made
the journey a *harsh* one.**

haugh·ty [hô´tē] *adj.* Thinking
of oneself as being better than,
or superior to, others: **Because
of her *haughty* ways she had
few friends.** *syn.* arrogant

head·land [hed´lənd] *n.* A high
point of land that overlooks
water, such as a cliff: **Sean
stood on the *headland* and
watched the ships sail away.**

hos·tile [hos´təl] *adj.* Opposing;
unfriendly: **The *hostile* nations
fought for many years.**

hu·mil·i·ty [hyōō·mil´ə·tē] *n.*
The quality of not being proud:
**After Susan won the spelling
bee, people were surprised at
her *humility*.**

headland

I

im·mor·tal [i·môr´təl] *adj.*
Living forever; never dying:
**Mr. Garcia recited the poet's
immortal words.**

im·plore [im·plôr´] *v.*
im·plored, im·plor·ing To beg:
**The students were *imploring*
the teacher to have a party on
the last day of school.**

in·ci·den·tal [in´sə·den´təl] *adj.*
Related but of little importance:
**Frank just wanted to compete;
winning was *incidental*.**
syn. minor

in·ci·sive [in·sī´siv] *adj.*
Sharp and direct: **May's
incisive wit kept everyone
at the table laughing through
the entire meal.**

in·com·pe·tent [in·kom´pə·tənt]
adj. Without ability or skill:
**The boss fired the lazy and
incompetent worker.**

in·crim·i·nate [in·krim´ə·nāt´]
v. To show to be guilty: **The
fingerprints at the scene of
the crime may *incriminate* the
suspect.**

in·dis·posed [in´dis·pōzd´] *adj.*
Not feeling well: **Mrs. Clark
was *indisposed* and could not
receive visitors.** *syns.* sick, ill

in·fect [in·fekt´] *v.* **in·fect·ed, in·fect·ing** To make ill by spreading germs or viruses: Janice stayed home so no one would become *infected* with her cold.

in·ten·sive [in·ten´siv] *adj.* Done with energy and concentration: Pablo made an *intensive* effort to score the winning goal.

in·ten·tion [in·ten´shən] *n.* Plan or purpose: Our *intention* is to learn some Chinese phrases before our trip to China.

in·ter·val [in´tər·vəl] *n.* The distance between two points: A football field is marked in *intervals* of ten yards.

in·tim·i·date [in·tim´ə·dāt´] *v.* **in·tim·i·dat·ed, in·tim·i·dat·ing** To frighten: The little poodle was *intimidated* by the big German shepherd.

in·tri·cate [in´tri·kit] *adj.* Containing many detailed parts: The patchwork quilt had a very *intricate* design.

K

ken·nel [ken´əl] *n.* A place where people house and raise dogs: Serena bought her puppy from a *kennel*.

L

lair [lâr] *n.* The home of a wild animal: My dad told us not to walk near the cave because it might be a bear's *lair*.

lapse [laps] *n.* A slip or fall, as from a better to a worse condition: A *lapse* in concentration caused Marcus to miss a good move in the chess game.

leg·en·dar·y [lej´ən·der´ē] *adj.* Very well known: Houdini was *legendary* for his escape act. *syn.* famous

M

mas·sive [mas´iv] *adj.* Very large; gigantic: Loc and his family were amazed at the sight of the *massive* volcano.

mis·chie·vous·ly [mis´chi·vəs·lē] *adv.* In a teasing or naughty way: Cary *mischievously* hid her father's slippers under the sofa.

mis·hap [mis´hap] *n.* Something that goes wrong: After his *mishap*, Lee's parents didn't let him help paint anymore. *syn.* accident

kennel

lair

a	add	o͝o	took
ā	ace	o͞o	pool
â	care	u	up
ä	palm	û	burn
e	end	yo͞o	fuse
ē	equal	oi	oil
i	it	ou	pout
ī	ice	ng	ring
o	odd	th	thin
ō	open	t͟h	this
ô	order	zh	vision

ə = {
a in *above*
e in *sicken*
i in *possible*
o in *melon*
u in *circus*
}

optimism The Latin word *optimus* meant "the best." Then the French expanded its meaning to "a person who thinks the best about everything."

pose

mon·u·men·tal [mon´yə•men´təl] *adj.* Great and important; like a monument: **The statue was** *monumental* **and impossible to ignore.** *syn.* impressive

N

no·mad·ic [nō•mad´ik] *adj.* Moving from place to place; not settled: **Many** *nomadic* **people live in tents.**

O

oc·cu·pa·tion [ok´yə•pā´shən] *n.* The taking and holding of land by military force: **During the** *occupation,* **there was little freedom.**

om·i·nous·ly [om´ə•nəs•lē] *adv.* In a way that points to something bad or frightening: **The clouds gathered** *ominously* **before the storm.**

op·ti·mism [op´•tə•miz´əm] *n.* The habit or ability of seeing the good side of things: **In spite of the problems, Greg never lost his** *optimism.*

o·ver·whelm [ō´vər•(h)welm´] *v.* **o·ver·whelmed, o·ver·whelm·ing** To overcome completely: **The avalanche was sudden, and soon the skiers were** *overwhelmed* **by the wave of snow.**

P

plun·der [plun´dər] *v.* **plun·dered, plun·der·ing** To steal things by force: **The police caught the robbers** *plundering* **the village.**

poised [poizd] *adj.* Ready to move or act: **Knees slightly bent and bat** *poised,* **Hugo waited for the pitcher to release the ball.**

pose [pōz] *v.* **posed, pos·ing** To sit or stand in a position for a picture: **The photographer would like Uncle Albert to** *pose* **behind Aunt Jenny.**

pre·cise·ly [pri•sīs´lē] *adv.* Exactly: **Thomas hit the ball** *precisely* **into the corner to win the tennis match.**

prej·u·dice [prej´ōō•dis] *n.* An unfair opinion formed without examining the available facts: **Some of the doctors had** *prejudices* **against the new medicine.**

pres·tig·ious [pres•tē´jəs *or* pres•tij´əs] *adj.* Honored and valued: **The Nobel Prize is one of the most *prestigious* awards.**

pri·or·i·ty [prī•ôr´ə•tē] *n.* Something that is first in order of importance: **Finishing your homework has *priority* over watching television.**

Q

quiv·er [kwiv´ər] *v.* **quiv·ered, quiv·er·ing** To make a slight trembling motion; vibrate: **Pete's knees *quivered* a little when he got up to give his speech.**

R

ra·di·ant·ly [rā´dē•ənt•lē] *adv.* Brilliantly; in a bright or glowing way: **Jamal smiled *radiantly* as he stepped up to receive first prize.**

re·lent [ri•lent´] *v.* **re·lent·ed, re·lent·ing** To become less severe and more gentle and cooperative: **The children finished their homework, so their parents *relented* and let them watch the video.**

rel·ic [rel´ik] *n.* Something remaining from a past culture or time period: **The *relics* from the lost city were displayed in the museum.** *syn.* artifact

res·i·dent [rez´ə•dənt] *n.* A person who lives in a certain place; not a visitor: **The *residents* of this neighborhood want a new park and cleaner streets.**

re·straint [ri•strānt´] *n.* The act of holding back: **The interior designer used *restraint* when decorating the room.**

re·stric·tion [ri•strik´shən] *n.* A limit: **The doctor gave her two *restrictions*: no fat and no sugar.**

re·trieve [ri•trēv´] *v.* **re·trieved, re·triev·ing** To get something back: **Mohammed *retrieved* the keys he had dropped into the swimming pool.**

re·vive [ri•vīv´] *v.* **re·vived, re·viv·ing** To bring back to consciousness: **The doctors *revived* the young girl who had almost drowned in the lake.**

ric·o·chet [rik´ə•shā´] *v.* To bounce off a surface: **Be careful if you play golf near trees, because a ball can hit a tree and *ricochet*.**

relic This word comes from the Latin word *relinquere*, meaning "to leave behind." In English it slowly developed two meanings. One of them is *relic*, and the other was "a widow," or a woman who was "left behind" after her husband's death. The second meaning is not used today.

ricochet

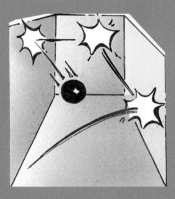

a	add	o͝o	took
ā	ace	o͞o	pool
â	care	u	up
ä	palm	û	burn
e	end	yo͞o	fuse
ē	equal	oi	oil
i	it	ou	pout
ī	ice	ng	ring
o	odd	th	thin
ō	open	th	this
ô	order	zh	vision

ə = {
  a in *above*
  e in *sicken*
  i in *possible*
  o in *melon*
  u in *circus*
}

spontaneously
The Latin word *sponte* originally meant "my will" or "a promise." Later the meaning became "of my own free will," or "something I do willingly." So, this word describes something you do on impulse, because you want to do it.

swerved

terminal

rig•or [rig´ər] *n.* Difficulty and discomfort; challenge: **Only a few people are able to handle the *rigors* of climbing Mt. Everest.**

S

scape•goat [skāp´gōt´] *n.* A person, group, or animal made to bear the blame for the errors of others: **There will be no *scapegoat* in this group because we are all to blame for missing the bus.**

se•rene [si•rēn´] *adj.* Peaceful; tranquil; unruffled: **The *serene* mood was shattered when a motorcycle roared past.**

slay [slā] *v.* **slew, slain, slay•ing** To kill violently: **More than three hundred people were *slain* in the battle that day.** *syn.* slaughter

spon•ta•ne•ous•ly [spon•tā´nē•əs•lē] *adv.* Naturally and without planning: **The winner of the contest *spontaneously* hugged the announcer.**

strive [strīv] *v.* **strove, stiv•en** [striv´ən], **striv•ing** To make a strong effort: **Wendy was *striving* to make her science project the best she had ever presented.**

sum•mon [sum´ən] *v.* **sum•moned, sum•mon•ing** To order to come: **The hotel clerk will *summon* a bellhop to help you with your suitcase.**

swerve [swûrv] *v.* **swerved, swerv•ing** To turn suddenly to one side: **Manisha had to *swerve* off the road to avoid hitting the deer.**

T

ter•mi•nal [tûr´mə•nəl] *n.* A bus, airplane, or train station at the end of a route: **Sylvia was to wait at the *terminal* for her Uncle Paul to pick her up.**

trend•y [tren´dē] *adj.* Of the latest fashion; popular for only a short time: **Barb wanted to buy those *trendy* new shoes, but they were very expensive.**

trib•ute [trib´yo͞ot] *n.* Respect and admiration: **The city paid *tribute* to the fireman who rescued the family from the burning house.**

tur•moil [tûr´moil] *n.* A condition of great confusion: **After the terrible hurricane, the town was in *turmoil*.**

U

un•eas•i•ness [un•ē´zē•nəs] *n.*
A feeling that there will be
trouble: **The house was too
quiet, and Sergio could not
shake his** *uneasiness* **about
being home alone.** *syn.* worry

un•wav•er•ing [un•wā´və•ring]
adj. Not faltering or failing: **No
matter what trouble the boy
got into, his mother's love was
unwavering.** *syn.* continuous

V

vast [vast] *adj.* Very large in size
or area: **The *vast* forest
covered thousands of acres.**
syn. huge

vir•tue [vûr´cho͞o] *n.* A good
quality or feature: **Honesty
and hard work are admirable
virtues.**

vi•tal•i•ty [vī•tal´ə•tē] *n.* Energy:
**Their *vitality* returned after
they had had a short rest.**

W

whim•per [(h)wim´pər] *n.* Soft
and broken crying or sobbing:
**The puppy's *whimpers* caught
the attention of its mother.**

vast The Latin
word *vastus* originally
meant that something
was "empty," like a
desert. Because
deserts are usually
very large, over the
years the meaning
of this word changed
to "huge."

virtue The ancient
Romans used the
word *virtus* to mean
"a man's strength."
Later this
word represented
"courage" and other
good qualities of both
men and women.

a	add	o͝o	took
ā	ace	o͞o	pool
â	care	u	up
ä	palm	û	burn
e	end	yo͞o	fuse
ē	equal	oi	oil
i	it	ou	pout
ī	ice	ng	ring
o	odd	th	thin
ō	open	t̶h̶	this
ô	order	zh	vision

ə = {
a in *above*
e in *sicken*
i in *possible*
o in *melon*
u in *circus*

INDEX OF
Titles and Authors

Page numbers in color refer to biographical information.

Printed in the United States of America

Acknowledgments

For permission to reprint copyrighted material, grateful acknowledgment is made to the following sources:

Editors of the Antioch Review: "On Watching the Construction of a Skyscraper" by Burton Raffel. Text copyright © 1960 by the Antioch Review, Inc. Originally published in the *Antioch Review*, Winter 1960.

Avon Books: Cover illustration by Patricia Mulvihill from *Bearstone* by Will Hobbs. Illustration copyright © 1989 by Patricia Mulvihill.

Bantam Doubleday Dell Books for Young Readers: From *Last Summer with Maizon* by Jacqueline Woodson, cover illustration by Leo and Diane Dillon. Text copyright © 1990 by Jacqueline Woodson; illustration copyright © 1990 by Leo and Diane Dillon.

Blackbirch Press, Inc.: Cover photograph from *Wilma Rudolph: Olympic Gold!* by Wayne Coffey. © 1993 by Blackbirch Press, Inc.

Bradbury Press, an Affiliate of Macmillan, Inc.: Cover photograph by Lyn Topinka from *Volcano: The Eruption and Healing of Mt. St. Helens* by Patricia Lauber. Photograph courtesy of United States Department of the Interior, U.S. Geological Survey, David A. Johnston Cascades Volcano Observatory, Vancouver, Washington.

George Braziller, Inc.: "fear" from *Dismantling the Silence* by Charles Simic. Text copyright © 1971 by Charles Simic.

Curtis Brown Ltd.: From "Elizabeth Borton de Treviño" in *PAUSES: Autobiographical Reflections of 101 Creators of Children's Books* by Lee Bennett Hopkins. Text copyright © 1995 by Lee Bennett Hopkins. Published by HarperCollins Publishers.

Richard Curtis Associates: "Freedom Ride" by Liz Fordred with Susie Blackmun.

Joan Daves Agency, on behalf of The Heirs to the Estate of Martin Luther King, Jr.: From "I Have a Dream" speech by Martin Luther King, Jr. Text copyright 1963 by Martin Luther King, Jr.; text copyright renewed 1991 by Coretta Scott King.

Delacorte Press, a division of Bantam Doubleday Dell Publishing Group, Inc.: From *The River* by Gary Paulsen, cover illustration by Neil Waldman. Text copyright © 1991 by Gary Paulsen; illustration copyright © 1991 by Neil Waldman. Cover illustration by Robert Hunt from *Cat Running* by Zilpha Keatley Snyder. Illustration copyright © 1994 by Robert Hunt.

Dell Books, a division of Bantam Doubleday Dell Publishing Group, Inc.: From *Where the Red Fern Grows* by Wilson Rawls, cover illustration by Robert McGinnis. Text copyright © 1961 by Sophie S. Rawls, Trustee, or successor Trustee(s) of the Rawls Trust, dated July 21, 1991; text copyright © 1961 by The Curtis Publishing Company; illustration copyright © 1989 by Robert McGinnis.

Dial Books for Young Readers, a division of Penguin Books USA Inc.: Cover illustration by E. B. Lewis from *The Baby Grand, The Moon in July, & Me* by Joyce Annette Barnes. Illustration © 1994 by E. B. Lewis.

Peter B. G. Duffy: Photograph of Liz and Peter Fordred by Peter B. G. Duffy from "Freedom Ride" by Liz Fordred with Susie Blackmun.

Dutton Children's Books, a division of Penguin Books USA Inc.: From "Four Generals" in *Shen of the Sea: Chinese Stories for Children* by Arthur Bowie Chrisman, cover illustration by Else Hasselriis. Copyright 1925 by E.P. Dutton, renewed 1953 by Arthur Bowie Chrisman.

Farrar, Straus & Giroux, Inc.: Cover photograph by Johnny Johnson from *Making Sense: Animal Perception and Communication* by Bruce Brooks. Photograph © by Johnny Johnson/Animals Animals. From *I, Juan de Pareja* by Elizabeth Borton de Treviño. Text and cover illustration copyright © 1965 by Elizabeth Borton de Treviño.

James Cross Giblin: "The Great Wall of China" from *Walls: Defenses Throughout History* by James Cross Giblin. Text copyright © 1984 by James Cross Giblin.

Greenwillow Books, a division of William Morrow & Company, Inc.: Cover illustration by Frank Modell from *Journal of a Teenage Genius* by Helen V. Griffith. Copyright © 1987 by Helen V. Griffith.

Harcourt Brace & Company: Cover illustration by Leo and Diane Dillon from *Aïda* by Leontyne Price. Illustration copyright © 1990 by Leo and Diane Dillon. "Photograph" from *Something Permanent* by Cynthia Rylant. Text copyright © 1994 by Cynthia Rylant. "The Challenge" from *Local News* by Gary Soto. Text copyright © 1993 by Gary Soto. Cover illustration by Goro Sasaki from *Pacific Crossing* by Gary Soto. Copyright © 1992 by Gary Soto.

HarperCollins Publishers: From *Julie of the Wolves* by Jean Craighead George, cover illustration by John Schoenherr. Text copyright ©1972 by Jean Craighead George; illustration copyright ©1972 by John Schoenherr. Cover illustration by Carl Burger from *Old Yeller* by Fred Gipson. Copyright © 1956 by Fred Gipson. Cover illustration by Stephen Fieser from *The Silk Route* by John S. Major. Illustration copyright © 1995 by Stephen Fieser.

Holiday House, Inc.: Cover photograph from *The Wright Brothers: How They Invented the Airplane* by Russell Freedman. Photograph courtesy of The Smithsonian Institution.

Houghton Mifflin Company: "A Song of Greatness" from *The Children Sing in the Far West* by Mary Austin. Text copyright 1928 by Mary Austin; text © renewed 1956 by Kenneth M. Chapman and Mary C. Wheelwright. From *Number the Stars* by Lois Lowry. Text and cover photograph copyright © 1989 by Lois Lowry. From *City* by David Macaulay. Copyright © 1974 by David Macaulay. From *Island of the Blue Dolphins* by Scott O'Dell, cover illustration by Ted Lewin. Text copyright © 1960 by Scott O'Dell, renewed 1988 by Scott O'Dell; illustration copyright © 1990 by Ted Lewin. Cover illustration by Troy Howell from *Apple Is My Sign* by Mary Riskind. Illustration © 1981 by Troy Howell.

Karen E. Hudson: From *The Will and the Way: Paul R. Williams, Architect* by Karen E. Hudson. Text copyright © 1994 by Karen E. Hudson.

Hyperion Books for Children: Cover illustration by Jeff Mangiat from *Stranded* by Ben Mikaelsen. Illustration copyright © 1995 by Jeff Mangiat. Cover illustration by Joe Burleson from *Climb or Die* by Edward Myers. Illustration copyright © 1994 by Joe Burleson.

Intellectual Properties Management, Atlanta, Georgia, as Manager for the King Estate: License to reprint image/likeness of Martin Luther King, Jr.

Kids Discover: From "The Pyramids of Egypt" in *Kids Discover: Pyramids*. Text © 1993 by Kids Discover. From *Kids Discover: Ancient Greece*. Text © 1994 by Kids Discover.

Alfred A. Knopf, Inc.: "On Hearing a Flute at Night from the Wall of Shou-Hsiang" by Li Yi from *The Jade Mountain*, translated by Witter Bynner. Text copyright 1929, renewed 1957 by Alfred A. Knopf, Inc. "City" from *Collected Poems* by Langston Hughes. Text copyright © 1994 by the Estate of Langston Hughes. Cover photographs from *Round Buildings, Square Buildings, & Buildings That Wiggle Like a Fish* by Philip M. Isaacson. Copyright © 1988 by Philip M. Isaacson.

Deborah Nourse Lattimore: Cover illustration by Deborah Nourse Lattimore from *Detectives in Togas* by Henry Winterfield.

Lerner Publications Company, Minneapolis, MN: From *Great Summer Olympic Moments* by Nate Aaseng. Text copyright © 1990 by Lerner Publications Company. From *The Vietnamese in America* by Paul Rutledge. Text copyright 1973 by Lerner Publications.

Little, Brown & Company: Cover illustration from *Walls: Defenses Throughout History* by James Cross Giblin. Cover photographs from *It's Our World, Too! Stories of Young People Who Are Making a Difference* by Phillip Hoose. Copyright © 1993 by Phillip Hoose. "Joan Benoit Samuelson" from *Champions: Stories of Ten Remarkable Athletes* by Bill Littlefield, illustrated by Bernie Fuchs. Text copyright © 1993 by Bill Littlefield; illustrations copyright © 1993 by Bernie Fuchs. Cover photograph from *Life in the Oceans* by Norbert Wu. Copyright © 1991 by Tern Enterprise, Inc.

Lodestar Books, an affiliate of Dutton Children's Books, a division of Penguin Books USA Inc.: Cover photographs by David Hautzig from *The Other Side: How Kids Live in a California Latino Neighborhood* by Kathleen Krull. Photographs copyright © 1994 by David Hautzig.

Lothrop, Lee & Shepard Books, a division of William Morrow & Company, Inc.: From *Hello, My Name Is Scrambled Eggs* by Jamie Gilson, cover illustration by John Wallner. Text copyright © 1985 by Jamie Gilson; illustration copyright © 1985 by John Wallner.

LRN Company: From Diego Rodriguez de Silva y Velásquez (Retitled: "The Art of Velázquez") by Ernest Raboff. Published by HarperCollins Publishers.

The Madison Press Limited: Cover photographs from *Into the Mummy's Tomb* by Nicholas Reeves. Photographs courtesy of The Robert Harding Picture Library and Lehnert and Landrock.

Alan Mazzetti: Cover illustration by Alan Mazzetti from *Taking Sides* by Gary Soto.

Margaret K. McElderry Books, an imprint of Simon & Schuster: "Volcano" from *A Tree Place and Other Poems* by Constance Levy. Text copyright © 1994 by Constance Kling Levy. Cover illustration by Kinuko Craft from *A Jar of Dreams* by Yoshiko Uchida. Copyright © 1981 by Yoshiko Uchida.

Morrow Junior Books, a division of William Morrow & Company, Inc.: Cover illustration by Derek James from *Tales of a Dead King* by Walter Dean Myers. Copyright © 1983 by Walter Dean Myers. From *The Star Fisher* by Laurence Yep, cover illustration by David Wiesner. Text copyright © 1991 by Laurence Yep; illustration copyright © 1991 by David Wiesner.

National Council of Teachers of English: "Foreign Student" by Barbara B. Robinson from *English Journal*, May 1976. Text copyright 1976 by The National Council of Teachers of English.

New Directions Publishing Corporation: "View from the Cliffs" by Tu Mu from *One Hundred More Poems from the Chinese* by Kenneth Rexroth. Text copyright © 1970 by Kenneth Rexroth.

Oxford University Press: "Hieroglyphics" from *Oxford Children's Encyclopedia*, Vol 3. © 1991 by Oxford University Press.

Puffin Books, a division of Penguin Books USA Inc.: From *The Golden Goblet* by Eloise Jarvis McGraw, cover illustration by Maureen Hyde. Text copyright © 1961, renewed © 1989 by Eloise Jarvis McGraw; illustration copyright © 1989 by Viking Penguin.

Random House, Inc.: "Passports to Understanding" from *Wouldn't Take Nothing For My Journey Now* by Maya Angelou. Text copyright © 1993 by Maya Angelou. Cover illustration by Jules Feiffer from *The Phantom Tollbooth* by Norton Juster. Illustration copyright © 1961, 1989 by Jules Feiffer.

Marian Reiner, on behalf of Lilian Moore: "Until I Saw the Sea" from *I Feel the Same Way* by Lilian Moore. Text copyright © 1967 by Lilian Moore; text © renewed 1995 by Lilian Moore.

Dominic C. H. Rieu, Executor of the Estate of E. V. Rieu: "The Paint Box" from *The Flattered Fish and Other Poems* by E. V. Rieu. Text copyright © 1962 by E. V. Rieu. Published by Methuen, London, 1962.

Rizzoli International Publications, Inc.: Cover from *The Will and the Way: Paul R. Williams, Architect* by Karen E. Hudson. Illustration copyright © 1994 by Rizzoli International Publications, Inc.; photograph copyright © 1994 by The Paul R. Williams Collection.

Scholastic Inc: Cover illustration from *The Lost Wreck of the Isis* by Robert D. Ballard. Copyright © 1990 by The Madison Press Limited. From *The Secrets of Vesuvius* by Sara C. Bisel. Copyright © 1990 by Sara C. Bisel and Family and The Madison Press Limited.

The Rod Serling Trust: "The Monsters Are Due on Maple Street" by Rod Serling. Text © 1960 by Rod Serling; text © 1988 by Carolyn Serling, Jodi Serling and Anne Serling.

Sniffen Court Books: From *Behind the Sealed Door: The Discovery of the Tomb and Treasures of Tutankhamun* by Irene and Laurence Swinburne. Text copyright © 1977 by Sniffen Court Books.

Troll Associates: Cover illustration by Richard Hook from *Growing Up in Ancient China* by Ken Teague. © 1994 by Eagle Books.

University Press of New England: "The Inner Tube" from *A Summer Life* by Gary Soto. Text copyright © 1990 by University Press of New England.

Walker and Company, 435 Hudson Street, New York, NY 10014: From *To the Top of the World* by Jim Brandenburg. Copyright © 1993 by Jim Brandenburg.

Albert Whitman & Company: From *Five Women Photographers* (Retitled: "Two Women Photographers") by Sylvia Wolf. Text copyright © 1994 by Sylvia Wolf.

Photo Credits

Key: (t) top, (b) bottom, (c) center, (l) left, (r) right.

Tim Kelly/Black Star/Harcourt Brace & Company, 43; Courtesy of MacIntosh & Otis, 107; Tom Sobolik/Black Star/Harcourt Brace & Company, 186; Dale Higgins/Harcourt Brace & Company, 315; Courtesy of Houghton Mifflin, 396; Courtesy of Farrar, Straus & Giroux, 465; Warren Faubel.Black Star/Harcourt Brace & Company, 507; Alinari/Art Resource, NY, 422 (t); Ancient Art & Architecture, 430-431, ;Ancient Art and Architecture Collection, 363, (r); Art Resource, NY, 423; David Austen/TSW, 121, (r); The Bettmann Archive, 340; Jonathan Blair/Woodfin Camp & Associates, 404-405, 407, 415, 418, 426 (t) ; Borromeo/Art Resource, NY, 121 (b); Margeret Bourke-White, Syracuse University Library, 475, Time Warner, 476-480; Jim Brandenburg, 580-607; Bridgeman/Art Resource, NY, 127, (br); Geoffrey Clifford/The Stock Market, 119, 128, (t); Original Art by Phil Colprit/Wood Ronsaville Harlin, Inc., 365, (b); Comstock, 184; Dennis Cox/ChinaStock, 176-177, 190-190; Culver Pictures, Inc., 365 (cl); William Curtsinger/Photo Researchers, Inc., 366 (b); Timothy Eagan/Woodfin Camp & Associates, 185; Thomas Eakins, The National Gallery of Art, Washington, D.C., Gift of Mr. and Mrs. Cornelius Vanderbilt Whitney, 70-71; Foto Marburg/Art Resource, NY, 364, (ct); Donald A. Frey/Institute of Nautical Archaeology, 367 (l); © Flor Garduno, 482-486; Giraudon/Art Resource, NY, 120-121, 362 (cl), 364, (c); The Granger Collection, 362 (lt), 362 (bl), 364(cb & b), 365 (tl), 365 (tr), 367 (b, the Schliemans); Farrell Grehan/Photo Researchers, Inc, 364, (tl); Robert Harding Picture Library, 152-153; © Adriano Heitmann, 472 (r), 491; Michael Holford, 361(b), 361(tr) ; Winslow Homer, The Metropolitan Museum of Art, Catherine Lorillard Wolfe, Collection, Wolfe Fund, 1906, 562-563; Courtesy of Karen E. Hudson, 492-504, 506, 510-511 (l, b, & r); Hulton-Deutsch Collection, 367, (b); Michael Jacobs/Woodfin Camp & Associates, 123, (t, c, & b, inset), 128, (b), 129, (b); J. Kerth/Leo de Wys, 367 (tr); Hiroji Kubota/Magnum, 182-183 ; Jacob Lawrence, The National Museum of American Art, washington, D.C., Art Resource, NY, 260-261; Erich Lessing/Art Resource, NY, 118, 120, 122, 124, (bl), 360 (l), 360-361 (c), 362, (br); LIFE Magazine © Time Warner, 472 (l), 490; Painting by Ken Marshall, Courtesy of Madison Press Books, 402-403, 408-409; O. Louis Mazzatenta © National Geographic Society, 405 (inset), 416-417, 421, 422 (b), 424-425, 426-427(b & r); Will & Deni McIntyre/Photo Researchers, Inc., 366, (l); George Munday/Leo de Wye, 358; NASA, 179; Katsushuika Oi, Museum of Fine Arts, Boston, Courtesy of William Sturgis Bigelow Collection, 470-471, ; Georgia O'Keefe, Columbus Muiseum of Art, Howard Fund II, 368-369; Courtesy of Oxford University Press, 126-127; John M. Roberts/The Stock Market, 186; Scala/Art Resource, NY, 120 (l), 122, 124-125, 359, 362, (tr & cr), 366 (c), 414; SEF/Art Resource, NY, 367 (tl); Julius Shulman, 505, 510-511 (c); SuperStock, 118, 129 (l), 124; Jean-Marc Truchet/TSW, 181; UPI/The Bettmann Archive, 351; Diego Velasquez, Scala/Art Resource, NY, 439-443 , 448 (b), 449 (c),Staatliche Museen zu Berlin-PreuBischer Kulturbesitz Gemaldegalerie, 444,449 (l), Christie's, London/SuperStock, 445, 449 (r), Erich Lessing/Art Resource, NY, 446, 448 (t) Luis Villota/The Stock Market, 123; Original art by Williams, Wood Ronsaville Harlin, Inc., 361-363;

Illustration Credits

Kazuhiko Sano, Cover Art; Rocco Baviera,108-109; Alaiyo Bradshaw, 46-69; Deborah Chabrian, 294-315, 318-319; Richard Cowdrey, 564-579; David Diaz, 466-467; Chris Duke, 400-401; Rick Farrell, 172-173,450-465, 468-469; Bernie Fuchs, 342-357; Jack Graham, 90-95; Darrin Johnston, 338-341; Hui Han Liu, 204-223, 226-227; Lori Lohstoetter, 96-107, 110-111; Roberta Ludlow, 228-251, 258-259; David Macaulay, 370-397; John Nickle, 262-287, 292-293; Guy Porfirio, 254-257; Edward Potthast, 534-535; Mike Reed, 72-89; Mark Reidy, 538-561; Oren Sherman, 130-147, 150-151; Peter Siu, 188-189; Heidi Stevens, 154-171, 174-175; Cynthia Torp, 290-291; David Wilgus, 326-337; Larry Winborg,22-45